# Lecture Notes in Computer Science

Vol. 352: J. Díaz, F. Orejas (Eds.), TAPSOFT '89. Volume 2. Proceedings, 1989. X, 389 pages. 1989.

Vol. 353: S. Hölldobler, Foundations of Equational Logic Programming. X, 250 pages. 1989. (Subseries LNAI).

Vol. 354: J.W. de Bakker, W.-P. de Roever, G. Rozenberg (Eds.), Linear Time, Branching Time and Partial Order in Logics and Models for Concurrency. VIII, 713 pages. 1989.

Vol. 355: N. Dershowitz (Ed.), Rewriting Techniques and Applications. Proceedings, 1989. VII, 579 pages. 1989.

Vol. 356: L. Huguet, A. Poli (Eds.), Applied Algebra, Algebraic Algorithms and Error-Correcting Codes. Proceedings, 1987. VI, 417 pages. 1989.

Vol. 357: T. Mora (Ed.), Applied Algebra, Algebraic Algorithms and Error-Correcting Codes. Proceedings, 1988. IX, 481 pages. 1989.

Vol. 358: P. Gianni (Ed.), Symbolic and Algebraic Computation. Proceedings, 1988. XI, 545 pages. 1989.

Vol. 359: D. Gawlick, M. Haynie, A. Reuter (Eds.), High Performance Transaction Systems. Proceedings, 1987. XII, 329 pages. 1989.

Vol. 360: H. Maurer (Ed.), Computer Assisted Learning – ICCAL '89. Proceedings, 1989. VII, 642 pages. 1989.

Vol. 361: S. Abiteboul, P.C. Fischer, H.-J. Schek (Eds.), Nested Relations and Complex Objects in Databases. VI, 323 pages. 1989.

Vol. 362: B. Lisper, Synthesizing Synchronous Systems by Static Scheduling in Space-Time. VI, 263 pages. 1989.

Vol. 363: A.R. Meyer, M.A. Taitslin (Eds.), Logic at Botik '89. Proceedings, 1989. X, 289 pages. 1989.

Vol. 364: J. Demetrovics, B. Thalheim (Eds.), MFDBS 89. Proceedings, 1989. VI, 428 pages. 1989.

Vol. 365: E. Odijk, M. Rem, J.-C. Syre (Eds.), PARLE '89. Parallel Architectures and Languages Europe. Volume I. Proceedings, 1989. XIII, 478 pages. 1989.

Vol. 366: E. Odijk, M. Rem, J.-C. Syre (Eds.), PARLE '89. Parallel Architectures and Languages Europe. Volume II. Proceedings, 1989. XIII, 442 pages. 1989.

Vol. 367: W. Litwin, H.-J. Schek (Eds.), Foundations of Data Organization and Algorithms. Proceedings, 1989. VIII, 531 pages. 1989.

Vol. 368: H. Boral, P. Faudemay (Eds.), IWDM '89, Database Machines. Proceedings, 1989. VI, 387 pages. 1989.

Vol. 369: D. Taubner, Finite Representations of CCS and TCSP Programs by Automata and Petri Nets. X. 168 pages. 1989.

Vol. 370: Ch. Meinel, Modified Branching Programs and Their Computational Power. VI, 132 pages. 1989.

Vol. 371: D. Hammer (Ed.), Compiler Compilers and High Speed Compilation. Proceedings, 1988. VI, 242 pages. 1989.

Vol. 372: G. Ausiello, M. Dezani-Ciancaglini, S. Ronchi Della Rocca (Eds.), Automata, Languages and Programming. Proceedings, 1989. XI, 788 pages. 1989.

Vol. 373: T. Theoharis, Algorithms for Parallel Polygon Rendering. VIII, 147 pages. 1989.

Vol. 374: K.A. Robbins, S. Robbins, The Cray X-MP/Model 24. VI, 165 pages. 1989.

Vol. 375: J.L.A. van de Snepscheut (Ed.), Mathematics of Program Construction. Proceedings, 1989. VI, 421 pages. 1989.

Vol. 376: N.E. Gibbs (Ed.), Software Engineering Education. Proceedings, 1989. VII, 312 pages. 1989.

Vol. 377: M. Gross, D. Perrin (Eds.), Electronic Dictionaries and Automata in Computational Linguistics. Proceedings, 1987. V, 110 pages. 1989.

Vol. 378: J.H. Davenport (Ed.), EUROCAL '87. Proceedings, 1987. VIII, 499 pages. 1989.

Vol. 379: A. Kreczmar, G. Mirkowska (Eds.), Mathematical Foundations of Computer Science 1989. Proceedings, 1989. VIII, 605 pages. 1989.

Vol. 380: J. Csirik, J. Demetrovics, F. Gécseg (Eds.), Fundamentals of Computation Theory. Proceedings, 1989. XI, 493 pages. 1989.

Vol. 381: J. Dassow, J. Kelemen (Eds.), Machines, Languages, and Complexity. Proceedings, 1988. VI, 244 pages. 1989.

Vol. 382: F. Dehne, J.-R. Sack, N. Santoro (Eds.), Algorithms and Data Structures. WADS '89. Proceedings, 1989. IX, 592 pages. 1989.

Vol. 383: K. Furukawa, H. Tanaka, T. Fujisaki (Eds.), Logic Programming '88. Proceedings, 1988. VII, 251 pages. 1989 (Subseries LNAI).

Vol. 384: G.A. van Zee, J.G.G. van de Vorst (Eds.), Parallel Computing 1988. Proceedings, 1988. V, 135 pages. 1989.

Vol. 385: E. Börger, H. Kleine Büning, M.M. Richter (Eds.), CSL '88. Proceedings, 1988. VI, 399 pages. 1989.

Vol. 386: J.E. Pin (Ed.), Formal Properties of Finite Automata and Applications. Proceedings, 1988. VIII, 260 pages. 1989.

Vol. 387: C. Ghezzi, J.A. McDermid (Eds.), ESEC '89. 2nd European Software Engineering Conference. Proceedings, 1989. VI, 496 pages. 1989.

Vol. 388: G. Cohen, J. Wolfmann (Eds.), Coding Theory and Applications. Proceedings, 1988. IX, 329 pages. 1989.

Vol. 389: D.H. Pitt, D.E. Rydeheard, P. Dybjer, A.M. Pitts, A. Poigné (Eds.), Category Theory and Computer Science. Proceedings, 1989. VI, 365 pages. 1989.

Vol. 390: J.P. Martins, E.M. Morgado (Eds.), EPIA 89. Proceedings, 1989. XII, 400 pages. 1989 (Subseries LNAI).

Vol. 391: J.-D. Boissonnat, J.-P. Laumond (Eds.), Geometry and Robotics. Proceedings, 1988. VI, 413 pages. 1989.

Vol. 392: J.-C. Bermond, M. Raynal (Eds.), Distributed Algorithms. Proceedings, 1989. VI, 315 pages. 1989.

Vol. 393: H. Ehrig, H. Herrlich, H.-J. Kreowski, G. Preuß (Eds.), Categorical Methods in Computer Science. VI, 350 pages. 1989.

Vol. 394: M. Wirsing, J.A. Bergstra (Eds.), Algebraic Methods: Theory, Tools and Applications. VI, 558 pages. 1989.

Vol. 395: M. Schmidt-Schauß, Computational Aspects of an Order-Sorted Logic with Term Declarations. VIII, 171 pages. 1989 (Subseries LNAI).

Vol. 396: T.A. Berson, T. Beth (Eds.), Local Area Network Security. Proceedings, 1989. IX, 152 pages. 1989.

Vol. 397: K.P. Jantke (Ed.), Analogical and Inductive Inference. Proceedings, 1989. IX, 338 pages. 1989 (Subseries LNAI).

Vol. 398: B. Banieqbal, H. Barringer, A. Pnueli (Eds.), Temporal Logic in Specification. Proceedings, 1987. VI, 448 pages. 1989.

Vol. 399: V. Cantoni, R. Creutzburg, S. Levialdi, G. Wolf (Eds.), Recent Issues in Pattern Analysis and Recognition. VII, 400 pages. 1989.

Vol. 400: R. Klein, Concrete and Abstract Voronoi Diagrams. IV, 167 pages. 1989.

Vol. 401: H. Djidjev (Ed.), Optimal Algorithms. Proceedings, 1989. VI, 308 pages. 1989.

Vol. 402: T.P. Bagchi, V.K. Chaudhri, Interactive Relational Database Design. XI, 186 pages. 1989.

Vol. 403: S. Goldwasser (Ed.), Advances in Cryptology – CRYPTO '88. Proceedings, 1988. XI, 591 pages. 1990.

Vol. 404: J. Beer, Concepts, Design, and Performance Analysis of a Parallel Prolog Machine. VI, 128 pages. 1989.

Vol. 405: C.E. Veni Madhavan (Ed.), Foundations of Software Technology and Theoretical Computer Science. Proceedings, 1989. VIII, 339 pages. 1989.

Vol. 406: C.J. Barter, M.J. Brooks (Eds.), AI '88. Proceedings, 1988. VIII, 463 pages. 1990 (Subseries LNAI).

Vol. 407: J. Sifakis (Ed.), Automatic Verification Methods for Finite State Systems. Proceedings, 1989. VII, 382 pages. 1990.

# Lecture Notes in Computer Science

Edited by G. Goos and J. Hartmanis

## 460

Jürgen Uhl
Hans Albrecht Schmid

# A Systematic Catalogue
of Reusable
Abstract Data Types

Springer-Verlag
Berlin Heidelberg New York London
Paris Tokyo Hong Kong Barcelona

**Authors**

Jürgen Uhl
Forschungszentrum Informatik, Universität Karlsruhe
Haid-und-Neu-Straße 10−14, W-7500 Karlsruhe, FRG

Hans Albrecht Schmid
Fachbereich Informatik, Fachhochschule Konstanz
Brauneggerstraße, W-7750 Konstanz, FRG

CR Subject Classification (1987): D.2.2, D.2.m, D.3.3, E.2


ISBN 3-540-53229-3 Springer-Verlag Berlin Heidelberg New York
ISBN 0-387-53229-3 Springer-Verlag New York Berlin Heidelberg

*Acknowledgments*

Our thanks are due to the institution and persons who made this work possible, and to our colleagues with whom we had fruitful discussions. Especially, we want to acknowledge

- the support of IBM and, in particular, of Albert Endres, who established the department of research and development in reusability at the IBM Böblingen development laboratory as early as 1983, and

- the base laid by Karl Kleine from FZI Karlsruhe, who made – under the contract of this department – the first steps into the land of catalogues and libraries of abstract data types as reusable components in 1984.

Jürgen Uhl, Karlsruhe
Hans Albrecht Schmid, Konstanz
May 1990

*Foreword*


More and more, people are starting to think of software as an investment. As a consequence, the concern is growing on how to develop software that can be maintained for long periods of time and adapted to new uses easily. This lead to a broad interest in software reusability. The motto "don't redo what is there already" is gaining support.

Reusability can be envisaged at the level of entire systems or at the level of individual pieces or components of a system. Source code can be reused, but also test cases, designs, specifications and even requirements. Software is considered reusable if it can be easily employed for applications it was not intended for originally.

The reuse technology that appears to be most mature is that of generalized components, frequently referred to as building blocks. Libraries of building blocks have been developed and successfully employed in several application areas. At the core of such libraries, particularly if they are intended for applications in system programming, are basic data structures. Ideally they are offered in the form of abstract data types.

The concept of abstract data types is one of the most successful and pervasive structuring concepts introduced into the software development practice. It embodies such software engineering principles as separation of interface and implementation information hiding, localization of functions, and parameterization. Their theoretical properties have been studied quite extensively and they are amenable to algebraic and axiomatic specifications. Designing with abstract data types fosters reuse because it encourages going from a special situation to the more general, or generic, case through classification and abstraction.

Building on a strong technical foundation laid by Kleine [8] several years ago, Uhl and Schmid have designed and implemented a new set of abstract data types that are described in this book. The implementations in this catalogue are done in the programming language Ada.

In contrast to previous similar efforts, Uhl and Schmid introduce two major new ideas. They try to achieve the utmost degree of consistency as far as the external interfaces are concerned. They then device a hierarchical relationship between the various data types which serves as the basis for the implementation, i.e. the more complex members are built out of the more elementary ones – reuse within reuse. The result of this is a very high number of variants that can be produced from a rather small code base.

Since the advantages of this approach in terms of development cost, code quality, learning effort and maintenance are quite obvious, I like to call this a second generation catalogue.

In addition to the catalogue itself, the authors give valuable practical guidelines on how to design using abstract data types. A comprehensive example at the end of the book illustrates the ideas through a realistic application.

Both authors have spent several years on industrial software projects or on joint studies between industry and academia. They have helped to introduce formal design methods and abstract data types. The entire text reflects this experience.

Albert Endres, Böblingen

# Contents

**1 Introduction**     **1**

**2 Motivation and Objectives**     **5**
    2.1   Simplicity of the Library Structure . . . . . . . . . . . . . . . . 6
    2.2   Functional Completeness . . . . . . . . . . . . . . . . . . . . 8
    2.3   Completeness of Implementation Variants . . . . . . . . . . . . 10
    2.4   Maintainability . . . . . . . . . . . . . . . . . . . . . . . . 12

**3 How to Reuse Abstract Data Types**     **15**
    3.1   Working With Data Structures – A Counter-Example . . . . . . . . 16
       3.1.1   Selecting a Data Structure . . . . . . . . . . . . . . . . . 17
       3.1.2   Designing the Operations on the Data Structure . . . . . . 17
       3.1.3   Conclusion . . . . . . . . . . . . . . . . . . . . . . . . 18
    3.2   Reusing Abstract Data Types . . . . . . . . . . . . . . . . . . 19
       3.2.1   Selecting "Low Level" Abstract Data Types . . . . . . . . 20
       3.2.2   Selecting the "Right" Abstract Data Types . . . . . . . . 23
       3.2.3   An Abstract Specification and Solution . . . . . . . . . . 25
       3.2.4   Selection of an Abstract Data Type Variant . . . . . . . . 27
    3.3   Reuse Paradigm . . . . . . . . . . . . . . . . . . . . . . . . 29

**4 Structure of the Catalogue**     **37**
    4.1   The Implementation Hierarchy . . . . . . . . . . . . . . . . . . 37
    4.2   The Abstract Data Types - an Overview . . . . . . . . . . . . . 39
       4.2.1   List . . . . . . . . . . . . . . . . . . . . . . . . . . . . 40
       4.2.2   Stack . . . . . . . . . . . . . . . . . . . . . . . . . . . 40
       4.2.3   Queue and Deque . . . . . . . . . . . . . . . . . . . . . 41
       4.2.4   Tree . . . . . . . . . . . . . . . . . . . . . . . . . . . . 41
       4.2.5   Order . . . . . . . . . . . . . . . . . . . . . . . . . . . 41
       4.2.6   Set . . . . . . . . . . . . . . . . . . . . . . . . . . . . 42
       4.2.7   Map . . . . . . . . . . . . . . . . . . . . . . . . . . . . 42

| | | |
|---|---|---|
| | 4.2.8 Bag | 42 |
| 4.3 | Variants of Building Blocks | 42 |

**5 Structure of the Building Blocks**            **45**

| | | |
|---|---|---|
| 5.1 | General Properties of the Data Types | 46 |
| | 5.1.1 Objects and Values | 46 |
| | 5.1.2 Structure Sharing | 47 |
| | 5.1.3 Compact and Dispersed Representations | 48 |
| | 5.1.4 Recursive Composition | 49 |
| 5.2 | Types | 50 |
| | 5.2.1 The Type STRUCT | 50 |
| | 5.2.2 The Type INDEX | 51 |
| | 5.2.3 INSERT_POSITIONs and REMOVE_POSITIONs | 53 |
| | 5.2.4 Structure PARTs | 54 |
| | 5.2.5 The Type ITERATION_ORDER | 54 |
| 5.3 | Operations | 54 |
| | 5.3.1 Constructors | 57 |
| | 5.3.2 Operations Based on Indices | 73 |
| | 5.3.3 Access by Position Count | 76 |
| | 5.3.4 Selector Operations | 77 |
| | 5.3.5 Iterators | 80 |
| | 5.3.6 Reduction | 86 |
| | 5.3.7 Find, Skip and Count | 89 |
| | 5.3.8 Existential and Universal Quantifiers | 90 |
| | 5.3.9 Order Dependent Operations | 91 |
| | 5.3.10 Hash Operation | 93 |
| 5.4 | Generic Parameters | 94 |
| | 5.4.1 Equal, Copy, and Transfer | 95 |
| | 5.4.2 Initialization | 95 |
| | 5.4.3 Deallocation | 96 |
| | 5.4.4 An Example | 96 |
| | 5.4.5 Key-Info Types | 98 |
| | 5.4.6 Accessed Elements | 98 |
| | 5.4.7 Bounded Collections | 98 |
| 5.5 | Variant Parameters | 99 |
| | 5.5.1 Classes of Element Types | 99 |
| | 5.5.2 Collection Management | 105 |
| | 5.5.3 Consistency Checking | 108 |
| | 5.5.4 Algorithms vs. Data | 108 |
| | 5.5.5 Summary | 109 |

**6 The Building Blocks**     **111**
   6.1   Linked Collections . . . . . . . . . . . . . . . . . . . . . 112
     6.1.1   Synopsis . . . . . . . . . . . . . . . . . . . . . 112
     6.1.2   Types and Operations . . . . . . . . . . . . . . 112
     6.1.3   Implementation Overview . . . . . . . . . . . . 113
     6.1.4   Specific Generic Parameters . . . . . . . . . . 114
     6.1.5   Specific Variants . . . . . . . . . . . . . . . . 114
     6.1.6   General Variants . . . . . . . . . . . . . . . . 114
     6.1.7   Representation of Linked Collections . . . . . . 116
   6.2   Tabular Collections . . . . . . . . . . . . . . . . . . . . 117
     6.2.1   Synopsis . . . . . . . . . . . . . . . . . . . . . 117
     6.2.2   Types and Operations . . . . . . . . . . . . . . 117
     6.2.3   Implementation Overview . . . . . . . . . . . . 118
     6.2.4   Specific Generic Parameters . . . . . . . . . . 118
     6.2.5   Specific Variants . . . . . . . . . . . . . . . . 119
     6.2.6   General Variants . . . . . . . . . . . . . . . . 119
   6.3   Hash tables . . . . . . . . . . . . . . . . . . . . . . . . 121
     6.3.1   Synopsis . . . . . . . . . . . . . . . . . . . . . 121
     6.3.2   Types and Operations . . . . . . . . . . . . . . 121
     6.3.3   Implementation Overview . . . . . . . . . . . . 122
     6.3.4   Specific Generic Parameters . . . . . . . . . . 123
     6.3.5   Specific Variants . . . . . . . . . . . . . . . . 123
     6.3.6   General Variants . . . . . . . . . . . . . . . . 126
     6.3.7   Combination of Variants . . . . . . . . . . . . 126
     6.3.8   Representation of Hash tables . . . . . . . . . 127
   6.4   Lists, Linked Lists, Tabular Lists . . . . . . . . . . . . 128
     6.4.1   Synopsis . . . . . . . . . . . . . . . . . . . . . 128
     6.4.2   Types and Operations . . . . . . . . . . . . . . 128
     6.4.3   Implementation Overview . . . . . . . . . . . . 138
     6.4.4   List Specific Variants . . . . . . . . . . . . . . 139
     6.4.5   General Variants of Lists . . . . . . . . . . . . 139
     6.4.6   Combination of List Variants . . . . . . . . . . 140
     6.4.7   Linked List Specific Variants . . . . . . . . . . 140
     6.4.8   General Variants of Linked Lists . . . . . . . . 142
     6.4.9   Combination of Linked List Variants . . . . . . 142
     6.4.10   Representation of Linked List by Linked Collections . . . . . . 142
     6.4.11   Tabular List Specific Variants . . . . . . . . . 143
     6.4.12   General Variants of Tabular Lists . . . . . . . . 146
     6.4.13   Representation of Tabular Lists by Tabular Collections . . . . 146
   6.5   Stacks . . . . . . . . . . . . . . . . . . . . . . . . . . . 148
     6.5.1   Synopsis . . . . . . . . . . . . . . . . . . . . . 148
     6.5.2   Types and Operations . . . . . . . . . . . . . . 148

        6.5.3   Implementation Overview . . . . . . . . . . . . . . . . . . . . 149
        6.5.4   Specific Variants . . . . . . . . . . . . . . . . . . . . . . . . 150
        6.5.5   General Variants . . . . . . . . . . . . . . . . . . . . . . . . 150
        6.5.6   Combination of Variants . . . . . . . . . . . . . . . . . . . 151
        6.5.7   Representation Specific Variants . . . . . . . . . . . . . . 151
        6.5.8   Representation of Stacks by Lists . . . . . . . . . . . . . 153
  6.6   Queues and Deques . . . . . . . . . . . . . . . . . . . . . . . . . . 154
        6.6.1   Synopsis . . . . . . . . . . . . . . . . . . . . . . . . . . . . 154
        6.6.2   Types and Operations . . . . . . . . . . . . . . . . . . . . 154
        6.6.3   Implementation Overview . . . . . . . . . . . . . . . . . . . . 155
        6.6.4   Specific Variants . . . . . . . . . . . . . . . . . . . . . . . . 155
        6.6.5   General Variants . . . . . . . . . . . . . . . . . . . . . . . . 155
        6.6.6   Combination of Variants . . . . . . . . . . . . . . . . . . . 156
        6.6.7   Representation Specific Variants . . . . . . . . . . . . . . 156
        6.6.8   Representation of Queues and Deques by Lists . . . . . . . . 157
  6.7   Trees, Linked Trees, Tabular Trees . . . . . . . . . . . . . . . . 158
        6.7.1   Synopsis . . . . . . . . . . . . . . . . . . . . . . . . . . . . 158
        6.7.2   Types and Operations . . . . . . . . . . . . . . . . . . . . 159
        6.7.3   Implementation Overview . . . . . . . . . . . . . . . . . . . . 167
        6.7.4   Specific Generic Parameters . . . . . . . . . . . . . . . . . 168
        6.7.5   Tree Specific Variants . . . . . . . . . . . . . . . . . . . . 168
        6.7.6   General Variants of Trees . . . . . . . . . . . . . . . . . . 169
        6.7.7   Combination of Tree Variants . . . . . . . . . . . . . . . . 169
        6.7.8   Linked Tree Specific Variants . . . . . . . . . . . . . . . . 169
        6.7.9   General Variants of Linked Trees . . . . . . . . . . . . . . 171
        6.7.10  Combination of Linked Tree Variants . . . . . . . . . . . . 171
        6.7.11  Representation of Linked Trees by Linked Collections . . . . . 172
        6.7.12  Tabular Tree Specific Variants . . . . . . . . . . . . . . . 173
        6.7.13  General Variants of Tabular Trees . . . . . . . . . . . . . . 174
        6.7.14  Representation of Tabular Trees by Tabular Collections . . . . 174
  6.8   Orders . . . . . . . . . . . . . . . . . . . . . . . . . . . . . . . . . 176
        6.8.1   Synopsis . . . . . . . . . . . . . . . . . . . . . . . . . . . . 176
        6.8.2   Types and Operations . . . . . . . . . . . . . . . . . . . . 177
        6.8.3   Implementation Overview . . . . . . . . . . . . . . . . . . . . 178
        6.8.4   Specific Generic Parameters . . . . . . . . . . . . . . . . . 178
        6.8.5   Specific Variants . . . . . . . . . . . . . . . . . . . . . . . . 179
        6.8.6   General Variants . . . . . . . . . . . . . . . . . . . . . . . . 179
        6.8.7   Combination of Variants . . . . . . . . . . . . . . . . . . . 180
        6.8.8   Representation Specific Variants . . . . . . . . . . . . . . 180
        6.8.9   Representation of Orders by Lists and Trees . . . . . . . . 183
  6.9   Sets and Maps . . . . . . . . . . . . . . . . . . . . . . . . . . . . 185
        6.9.1   Synopsis . . . . . . . . . . . . . . . . . . . . . . . . . . . . 185

| | | | |
|---|---|---|---|
| | 6.9.2 | Types and Operations | 185 |
| | 6.9.3 | Implementation Overview | 187 |
| | 6.9.4 | Specific Generic Parameters | 188 |
| | 6.9.5 | Specific Variants | 188 |
| | 6.9.6 | General Variants | 188 |
| | 6.9.7 | Combination of Variants | 189 |
| | 6.9.8 | Representation Specific Variants | 189 |
| | 6.9.9 | Representation of Sets and Maps | 193 |
| 6.10 | Bags | | 194 |
| | 6.10.1 | Synopsis | 194 |
| | 6.10.2 | Types and Operations | 194 |
| | 6.10.3 | Implementation Overview | 195 |
| | 6.10.4 | Specific Generic Parameters | 196 |
| | 6.10.5 | Specific Variants | 196 |
| | 6.10.6 | General Variants | 197 |
| | 6.10.7 | Combination of Variants | 197 |
| | 6.10.8 | Representation Specific Variants | 197 |
| | 6.10.9 | Representation of Bags | 198 |

**7 Technical Issues** — **199**

| | | | |
|---|---|---|---|
| 7.1 | Selection of Building Block Variants | | 199 |
| 7.2 | Ada Design Decisions | | 200 |
| | 7.2.1 | Dispersion of Structures Objects | 202 |
| | 7.2.2 | Composition of Data Types | 204 |
| | 7.2.3 | Storage Management | 205 |
| 7.3 | Deficiencies and Open Problems | | 206 |

**8 Case Study: A File Compression System** — **209**

| | | | |
|---|---|---|---|
| 8.1 | The Overall Task | | 209 |
| 8.2 | Search for Reusable Building Blocks (Phase 1) | | 210 |
| 8.3 | Functional Decomposition (Phase 1) | | 210 |
| 8.4 | Modular Decomposition | | 211 |
| | 8.4.1 | Words, Codes and Items | 212 |
| | 8.4.2 | The Word-Frequency Collection | 214 |
| | 8.4.3 | The Word-Code Map | 215 |
| | 8.4.4 | The Code-Word Map | 216 |
| 8.5 | Search for Reusable Building Blocks (Phase 2) | | 217 |
| | 8.5.1 | Words, Codes and Items | 219 |
| | 8.5.2 | The Word-Frequency Collection | 219 |
| | 8.5.3 | The Word-Code Map | 223 |
| | 8.5.4 | Decompression | 224 |

**Bibliography** 227

**A  Appendix:  Ada Specifications** 229
  A.1  Building Block Utilities . . . . . . . . . . . . . . . . . . . . . 229
  A.2  Generic Parameters . . . . . . . . . . . . . . . . . . . . . . . 232
  A.3  Linked Collections . . . . . . . . . . . . . . . . . . . . . . . . 234
  A.4  Tabular Collections . . . . . . . . . . . . . . . . . . . . . . . 236
  A.5  Hash Tables . . . . . . . . . . . . . . . . . . . . . . . . . . . 238
  A.6  Lists . . . . . . . . . . . . . . . . . . . . . . . . . . . . . . . . 243
  A.7  Stacks . . . . . . . . . . . . . . . . . . . . . . . . . . . . . . . 259
  A.8  Queues and Deques . . . . . . . . . . . . . . . . . . . . . . . 271
  A.9  Trees . . . . . . . . . . . . . . . . . . . . . . . . . . . . . . . 282
  A.10 Orders . . . . . . . . . . . . . . . . . . . . . . . . . . . . . . 294
  A.11 Key-Info Orders . . . . . . . . . . . . . . . . . . . . . . . . . 304
  A.12 Sets . . . . . . . . . . . . . . . . . . . . . . . . . . . . . . . . 318
  A.13 Maps . . . . . . . . . . . . . . . . . . . . . . . . . . . . . . . 326
  A.14 Bags . . . . . . . . . . . . . . . . . . . . . . . . . . . . . . . 338

# Chapter 1

# Introduction

Reusability is one of the most promising issues in today's arena of software engineering. Some people expect it to put an end to the "software crisis"; others, however, consider it a technique that has been practiced since the beginning of software development and do not expect dramatic impacts. We believe and have experienced ourselves that reuse in the area on which we will focus here, can significantly decrease the cost of software development and maintenance and can improve essential system properties, like modularity and reliability.

Reuse comes in many different flavors. Biggerstaff describes the following framework for reusability technologies in [3]:

| Features | Approaches to Reusability | | | | |
|---|---|---|---|---|---|
| Component Reused | Building Blocks | | Patterns | | |
| Nature of Component | Atomic and Immutable Passive | | Diffuse and Malleable Active | | |
| Principle of Reuse | Composition | | Generation | | |
| Emphasis | Application Component Libraries | Organization & Composition Principles | Language Based Generators | Application Generators | Trans- formation Systems |
| Typical Systems | Libraries of Subroutines | Obj. Oriented, Pipe Archs | VHLLs POLs | CRT Fmtrs File Mgmt | Language Transf. |

Our focus is on a rather specific and narrow class of reusable components, namely on basic abstract data types, like lists, stacks, trees or sets. On the first glance this falls into the left-hand side categories of Biggerstaff's classification. However, the work also touches some aspects from the right-hand side as we will soon explain.

Our work was triggered from experience which the second author made with IBM where, in systems programming projects, abstract data types formed a considerable part of the components reused [12]. Therefore, he initiated a project that produced a catalogue of abstract data types [8]. This is, to our knowledge, the first published collection – though only internal to IBM – of reusable abstract data types. As such, it had some deficiencies which were the reason and gave the motivation to start this work.

The main objective of our work is to present a practically useful library of efficient components that include the major data structures, which are known and used across different areas, in particular, in systems programming. The sub-objectives and goals that we derived from these objectives will be discussed in chapter 2.

The components are specified and implemented in Ada and can thus be used for realistic applications.

The research on organization and composition principles was not one of our primary objectives. Nevertheless, we had to do some considerable work in this field during the search for an appropriate structure of the library. Our focus was on defining an orthogonal structure that should ease the search, the use and the exchange of components.

Let us summarize here the main features, which distinguish our catalogue of abstract data types from existing work:

- A clear and strict separation between functional aspects and implementation or performance oriented aspects:
  - The functional behavior is defined by around ten abstract data types, which have a standardized interface across all data types.
  - Every abstract data type has in the order of thousand different implementations to be accessed by one uniform interface.

    There are general variations of reusable components with respect to space bounds or potential concurrency, as Booch describes them in [4], which we have defined in a similar way (though we have lesser subclasses and are not interested in concurrency in this book). In addition, the objective of efficiency leads to a large amount of abstract data type specific implementation variations.

We call both of them variants, which are considered as points in a library space that is spanned by (mainly orthogonal) basic properties.

According to modern software engineering principles, an abstract data type and its implementation should be determined stepwise. First, the problem "specification" should be stated thus abstracting from the efficiency related properties ("implementation details"). With our catalogue, the abstract data type is to be selected only on the base of this specification.

In terms of this specification one has to reason about the implementation properties, which results in the selection of the variants.

Under this viewpoint the nature of the building blocks as a whole is no longer atomic and immutable (as Biggerstaff puts it in his framework), but becomes similar to a transformational approach. This transformational approach has also been suggested for the use in very high level languages (VHLL), in particular in the area of high level data types. By making the implementation properties of the variants in our catalogue explicit, we hope to contribute to the areas of VHLLs and program transformation paradigms.

- The definition of an (implementation) hierarchy of abstract data types that allows,

  - from the user viewpoint, to select the most general abstract data type suitable for the application. At the same time, it is guaranteed that one can select among all implementation variants that might be available with a less general abstract data type.
  - from the implementor's and maintainer's viewpoint, to implement every data representation and access algorithm only once, but have it available for every suitable abstract data type ("reuse within reuse").

With these features, we are able to meet general requirements to a catalogue of abstract data types, which are derived from the reuse paradigm presented in section 3.3.

How is our attempt related to other areas of reuse? It seems that the reuse of data types is at the lower end of the scale of reusable software, with regard to the size of a single component. Therefore, it may be hard to apply our experience to other, higher level areas of reuse. On the other hand, such higher level components might reuse the lower level ones and we have to consider the impact of reusing the low level components on reusability on the higher level.

The gain from a library of reusable components is equal to the product from the gain of a single reused component and the frequency of actual uses. For the class of basic data types the gain from reusing a single component is small, compared to the gain of reusing more complete, application oriented solutions. However, these data types are so frequently used that the overall gain is expected to become substantial.

This book is divided into two parts. The first part (chapters 2 - 4) discusses the motivation, suggest a general strategy for reusing abstract data types and gives a language independent introduction to the structure and functionality of our library. The second part is devoted to the realization of these ideas in Ada. It discusses the essential means provided by Ada and the specific design decisions that were based on the language. An extended example shows the use of the catalogue and finally we present the complete specifications of the library components.

# Chapter 2

# Motivation and Objectives

Data types are being developed in two different forms: as "data structures and algorithms" that are – more or less precisely – described on paper, and as library modules for an immediate application within a programming language. The first form we will call "theoretical", the second one "practical". [9], [10], [1], [13], [6], and [16] are only a few of numerous books that represent the theoretical form. Some of these publications present the algorithms in some programming language, thus showing a strong tendency towards the practical form. However, many of the algorithms cannot immediately be used, because they do not provide an appropriate modularization and interface. [4], [8], [11], and [14] are recent examples of the practical form. The idea of data type libraries, however, is already found in common programming languages, like Common Lisp [15], SETL [7], or even C (with the Unix library functions) [2].

Both forms have their strengths and their weaknesses. The theoretical forms mostly provide an in-depth discussion of all kinds of implementation variants. So they can offer data structures and algorithms that serve high efficiency requirements. On the other hand, finding the right data structure for a given problem is not always simple. There is little methodology for this retrieval procedure. Beside this difficulty, the choice for a data structure must be made before the coding phase. A replacement of one data structure by another is often impossible because the functional interfaces of different data structures do not match.

The practical forms make the selection easier. However, mostly they do not provide a rich selection of different representations and implementations, and thereby cost possibly considerable efficiency. Even for many practical libraries, a replacement of modules during the coding phase is impossible due to the interface deficiencies mentioned before.

The motivation for the work that is presented in this book was to bridge the gap between theory and practice, bringing together the two advantages of

- ease of retrieval and use, and
- high efficiency.

Both goals must be reached to make reuse actually happen. In particular, the lack of efficiency is often a killer argument against reuse (even if it is only pretended in order to cover the not-invented-here syndrome).

In order to achieve the major goals, we focussed on the following objectives:

- simplicity of the library structure,
- functional completeness, and
- completeness of implementation variants.

Simplicity of the library structure will allow a manageable retrieval process; functional completeness will ease the use and implementation completeness is the key to efficiency. Besides these primary objectives, that are directed towards the user of our library, maintainability of the library itself turned out as a non-trivial necessity.

Let us discuss in detail what these objectives mean, and what we have done to meet them.

## 2.1   Simplicity of the Library Structure

To obtain a clear library structure, we have separated the functional issues from the performance issues. We provide a relatively *small number of abstract data types* (around ten) each of which is defined only by its functional interface. There is one so-called building block to implement each abstract data type.

Thus, a user of our library has to base his or her first selection only on the functional requirements of the application. As a consequence, the selection should be fairly simple, which is – in addition – supported by the fact that the number of abstract data types is quite small.

Completeness of implementation variants requires a very large number of variants of each building block, which is in a magnitude of several thousands. These variants embody different implementations of data structures or algorithms.

Let us emphasize that the interface of an abstract data type is the same, i.e. uniform, for all variants. This means that the same set of operations is applicable to all variants, and that the syntax and semantics of all operations is identical for all variants.

In order to manage the selection between such a large number of variants of a building, we have defined standard properties that apply to all building blocks (described in section 5.5). Besides the standard properties, there are abstract data type specific properties (described in chapter 6). For all of these properties, we have defined an orthogonal scheme with mostly binary or ternary properties (wrapped vs. non-wrapped, diluted vs. non-diluted, pointered vs. non-pointered, precondition-check vs. constraint-check vs. no-check, etc.) to make the search only logarithmic in the number of components in the library.

In general, we see that a long term standard that is taught to software engineers and slowly becomes common knowledge could enable the user to think in terms of such a library and, in particular, in terms of standard properties.

*Uniformity of the interface* is not only achieved for the different variants of one building block but also across building blocks. This means that the same set of operations is applicable to all abstract data types or to a large subclass of them.

This uniformity was a result of the attempt to identify the basic functional concepts that are common to all abstract data types of our catalogue, or to a large subclass of them. For example, there is a class of abstract data types for which the position at which an element is inserted is relevant and can be chosen freely. For this class, there is an insert operation that takes the element to be inserted and the insert position. Lists and trees both belong to this class and thus have an identical interface for the insert operation; they only differ in the way, the insert position is characterized.

A second aspect of the uniformity of interfaces is if only a single semantics – either share or copy semantics – is used across all data types. For some of the data types, as for example trees, the share semantics may seem more natural, and for large, dispersed elements of a data type (which may be abstract data types themselves) it is usually much more efficient. For other data types , as for example stacks, the copy semantics may seem more natural, and it is more efficient for compact small elements (as for example, integer values) which are used very frequently. Other catalogues, for example [4], do mix both semantics. Our solution is to use only one semantics, namely the copy semantics, but to provide (uniform) operations that allow to move elements without copying them (compare section 5.1).

A uniform interface provides both ease of learning and ease of use, and it supports the interchangeability of building blocks. In particular, the set of different operations for all the different building blocks becomes smaller and the user does not have to care about the existence of certain operations when making his choice, since either all or none of the eligible building blocks provide the operation. Uniformity may increases the size of the interface of a single building block. However, this appears only as a technical problem because the user should know about all the operations of all the different building blocks, anyway. This total number is even decreased by the uniformity.

Besides these structural considerations, modern software engineering principles, like modularization, information hiding and strong typing, must be applied to achieve clarity and ease of use. A formal specification of the provided modules would certainly improve the usability, however, it is beyond the scope of this book.

# 2.2   Functional Completeness

Functional completeness means that all functions that could be useful for a user of a data type are available from the reused building block. It is not sufficient to provide a minimal orthogonal set of operations, as it might be used for specification purposes.

The **FIND_OR_INSERT** operation is a typical example. Though it is useful in many applications (see, for example, chapter 3) it could be composed from a **FIND** operation and an **INSERT** operation. However, this would cause a major inefficiency in may cases, since each of these operations searches though a given data structure. Having to search a data structure twice instead of once could be a severe argument agains reuse in practical applications. Introducing the **FIND_OR_INSERT** operation, which searches the data structure once, copes with this problem.

As another kind of example, consider the basic list traversal operations. It is theoretically sufficient to provide a FIRST and a NEXT operation, because they allow to access all elements in the list. In particular, they allow the access to the last element of the list or to the element that is previous to a given one. However, not providing the LAST and PREVIOUS operations would be unacceptable from an ease of use point of view. Furthermore, in the case of a doubly linked, double anchor representation of a list, it would sacrifice efficiency. LAST and PREVIOUS are implemented with constant time, whereas the iteration using FIRST and NEXT to get the last or previous element takes linear time.

Functional completeness is closely related to the desire of including *different implementation variants* into a single building block, and to the *uniformity of interfaces*. They all lead to the situation that functions are provided for an abstract data type that may not be specific or typical for it.

An often heard argument says that reuse and *information hiding* are contradicting goals. As a typical example the following situation is constructed: "Assume you have an available stack module with the common operations EMPTY, PUSH, POP, TOP and IS_EMPTY. You want to reuse this module to implement a real-world stack, let's say a pile of documents on your desk. After having done so, you want to implement a function that inspects the pile for whether it contains a certain document. You can only do so by using a second stack, popping all documents from the given stack to the new stack, thereby inspecting them and finally transferring the elements back to the original stack." The argument is now as follows: "If you had the stack implementation available, which is of course a linked list or an array, you could easily inspect all the elements without bothering with the auxiliary stack and the obvious loss of efficiency."

Our answer to this argument is that, instead of giving up information hiding, the problem can also be avoided by functional completeness. Our stack module provides all sensible operations (that we could think of) that are applicable to a stack. In particular, it provides an iteration operation that allows inspection of all elements.

It is difficult to determine which degree of functional completeness we have reached with respect to ease of use. It is hard to guess what some future applications might look for. The degree of functional completeness, with respect to efficiency, is easier to determine.

Here, functional completeness means that the structural specialities of all implementation variants are accessible, though on a logical, implementation independent level. The NEXT, PREVIOUS operations, given as an example, follow this rule with respect to doubly linked lists.

Another example is the linearly or circularly linked representation of lists. For a
linear representation, the last element has a null pointer, whereas for a circular representation, it points back to the first element. Independent of the implementation
choice, our catalogue provides two kinds of NEXT operations: one that yields null when
applied to the last element (the linear NEXT), and another one that yields the first
element (the circular NEXT). Functional completeness and uniformity of the interfaces
require that both operations are provided for each list variant.


# 2.3   Completeness of Implementation Variants


Completeness of implementation variants means that at least the common implementation techniques for data structures, as they are known from the literature, are
available for each abstract data type. We have included most of the techniques that
are used across all areas of systems programming and that are described in the literature.

Completeness of implementation variants is the key to *efficiency*. Take, for example,
a list of about 1.000 elements. Suppose that it is used by an application which needs
to count the elements in the list after about 10 insertions or deletions have been
done. Reuse of the abstract data type list, if there does not exist an implementation
variant that keeps a length counter for the list (thus performing the count operation
in constant time), would cost a considerable time performance overhead, compared
to an implementation that uses a length counter. This would be a valid (technical)
argument against reuse.

On the other hand, if a length counter would be kept in all list implementations
variants, the same argument would be applicable (time overhead to increment or
decrement the counter) for different applications, namely such ones that does not
require the count operation, or that use it very infrequently in comparison to insertions
and deletions. The consequence is that both implementation variants have to be
provided such that the appropriate one can be selected.

Note that an object oriented "reuse by inheritance", where the counter is added by
the user, would also be a costly undertaking, since the counter increment/decrement
takes place in several operations. Take, for example, the REMOVE_ALL operation,
which removes all occurrences of a given element value; this operation would have to
be completely rewritten in the counter variant.

The situation of reuse is comparable to that of very high level languages. The benefit of standardizing certain application patterns is commonly paid with the loss of immediate access to the lower level concepts. The set-oriented language SETL [7] is an example. It tries to solve this problem by providing the concept of representation specifications which allow the user to specify how a given data type shall be implemented.

The representation specification is made in the form of implementation variants for the building blocks of our library.

Our library provides a large number of variants, each with a specific *performance profile*. We have tried to achieve completeness with respect to the possible performance profiles. New performance profiles mostly originated from the attempt to make a certain operation or a class of operations more efficient. For example, making the PREVIOUS operation for lists more efficient results in the variant of doubly linked lists; making the COUNT operation more efficient results in the counted variant, and so on.

Certainly, a library cannot foresee all possible applications. There seems to be a good chance to cover most possible implementations of a single abstract data types. But this seems not to be true for combinations of data types.

There seem to be always be problem specific data structures that are more efficient than any combination of reusable components. A typical example is a compiler's definition table for a block structured language. In terms of our catalogue, this data type is a map from symbols to stacks of descriptors (where the top element describes the currently visible definition of the corresponding symbol) together with a stack of sets of symbols (where the top element describes the symbols defined within the current block). The typical implementation of this data type consists of a sophisticated mix of both, the map of stacks and the stack of sets, that cannot be achieved by systematically combining the data types from our catalogue. However, it would be possible to reuse our map and stack module and "encode" the set by hand, thus reaching the common definition table structure.

In practice it can often be observed that data structures are chosen which are far from the optimum just because they are easier to implement. And even if some time is spent on the design of a particularly well-suited data structure it is not guaranteed that this structure really achieves the optimal behavior. The reuse of existing components eliminates the ease-of-implementation argument. In addition, a systematic structure of the library may even help to systematically find the most appropriate solution.

## 2.4   Maintainability

From the above considerations we can expect to get quite a large number of different
variants for most abstract data types. A list, for example, may be based either on
linear or circular links of the elements, it may have either only single links to the next
element or double links to the next and the previous one, and it may have either a
single anchor or a double anchor pointing to its first and last element. With four
binary implementation alternatives, we get $2^4 = 16$ implementations, of which the
four implementations with both double anchor and circular links are not of interest,
since circular lists always point to the last element only.

In addition, there are standard variants like precondition-check, constraint-check, no
check, or object-bounded, collection-bounded, unbounded, etc., that are common to
practically all abstract data types of our catalogue. They will be discussed, in detail,
in chapter 5. Nearly all of these alternatives are *orthogonal*, so they can be combined
freely. As a result, there may be thousands of different variants for one abstract data
type.

Handling them as different program variants, by hand, is impossible. Use of tools like
"cpp" will ease the task. However, we have tried to alleviate this problem as much as
possible by a suitable internal structuring of the implementation of an abstract data
type.

Introducing *several layers of abstraction*, where each layer encapsulates implementation alternatives, is a well-known technique to reduce the number of variants. The
interface of a layer must be one and the same independent from the implementation
alternative that is actually selected. That is, the lower layer itself is to be considered
as an abstract data type that provides more low-level operations.

We have applied this technique where possible. As a result we were able to define
a hierarchy of abstract data types, and a corresponding hierarchy of building blocks
(for a description, see section 4.1),

- that allows us to select freely any meaningful combination of implementations
  for any abstract data type,

- though we have to provide each basic implementation only once in this hierarchy.

The application of this technique has shown great advantages. First, the development and maintenance effort is widely reduced. The number of different programs to be handled equals the sum of implementation alternatives in each layer, instead of the product of alternatives. Second, were able to get a clearer structure and a separation of concerns. Last but not least we practice reuse ourselves.

However, there was also a large number of cases where this technique could not be applied, since the implementation alternatives to be factored out depended on each other, as for example, the 16 implementation alternatives for a list as described above. A macro preprocessor was used in these cases. A building block implementation contains macros that depend on the selected variant. Thus, different code is generated for different variants by the macro preprocessor.

If we had to generate, for example for the list, 16 different pieces of code (one for each variant) for each list operation, we would not gain anything compared to providing 16 separate implementations. However, since the 16 variants are derived from four orthogonal properties, most list operations only distinguish two cases that are based on one property, such that the application of the macro technique provides a considerable advantage.

# Chapter 3

# How to Reuse Abstract Data Types

In this chapter, we will study how to reuse abstract data types. In particular, we demonstrate that it is very important to select abstract data types from the right level of abstraction (i.e. from one that is adequate to the problem to be solved) to gain all possible advantages from reuse.

An example is given to illustrate how reusable abstract data types are to be selected, and how our catalogue is intended to be used. We start, as a counter-example, with the conventional data structure oriented approach, where unencapsulated data structures are accessed directly. As a second counter-example, we show the problems that are caused when using abstract data types in the same way as data structures, that means when they are selected from a too low abstraction level. Finally, we demonstrate the selection from the right abstraction level, both in a top-down and a bottom-up approach.

We generalize this experience into a paradigm for the reuse of abstract data types, and derive from this paradigm

- two criteria for the selection of abstract data types
- two requirements for the structure of a catalogue of reusable abstract data types.

The reuse of abstract data types is a specific area in the reuse of software components. Some of the results obtained in this area may possibly not be applied in general to reuse in other contexts. However, we believe that our paradigm, and in particular its aspects of abstraction and standardization, are applicable in a wide range of the reuse spectrum.

In this chapter, we use a part of the text file compression system example from chapter 8. The part is the task of finding the n most often occurring words in a set of files, called "word frequency collection". One might look for a single reusable component that provides this function, if one has a corresponding application library of reusable components at hand. Let us assume that such a component does not exist in our reuse library, and that we have to develop it from our data type catalogue.

The word frequency collection is used to collect words from text files, and the frequencies with which a word occurs. When scanning through the text files, we want to add single words to this collection. Adding a word means: If the word is already in the collection, its frequency count is increased by one; otherwise, it is stored into the collection with a frequency count of one. When the scanning of the text files is finished we want to get the n (let's say 256) most often occurring words out of the collection, ordered according to their frequencies (the most frequent first).

Let us note that the number of words to be collected is not known in advance. It depends heavily on the number, the size, and the contents of the text files that are scanned. It also depends on the application area: programs and English texts have quite a different vocabulary. However, we can guess that it will be in the order of hundred to thousands of words.

# 3.1   Working With Data Structures – A Counter-Example

We start by looking for a data structure to accommodate the application requirements which we have described.

### 3.1.1 Selecting a Data Structure

With the data structures of classical programming languages in mind, the simplest structure to be used is an array of records, each consisting of a word and its frequency count. The array should be ordered on the words to make adding of a word fast. This allows us to use binary search to find out if a given word is already in the collection, and to return the index of the record. If the word is not yet there, the search returns the spot where a new record needs to be inserted into the array. However, inserting a new record into the array requires to shift all the records that come after it. Since there are a few hundred words to be shifted on an average, according to our estimate, this causes quite an overhead. Even when we notice that this overhead will not come about with every word that is added, but only with the words that are new to the collection, we should look for another data structure to avoid this overhead.

An ordered binary tree allows a fast logarithmic search, too. It avoids the shifting when a new word frequency record is to be inserted, at the cost of two additional pointers, to the sons in the tree, with each word-frequency record. This yields a space overhead in the order of thousand to ten thousand bytes, when we assume that each pointer requires four bytes. We can tolerate this space overhead, it is not a concern with the storage sizes of today.

A hash table allows even a faster search than tree and array. An argument against its use is the variable number of word-frequency records to be stored, since hashing requires a fixed hash table size. This argument is not really valid, as we will see later, but based on it, many software developers would, probably, exclude a hash table implementation from any further consideration, having the complexity of implementing a hashing method in the back of their minds.

Therefore, let us suppose that we select a binary tree as a data structure to represent the word-frequency collection.

### 3.1.2 Designing the Operations on the Data Structure

Now, we have to consider how to implement the operations, which our application requires, on the data structure of a binary tree.

First let us consider how to add a word. The algorithm for searching for a word is well-known (see, for example, [10]). It starts from the root and compares the given word to the word contained in the current node, whether it is equal, less or greater. When the words are equal, the search is successful and it delivers a node the frequency count of which is increased. When the word is not equal to the word in the node, one continues, if it is less, with the left son, else with the right son. The search is unsuccessfully terminated if there is no more son in the selected direction.

After an unsuccessful search, if the word is not yet in the tree, a new word-frequency record has to be inserted. How to do this? One could start from the root again and apply the algorithm to insert a new node into the tree, which is also well-known. However, this would mean to search the tree twice and, hence, would not be very efficient. To avoid this, one needs to keep track of the last node at which the search was terminated. The new node is to become left or right son of this node, depending on the result of the word comparison. The word, and a frequency count of one, are set in the new word-frequency record.

Similar considerations apply to the second operation, which is to get each word and its frequency out of the tree, ordered according to descending frequencies. The first step is to reorder the tree (which is ordered according to the word component of a node). We can use an algorithm to order binary trees that is available from the literature. The next step is to visit all nodes of the tree in descending order which is called an inorder traversal. An algorithm to do this is available, too.

To summarize our considerations from the design of the tree operations: The operations required are relatively simple, such that we can reuse existing tree algorithms. However, there are quite a number of detailed considerations involved in the algorithms, which we have to learn and understand. Further, there is a number of details which may cause errors during the implementation.

During the implementation, one will define the data types and structures for the tree and then reprogram the algorithms for them. Inline code or, better, procedures accessing the tree data structures will be developed, dispersed over the modules that include the operations on the word-frequency collection.

## 3.1.3   Conclusion

Let us sum up the way in which we have been proceeding: First, we made a selection among different data structures based on performance criteria. After a data structure was selected, we started thinking in terms of this data structure, the binary tree in our example, to understand and develop the required algorithms.

## 3.2     Reusing Abstract Data Types

Let us contrast the data structure oriented proceeding with the approach of reusing abstract data types.

Our catalogue provides ten primary (abstract) data types: lists and trees - both general, linked and tabular -, orders (that include lists and trees with sorted elements), sets, maps and bags. They will be introduced in detail in chapter 4.

What we need to know for the rest of this chapter is the following: lists and trees are structures for arbitrary insertion; the insert position is relevant and determined by the user with the insert operation. For orders, the order of the elements is relevant, but determined by the operation itself (no choice for the user). For sets, maps and bags the order is irrelevant. Elements of hash tables, orders and maps consist of two parts, a key and an info; for hash tables and orders, the info part is optional; the usual properties of the structures (like ordering) hold with respect to the key part.

When reusing data types, we do not concentrate upon the data structures, but on the operations that encapsulate these structures.

Two operations on the word-frequency collection are required in our application, adding a word, and getting a word-frequency pair back.

Adding a word can be split up into a combination of simpler, "more standard" operations, when a reusable data type does not offer this relatively complex operation: finding a word-frequency pair and incrementing its frequency count if the pair containing this word is already in the collection, and inserting a new pair if the pair is not yet in the collection.

Getting n pairs back ordered according to their frequency count can be split up – for the same reason – into getting all pairs back in a deliberate sequence, and selecting n pairs with the greatest frequency counts. In the sequel, we will consider if, and how well, the operations provided from different abstract data types do fit to the required ones.

Though an abstract data type is encapsulated, and we follow the principle of information hiding, we may have in mind a model of the encapsulated data structure for its visualization.

It seems beneficial to us, that one can visualize a structure. One can do this perfectly for structures like, for example, arrays and trees. Arrays are collections of adjacent cells (horizontally placed), each cell having a number (running from left to right) through which it can be directly accessed. Binary trees are collections of cells each having two son-cells, which are positioned left and right below the cell itself. Stacks are (almost) always visualized as piles of car tires.

Although these visualizations are overspecifications, that means, they express more than necessary for the behavior of the data type, they are useful because one immediately associates certain properties of the operations (have you ever tried to remove a car tire other than the top from a pile – or, even worse, to insert one?). The human brain can apparently automatically abstract from these details.

Unfortunately, not all properties of data types can be visualized as nicely as the given ones for arrays, trees and stacks. In particular, the absence of properties is often hard to grasp, for example the property of sets, not to be ordered, because visualizations of sets are likely to somehow place the elements and thereby imply some ordering.

Really "abstract" data types, as specified in an axiomatic way, may be helpful in certain areas of program development, but are not supporting our idea.

## 3.2.1   Selecting "Low Level" Abstract Data Types

As mentioned, we will proceed from "low level" abstract data types that encapsulate the data structures presented in section 3.1, because there is a good chance that somebody not experienced in the use of abstract data types might proceed in this way. As the conclusion of this section, we will show why this is not the right approach.

The data type list can be subdivided in the data types tabular list and linked list. The operations on all three data types are identical, except for one difference which is not of concern here. Let us discuss the list operations that might allow to implement the required operations on the word-frequency collection.

FIND allows the search for an element with a given value, MODIFY_ELEM allows the modification of a given element, and INSERT allows the insertion of a new element at a given position. These are the simple operations, which need to be combined to add a word. This causes a certain effort for the user, and, worse, a performance overhead since both FIND and INSERT search the list. This effort and overhead may be avoided with the FIND_OR_INSERT operation that comes very close to the one required. It returns the index of an element with a given value, if it is in the list, otherwise it inserts a new element with this value. What remains to be done is to modify (with MODIFY_ELEM) the frequency count if the element is in the list.

Unfortunately, both the FIND and the FIND_OR_INSERT operations work on the complete element. They do not allow to refer to the part of an element, as it is required to search for a given word. Therefore, we cannot use these operations, we have to use FIND_PROPERTY that allows to search for an element with an arbitrary property.

Another point to be considered is that a list is, a priori, not sorted. We need to sort it ourselves, which means we have to determine the position at which an element is to be inserted into the list. We cannot determine this position by using FIND_PROPERTY because this operation does not return a position if no element is found. For insertion of a new element, the position of the element next (with regard to the property) to the given new element is required. The operation ITERATE may be used to iterate through all elements until the given element or the element next to it is found, such that the given element can be inserted in the sorting sequence. However, using ITERATE does not exploit that the list is sorted since all elements are visited sequentially. A binary search operation is not offered by lists (since they are not sorted). We can implement a binary search using the position based operation GET_ELEM, that allows the access to the n-th element of a list. Obviously, this makes no sense for linked lists since these operations have a linear time performance there.

The operation ITERATE is used to implement the second operation on the word-frequency collection, to retrieve all pairs from the collection.

To summarize, all three data types list provide operations, but not very straightforward ones, to implement the word-frequency collection. The operations FIND and FIND_OR_INSERT cannot be used to search for a given word, since they allow only to search for complete elements. ITERATE, or GET_ELEM must be used instead of them together with INSERT.

Next, let us consider the data type tree, which can be subdivided in the data types tabular tree and linked tree. The operations on all three data types are very similar to the list operations. The main difference is that the position of an element to be inserted is in "hierarchical" tree terms, and not in "linear" list terms. Trees are, same as lists, not ordered.

As a consequence, the functional considerations are the same as for lists. Consequently, a tree can be used as well as a list (from a functional point of view) to implement the word-frequency collection. We need not repeat the functional considerations and study in detail the tree operations offered by the catalogue. This advantage is due to the consistent interface that the reusable data types of our catalogue have.

The next data type of interest is the order, which is a sorted (or ordered) collection of elements, in contrast to lists and trees that are not sorted. Note that we did not discuss a data structure in section 3.1 that is directly equivalent to the data type order. There are the data structures array and tree, for both of which an ordered and unordered organization exists.

A new element is inserted in an order automatically at its position with regard to the given order relation. Further, an order, called "key_info_order", allows one to split up an element into two parts, a key part and an info part, where only the key is relevant as the order criterion. Obviously, we use the key to store the word, and the info to store its frequency count. Both these properties of an order correspond well to requirements of our application.

This means that we use `FIND_OR_INSERT` to search for an element with a given word as the key (setting the info to one). The element is automatically inserted according to the order when the word is new. Otherwise, the index to the found element is returned, and we use `MODIFY_ELEM` to increment its info part. When all word-frequency pairs are collected, `ITERATE` is used as described for lists and trees to retrieve them.

As a conclusion, the data type order provides operations that are much more suitable to the solution of our application problem than lists and trees.

A precondition for its selection is that there is an order relation defined on the key part of the element. This is true for the type word of our application. Another implication of selecting an order is that an ordered tree or an ordered list implementation is used to store the collection. The performance considerations of section 3.1.1 show that this is not necessarily the best choice, since the use of a hashing method might provide a better performance.

The data type hash table is provided only as an auxiliary data type in our catalogue, that means it is provided rather for the implementors of the catalogue – to implement other data types on top of it – and not for its users, for reasons that will be explained in the next section, and in section 4.1.

A hash table provides, similarly to an order,

- the key-info structure of its elements
- the position at which an element is inserted to be determined by its key
- the operations `FIND_OR_INSERT`, `MODIFY_INFO`, and `ITERATE` to be used in the same way.

Therefore, it would be suited as well as an order to implement the word-frequency collection, based on the condition that a suitable hash function on the key can be defined, which is true for words.

Let us summarize the results, and analyze the way in which we proceeded in this section and in section 3.1. We picked a data structure, namely an array, or, respectively, an abstract data type with similar features, a (tabular) list. We modeled our problem in terms of this structure and reasoned about the operations. We found a problem with this structure (resulting from unacceptable inefficiency or operations not fitting well to the requirements) and switched to another structure or abstract data type, a tree, repeating the process. Then we switched to a hash table, repeating the process another time, not to forget the order, which we considered also in this section.

Intuitively, there seems to be something wrong with this approach; but what is it? It is not the case, that the structures (arrays and trees) are no abstract data types. In fact they are abstract data types (or can at least be described in an abstract manner) like any other abstract data type.

So if the kind of abstraction is right, what is wrong? It is the level of abstraction! The chosen data types have properties that are irrelevant for the specification of our problem and its solution (at least in the first design step). In other words, our selection was too much implementation oriented and not abstract enough. This is the reason why we had to switch between data types rather arbitrarily and with little direction and guidance. The next section will show that a selection among the higher level, more "problem oriented" data types like set, map, and bag removes this problem.

## 3.2.2  Selecting the "Right" Abstract Data Types

Starting with the right level of abstraction just determines the properties that are relevant for the current step. In most cases, this leaves many choices for the (more concrete) ultimate representation. These choices have, of course, to be made even if they are postponed. However, they will be made in terms of properties which determine (only) the performance of the given operations, but not the functional behavior.

Let us examine this at our example. The word-frequency collection associates word counts to words. Thus we may consider it as a mapping from words to word counts, and use the data type map to represent it.

A map has elements consisting of a key part an an info part. Similarly to an order, the operations FIND_OR_INSERT, INSERT, MODIFY_INFO and ITERATE are used to implement the operations on the word frequency collection.

Thus, we have found and selected a data type that is on a more abstract level than an order and, even more, than a list, a tree and a hash table, which we have considered.

A map is on a more abstract level than these data types since it is left open how a map is represented. We will see in the chapters 4 and 6 that a map can be represented either by an order, by a hash table or by an (unordered) list or tree. From a functional viewpoint, all these different representations of a map are identical (that means they support the same operations with the same semantics). What is different, is the performance of the operations. With the selection of a map, we postpone this performance oriented decision, and keep us the freedom of this choice up to a later stage in the development cycle.

Are there other of the more abstract data types that seem suitable to implement the word-frequency collection? Neither the data types set or bag seem to be useful to represent it, at a first glance, since both of them do not have elements split in pairs. Let us terminate our considerations, for the moment, with this argument (though we will take them up again in the next section). Our conclusion is that a map is the right data type to represent a word-frequency collection.

To find the right level of abstraction one must have some knowledge

- of the available abstraction levels
- of the data types (or structures) on each level
- and of their relevant properties.

We consider it as one of the major benefits from a catalogue of reusable data types, which comes as a side effect if the catalogue is structured appropriately, to provide a standard framework in which the designer or the programmer can think in order to find what he seeks.

There is usually a large amount of properties which, unfortunately, cannot all be structured in a hierarchical or orthogonal manner. For example, the properties of being ordered and of containing each element at most once, are not combined, in our catalogue, in a single data type. They are rather the combination of two data types, namely of orders and of sets. It therefore takes some experience to find out which data type (combination) is the right one to start with, allowing a directed procedure to find an efficient realization. Since no catalogue of reusable data types can represent the cartesian product of all possible properties, the chosen starting point is, in most cases, a slight overspecification.

### 3.2.3   An Abstract Specification and Solution

Now let us reconsider the problems associated with finding the right abstraction level, selecting a different approach, namely to start from a more abstract specification of our application: its input is a set of files, each consisting of (linear) list of words. The output is a list of n word-frequency pairs, ordered by decreasing frequency.

Note that for the description of our application, we might want to abstract from the fact that the words are ordered within the files, and that they are split into files. On the most abstract level, all the input files together could be considered as a so-called "bag" of words. (Bags are similar to sets in that there is no order of the elements defined; in contrast to sets, however, an element can occur more than once in a bag.)

Although this structure is conceptually simpler than the set of lists, we have to stay with the "set-of-list-view", because this is the actual representation of our input, and we need it (at least the list view) in order to reason about the performance characteristics of our solution.

With these structures in mind, a first abstract solution to our problem can be formulated as follows: find out for each word, occurring in the input, how often it appears; then find the 256 most often occurring words and deliver them ordered by their frequency.

A straightforward procedure is given by this problem formulation: the problem is solved in two phases where the first phase (frequency count) produces some data structure that represents the word frequencies and that is consumed by the second phase (selecting the most often occurring words). The second phase produces a data structure that represents the most often occurring words ordered according to their frequencies. What are the properties of the data structures produced by each phase?

The first structure has two major properties, where the first one is mainly determined by the problem statement and the second one is mainly determined by the processing: The first structure must

- associate to each word the number of its occurrences within the input, and
- represent the occurring words as a set rather than a list with multiple occurrences, since for finding the most often occurring words, we want to inspect each word at most once.

Both properties are fulfilled by exactly one data type in out catalogue: a map. A map associates to each key (i.e. word) an info (i.e. frequency) representing each key at most once.

The second structure must represent the words ordered according to their frequencies. This is a typical (key-info) order with the frequency as key and the word as info.

The procedures for constructing the data structures are simple: The first phase iterates over all words in the input; if the current word is already in the map, its associated frequency count is incremented by one, otherwise it is inserted with the frequency count one. The second phase iterates over all word-frequency pairs in the map and inserts them into the order, with the frequency (i.e. map-info) as key and the word (i.e. map-key) as info.

We hope that the difference to our original approach has become clear. Arrays and trees overspecify the solution in a way which does not help to visualize it. These structures even complicate the modeling and preclude decisions which are left open with the more abstract approach.

We have also seen, that the abstract data type choice is not only influenced by the problem statement but that certain (high level) algorithmic considerations are already taken into account. The finer the distinction between data types, the more complicated is the search for the right abstraction. Suppose we had an extra data type for "priority queues" that supports a particularly efficient removal of the least element, but no removal of any other element (and therefore would be different from the data type "order"). With the following considerations, this would have to be the data type of our choice: Since only the 256 most frequently occurring words are sought, the order structure can be bounded to 256 elements. Therefore, before a new frequency-word pair is inserted, it is checked whether the order is full and, in case the frequency to be inserted is greater than the least frequency in a full order, this least frequency-word pair is deleted. We see that the choice between an order and a priority queue (if it were present in our catalogue) would require a deeper algorithmic insight into the phases. This was one of the reasons why we omitted the priority queue as an extra data type, but rather provide representations of ordered structures that have the performance characteristics of priority queues.

## 3.2.4   Selection of an Abstract Data Type Variant

Let us now look at the possible representation and implementation alternatives, called variants, for maps and orders in order to determine those with the optimum behavior.

We do not know exactly yet, how words will be represented. We know that words have no discrete type (in Ada terms), but there is a straightforward ordering (i.e. lexicographical) on words, and there exist suitable hash functions.

This leaves two implementation alternatives of interest for the abstract data type map (compare section 6.9.3), the tree-ordered map, and the hashed map. All other alternatives are excluded for the following reasons: Words being not discrete excludes the array representation of maps (where the key component of a map is used as an array index, and the info component as the corresponding array value). (Ordered) tabular and linked list implementations are excluded due to linear complexity for insertion, (unordered) tabular and linked list implementations are excluded due to linear complexity for searching.

Let us first have a look on the implementation choices for the tree-ordered map (compare section 6.9.8.2). For a (binary search) tree, there is one major implementation choice between plain (unbalanced) trees and AVL-trees.

The unbalanced tree may degenerate to a worst case insert performance of O(n). This is avoided with the AVL-tree that always provides an access performance of O(log n), at an additional (constant factor) cost for insertions and deletions to balance the tree, if required. Although the big-O-calculus determines a definite winner (namely AVL

with O(log n) over unbalanced with O(n)) this is only a worst case analysis which is
not reasonable in many practical cases.

A more detailed reasoning depends on two characteristics of the sample texts. First,
how are the words placed in the sample text? The more they are ordered (according to
the order with which the tree is organized), the less balanced the plain tree becomes.
We assume that there is no implicit ordering on the sample files, so the plain tree
should be almost balanced. The second question is now, how many different words
occur in the sample texts? If the quotient of the number of actual insertions and the
number of searches is small (that means a high average word frequency) the additional
cost of the AVL-balancing becomes less important.

These factors are hard to guess or to determine analytically. It seems most appropriate
to simply try both solutions and see which one works best. In any case the estimated
time complexity for inserting all the O(n) words from the sample (with a cost of O(log
n) for each insertion) is O(n * log n). The space complexity is O(n).

The selection between a **linked** and a **tabular** variant is, fairly obviously, that of the
**linked** tree variant, due to the many insertions of word-frequency pairs. Since the
tree is searched with every **FIND_OR_INSERT** operation from the root (and there are
no operations going from a son to the parent), the **single_link** variant is selected.

From the general variants (see section 6.9.6), the following one are selected:

- **variable_elements**, since the words in the word-frequency pairs have variable
  length.

- **unbounded**, such that the map may become as large as necessary and possible

- **no_counter**, since the number of elements in the map is not of interest

- **precondition_check** in the test phase, and **no_check** when the program is in
  production.

The implementation alternatives for a hash table solution are considered in a similar
way (compare section 6.9.8.3). The worst case insertion complexity for hash tables is
O(n). The average complexity depends on the quotient of the the hash table size and
the actual number of different words and on the distribution of the hash function. For
a sufficient size quotient and equal-distribution hash function the average insertion
complexity is O(1).

The primary selection is between open-addressing implementations, which have a fixed maximal number of elements, and hash-chaining implementations, which allow for a dynamic number of elements. The latter might seem suitable for our application, since we do not know the number of words in advance. However, if the collision lists become too long (compare section 6.3.5, also for the following considerations), the search performance of hash-chaining implementations degenerates to $O(1)$.

This means that both for open-addressing and for hash-chaining, we need an estimate of the number of different words in the text files. Counting the words in the files, before we proceed, is no help since it yields the number of all words. This is a very rough upper boundary for the number of different words. For open-addressing, the estimate must be larger than the actual number. For hash-chaining, it can be smaller, even by a factor five to ten, without serious performance degradations.

Since we do not have a good estimate of the number of hash table elements, we select the `hash_chaining` variant, setting the number of elements equal to the expected number of different words.

The only remaining variant parameters still to be selected are the general variants. We select the same general variants as for the tree implementation, for the same reasoning as there.

Summarizing, the complexity for the hash solution (with a cost of $O(1)$ for each insertion of a word for n words) will be $O(n)$, for time as well as for space. This makes it superior to the tree solution.

## 3.3  Reuse Paradigm

Let us reconsider the steps we made working at our example in the last section, and our way of proceeding. The objective is to generalize our approach, and to develop a paradigm for reusing abstract data types.

The proceeding explained in section 3.2 (without section 3.2.3) follows a top-down approach that is also viable for a not very experienced developer. It is structured into the six following steps. An experienced developer may combine the steps one to four of our paradigm into one single step, as illustrated in section 3.2.3. This is a kind of bottom-up approach.

## 1. Identifying an application object as reuse candidate

The starting point is that the usual top-down design has identified an application object, consisting of a collection of data items, which is a candidate for implementation by reuse of an abstract data type. In our example, the word-frequency collection was the reuse candidate.

## 2. Determining the application operations on the object

The second step is to determine the operations that are performed by the application on the collection of data items. The result of the second step is a list of operations, including a knowledge of the input and output parameters, and of the intended semantics of each operation.

Let us emphasize that the operations are not to be considered from a data structure oriented point of view. Rather, one should take an application oriented viewpoint and consider which operations are required by the application. This means that we consider the data item collection as an object, and ask ourselves which transformations need to be performed on this object, and which information is to be got from it in our application. Therefore, this could be called – with Booch [4] – an object-oriented point of view.

For the word-frequency collection, two operations were required from our application:

- adding a word, and
- retrieving each word and its related frequency.

## 3. Abstraction from the application specifics of the operations

To be able to find generally reusable building blocks, we need to abstract first from the application specifics of the operations. These include application specific types of the data items. However, in some cases, this abstraction may not (or only partially) be required. A reuse library for a specific application domain might contain building blocks with element types that fit to a given application from this area.

In our example, the data types word and word count are application specific. They are to be considered as two separate data items since the operation of adding a word does treat them differently. We would consider the pair as only one data item if all operations would use the whole pair as a parameter.

If the operations on the application objects are application specific also in other regards, we need to abstract from these specifics. For example, if the application operations are quite complex, they might need to be split into a sequence of simpler operations. The reason is that the chances might be not good to find an abstract data type that provides a complex application specific operation.

Let us take the operation to add a word, and count its frequency as an example. It might often occur in statistical text-processing applications, so there are good chances we might find it in a reusable library from this area.

Otherwise, the following abstraction is to be done: The part of the operation that increments the word count, when the word is in the collection, is application specific. Abstracting from this specifics means to have a data item that is associated to a key (i.e. the word), and to modify this data item when the key is found. The other part of the operation is also application specific in inserting the key and the specific value one, when the key is not found. Abstracting from this means that the key is to be inserted together with a given value.

There are good chances we might find this abstracted operation in a statistical library. We will probably not find it in a catalog of general abstract data types. So we need to split it into simpler operations. There are three simple operations into which we split this complex operation, searching a pair, modifying its second component, and inserting a pair. However, we have seen that our catalogue provides an operation that combines finding and inserting.

## 4. Selection of an abstract data type with matching operations

Now, we can search for an abstract data type that provides exactly the operations, or operations similar to those that we have identified. Let us note that we do not yet consider implementation issues at this stage.

Note:

As mentioned already, steps one to four may be combined from an experienced developer, if the application problem is not very complex, into one single bottom-up step. This step proceeds in the following way:

Instead of defining an application object, the developer selects an abstract data type, which might fulfill, from his knowledge and experience, the application requirements. Then he or she analyses, how well the data type operations can be used to implement the application operations (instead of defining the application operations explicitly).

The whole is an iterative process, which might have to be repeated until a matching data type is found. If several matching ones are found, the same considerations apply as in the top-down approach, which are given in the following.

If we find only one abstract data type with matching operations, we select this one. But on which criteria do we base the selection if we find more than one?

In our example, we had first found the list, tree, order and hash table. Though the list and tree could be used, their operations did not fit as well as those of the order or the hash table. In particular, no element structure in a pair of data items was provided with the list and the tree, such that no operations like search for the key component of the pair and modification of its second component were offered. For these reasons, we excluded list and tree from our selection.

The *first criterion* for selection among several abstract data types is:

> How well do the operations of an abstract data type match the required operations on the application object?

The first criterion may still leave several abstract data types the operations of which match equally well to the desired ones. In our example, the data types order, hash table, map and bag did provide equivalent operations.

The *second criterion* to be applied is:

> Select the most general abstract data type!
>
> The arguments for selecting the most general data type are that

- we keep more freedom of selection up to a later point of time in the development cycle,
- the data type implementation can easier be exchanged during the maintenance phase if the environment changes.

Though perfectly valid from an abstract point of view, the second criterion can only be applied in practice if the following assumption is fulfilled. In our application example, we selected a map (or a bag) following this criterion and excluded an order, a list, a tree or a hash table. What would happen if, for performance reasons, a tree implementation is required in our application, but the catalogue of reusable data types would offer no tree representation of a map? The answer is simply that we either loose performance, or we cannot select the data type which is adequate from a functional viewpoint. Both of this is not acceptable.

As a consequence, we formulate a requirement for the structure of a catalogue of reusable data types that we call the *exhaustive representation requirement*:

> A more general data type must provide representation alternatives that are equivalent to those of all corresponding less general data types. That means an implementation of a more general data type must meet the performance requirements of an application equally well as that of a corresponding less general data type.

In our catalogue, we have made sure that any more general data type provides all possible meaningful implementations which a more special data type provides. Thus, we are sure that the uniformity of abstraction and representation hierarchy requirement is always fulfilled, when we select the most general data type in our selection. With regard to our example, chapter 6 shows that all different order, list, tree or hash table implementations are also available as implementations of a map or a bag.

No other catalogue of reusable abstract data types that we know about (for example, [4], [11]) does fulfill this requirement. For example, [4] offers for sets and bags only an unordered linked list implementation (in the unbounded case) and an unordered tabular list implementation (in the bounded case). This means one could not select a bag over a tree and a hash table, even if it would be the most general appropriate data type, if one would not be willing to accept very severe performance penalties resulting from the list implementation. This observation is also true for other samples from this catalogue.

## 5. Selection of the abstract data type variant

This step selects the representation and implementation, which we call the variant of an abstract data type.

Steps one to four take place early in the development cycle at the system design stage, when a component (or a large module) is refined into smaller modules, and the interfaces of these modules are defined. Obviously, this may be an iterative process.

Step five takes place late in the development cycle, at the implementation stage, when the modules are implemented. Now, we have a better knowledge of the application and its performance requirements, and we know exactly and in detail, which operations of an abstract data type we are going to use.

Therefore, we can select the appropriate variant of the abstract data type (which was selected at design time) based on the following criterion:

> Which variant of the abstract data type does yield the best application performance?

> Some operations of a data type may be executed very frequently, others infrequently in a given application. Thus, we can, for example, optimize the overall time performance by selecting an variant, which provides a very good time performance for the operations that are executed frequently. Formally, we minimize the sum of the execution time of an operation, multiplied with its frequency, over all operations.

> In our example, adding a word is done much more frequent than returning each word and frequency count, which is done only once for each word. Therefore, our selection of the implementation needs to consider primarily how fast a word is added. This depends mainly on the search time performance, and to a lesser degree on the insertion time performance (because an insertion is done only if a word is added the first time). A hash implementation provides the best search performance. We did select it, because it met also our other constraints (regarding the unknown number of words and the storage size).

Though perfectly valid from an abstract point of view, the criterion for the selection of a variant can be applied only if the catalogue of reusable data types fulfills a second requirement. Take for example, that a variant is selected according to the application performance criterion, but that is does not support an operation, which is required by the application. In this case, one would be urged to select a variant that does not have optimal performance characteristics, but offers all operations required from the application.

This results in the second requirement for a catalogue of reusable data types that we call the *variant uniformity requirement*:

> Each variant of a data type must offer all operations that define the interface of the data type.

We have made sure in our catalogue that this criterion is fulfilled for all data types.

No other catalogue, which we know, does fulfill this requirement. For example, the **PREVIOUS** operation for linked lists is provided in other catalogues (for example, [4]) only for doubly linked implementations.

## 6. Exchanging the abstract data type implementation

During the life time of a software system, very often its environment changes. These changes make, usually, a modification of the system itself necessary. Very frequently, the performance characteristics and requirements of an application change. For example, collections of data items grow in size. "Nobody could anticipate that there will be 10.000 items, instead of 100. As a consequence, we need to change everything" is a statement quite common among software developers.

When we use abstract data types to encapsulate data structures, modifications that are due to such changes will mainly be confined to the implementation of the data type, leaving its interface unchanged. Very often, one may have to exchange only one variant of a data type against another.

Take for example the word-frequency collection. Suppose that we had a small collection of about 100 word-counts in the beginning, and that we had selected the ordered tabular list implementation of a map. Its binary search performance, taking about seven steps, was good enough, and shifting of fifty words, on an average, with an insertion was a negligible effort.

Whith a growing size of the map, the performance of adding a word is getting worse and worse. Its performance is not acceptable any longer, when the map contains, for example, 1.000 to 10.000 word-counts. The performance problem is solved by exchanging the current implementation against an ordered tree implementation of a map.

With our catalogue, this means only exchanging one variant against another. Since our catalogue fulfills the requirement of variant uniformity, this exchange requires no modification of the program, just the variant name must be changed. (Note that exchanging the current variant against a hash variant might require to add the definition of a hash function to the program.)

With these six steps, we have focused on those parts of the software life cycle that are relevant to the reuse of software building blocks. A paradigm for reusing abstract data types has been given, criteria for the selection of the data types have been stated, and requirements to the structure of a catalogue of reusable data types have been derived.

The paradigm can easily be extended to the reuse of other kinds of building blocks. The only assumption to be made is that a building block is separated into

- a functional description that encapsulates its representation and implementation, and

- an implementation that determines its performance characteristics.

# Chapter 4

# Structure of the Catalogue

As we have seen in the previous chapter, a clear and simple structure of the catalogue is a major prerequisite for a successful retrieval of building blocks. Building blocks can be classified according to different properties and depending on the choice of these properties we get different views of the catalogue structure.

## 4.1 The Implementation Hierarchy

The structural aspect under which we will present our catalogue in this chapter is based on a view of abstract data types as data structures. This aspect induces a hierarchy where lower levels are used to (conceptually) implement higher levels. The lower the level, the more concrete can a visualization of the data structure be. On the level of lists and trees, programmers have a rather detailed understanding of the data structures and their impacts on the cost (or at least complexity) of operations. On the higher levels, like ordered structures or sets, this understanding is mostly gained by considering the possible implementations. The catalogue structure presented in figure 4.1 shall provide a framework that supports such considerations.

We want to note that this hierarchy is mainly justified from a data structure point of view. With an axiomatic view the dependencies are circular: most data structures can be defined in terms of higher level structures. An array can, for example, be viewed

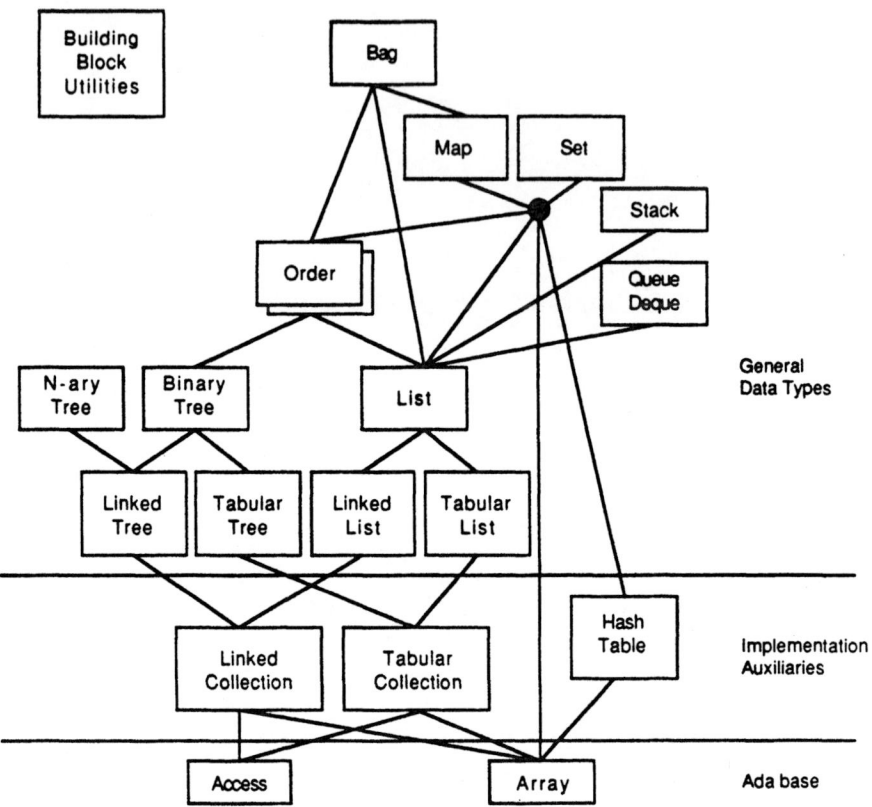

Figure 4.1: Catalogue structure

as a map from an integer range to the element type.  Under this aspect, our choice
of a hierarchy seems somehow arbitrary. We experimented with different layers, for
example, first viewing a set as a map (to boolean) and then viewing a map as a set (of
pairs), until we came to the given picture. We find it hard to formally argue why this
is more appropriate than others. Nevertheless, this hierarchy proved very valuable,
not only from an implementation viewpoint, but also our thinking of data structures
became clearer. Now we could associate models to our different data types that could
be refined to lower levels without spinning in circles. This model oriented view is
what we mean when we talk about "data structures".

Within our hierarchical structure we distinguish the following classes of building
blocks:

- *Implementation auxiliaries* are building blocks that should not be applied by the ordinary catalogue user. They are used for manufacturing the remaining blocks in the catalogue. The operations provided by blocks in this class differ to a large extent from the operations provided by the other building blocks. Linked and tabular collections as well as hash tables belong to this class.

- *General data types* provide common operations from a catalogue-wide framework. They are intended for general use.

- The BUILDING_BLOCK_UTILITIES define standard entities, like types or exceptions that are common to all building blocks. In addition they provide utilities that can be used to instantiate building blocks with more complicated element types.

We shall now give a rough overview of the different abstract data types before we return to further classification aspects.

## 4.2 The Abstract Data Types - an Overview

The general abstract data types contained in the catalogue are:

- list (linked and tabular)

- stack

- queue and deque (double ended queue)

- tree (linked and tabular, binary and N-ary)

- order

- set

- map

- bag

The values of all these data types are finite compositions of values of some element type. The main distinction between the data types can be explained in terms of structural relationships of the element values within the composite values. We therefore call the data types in the catalogue *structures*. Structures can be imagined as collections of *occurrences* of element values together with certain relationships between these occurrences. For orthogonality reasons we introduce the notion of occurrences for all structures, although for some it is irrelevant (as for sets) or can be weakened (as for bags, where only the number of elements is interesting). We use the term *index* as a reference to an occurrence of an element. We will omit the term occurrence just speaking of *elements* and hope that it becomes clear from the context.

Most implementation lines in the figure for the catalogue structure should be clear from the well-known literature on data structures. They will be discussed in detail in chapter 6.

## 4.2.1   List

The elements of lists have a linear, acyclic structure with a first and a last element. This structure is explicitly determined by the constructor operations. They specify the position of an element to be inserted. Elements may be inserted at or removed from any position within a given list.

The difference between linked and tabular lists is the relation between indices and elements. For elements in a linked list, this relation is not changed by insertions or removals of other elements, whereas for tabular lists the elements are "shifted" relative to the indices. Access and array implementations provide the typical model.

## 4.2.2   Stack

Stacks are basically lists with a restricted set of insert and remove operations. The operations grant insert or remove access only to the first element of the structure. This restriction can nicely be expressed by restricting the concept of insert and remove positions. Furthermore there is no possibility to modify elements within the structure.

Due to these restrictions, stacks can easily be implemented by using structure sharing, which is more difficult (and not implemented) for all other data types. Note that structure sharing cannot be observed through the data type's interface, but only through performance observations.

### 4.2.3 Queue and Deque

Like stacks, also queues and deques are lists with a restricted set of insert and remove operations.

A queue provides insert access to the first and remove access to the last element; a deque provides insert and remove access to both ends. Structure sharing is not as simple as for stacks, since queues and deques require doubly linked structures; it is therefore not implemented.

### 4.2.4 Tree

The elements in trees stand in a father-son relationship. Each son has at most one father and the father-son relation is acyclic. There is exactly one element (the root) that does not have a father. As for lists, elements can be inserted and removed at arbitrary positions within a tree.

The difference between the linear and the tabular case is like for lists.

We distinguish between binary and N-ary trees because binary trees provide certain facilities that are difficult to generalize, like infix traversal, threads, or tabular representation.

### 4.2.5 Order

The elements of an order are arranged by means of a total ordering relation given for the element type. Thus the position of an element to be inserted is always implicitly determined by its value, modulo the position within a row of equal element values. There is no sensible unique picture that can be used to visualize the structure of orders. The implementation can be in terms of lists and trees as well.

For orders, we distinguish the special case that the order is defined on only a part of the element. We call this part the "key" and the rest the "info" part. Special operations are provided for the key type. A similar distinction is made for hash tables.

### 4.2.6   Set

Sets are collections without an internal structure. Each element in a set occurs exactly once. This is important for the semantics of iteration. Special operations for set union, intersection, etc. are provided.

### 4.2.7   Map

Maps are representations of finite functions from a "key" type to an "info" type. Maps are related to sets in a similar way as key-info orders are related to ordinary orders.

### 4.2.8   Bag

Like sets, bags have no internal structure, but elements may occur more than once.

# 4.3   Variants of Building Blocks

The hierarchical structure of the catalogue implies that for each point in this hierarchy there are several implementations possible. With the axiomatic view, each point represents the weakest semantics that is common to all possible implementations. Lists, for example, abstract from the property of index invariance in order to provide a common model for linked and tabular lists which can be used for its implementation.

A variant for a building block is determined by two factors,

- the lower level building block that is chosen for its actual implementation, and
- the way in which the structures of the lower level building block are used to represent the structures of the higher level.

An examples that illustrates the second factor is the alternative to implement a linked lists using single links or double links (both use linked collections).

The choice of variants for a given point is of course recursive in the sense that for the implementation again there may be several variants: for a set that shall be represented by an order it must be determined whether the order shall be implemented by a list or a tree, and so on.

The more implementation details are determined, the more concrete becomes the understanding of the resulting variant's performance. However, due to the technical facility of information hiding, these more concrete aspects cannot be observed or exploited through the higher level interface. Therefore, we believe that thinking in the more concrete structures is not harmful.

One of our objectives was to keep the number of building blocks small. The method by which the number of building blocks can be reduced is to summarize similar structures in one abstract data type. This ADT must provide operations that exploit the properties of all summarized structures. Let us illustrate this procedure by an example. For linked lists we can imagine two distinct structures, one for which the elements are linked in a way where the last element does not refer to a next element, and one for which the last element refers back to the first element and the anchor of the list points to the last element (so the last element can be distinguished). If we made this structure visible by providing an operation to inspect the next pointer, the semantics of both lists would be different (in the first case the next pointer of the last element is null, in the second case it points to the first element). Instead, we provide two, logically different operations: a NEXT operation that always yields null if applied to the last element, and a CIRCULAR_NEXT operation that yields the first element in this case. Now, both variants have the same semantics. However, NEXT is slightly more efficient for the first variant, and CIRCULAR_NEXT for the second; both need an additional check in the worse case. The same procedure can be applied to several other variant alternatives, like for single and double links or single and double anchors.

The technique of subsuming different variants under one abstract data type often requires additional parameters for the operations. In our example, the next operation needs the whole list structure as a parameter, since for the circular variant the list is needed to distinguish the last element. We believe that this is in most cases even an advantage since it defines uniform dependencies between arguments and results. From the efficiency point of view the additional parameters are mostly irrelevant since they are eliminated by simple state-of-the-art optimizations.

Generally speaking, the summary technique shifts structural and functional considerations to efficiency considerations. The benefit is that efficiency considerations can be delayed until (part of) a larger system is implemented and can be tested and an operation profile can be determined. The profile information can then be used to select a more efficient variant. However, there are also drawbacks that shall not be concealed. Modern software engineering methods tell us not to worry about efficiency when writing our specifications and then gaining efficiency by (stepwise) refinement. However, playing this game has its limits when it comes to implicit algorithmic considerations within the specification. No known specification method is free of such aspects. The choices of algorithms and data structures influence each other and the more "loose ends" one has to manage, the more difficult the refinement process becomes. So we recommend a view of abstract data types that is somewhere between the view of its possible implementations and the view of its abstract properties. Finding the right level at a given time in the development process is one of the keys to a well-designed and efficiently implemented system.

# Chapter 5

# Structure of the Building Blocks

This chapter will explain the general properties of building blocks. It will discuss the general parameters that are used to select variants and the general classes of types and operations that are provided by the building block interfaces.

Selection of a variant is technically done in two steps: first the implementation structure of a building block is determined by so-called *variant parameters*. The building block is processed by a macro processor and the result of this first step is an Ada generic unit. From this unit instances can be created by providing actual *generic parameters*.

The interfaces of all generic abstract data types that can be selected from our catalogue are structured in the same way. They consist of

- the generic (formal) parameters, which are used to create an instance of a building block,

- the type definitions and

- the specifications of the operations that are provided by the interface of such an instance.

The general variant parameters, generic parameters, types and operation classes, that will be introduced in this chapter, are common to most of our building blocks, not necessarily to all. In addition, there are specific ones that will be explained in the sections in chapter 6 that are devoted to the discussion of the particular abstract data types.

After introducing general properties of the catalogue's data types, we will first discuss the general types and operations. This discussion will lead us to the required generic parameters and the variant parameterization.

# 5.1    General Properties of the Data Types

All data types of our catalogue model composite data. We call an object or value of such a composite type a *structure* object or value.

## 5.1.1    Objects and Values

Our data types are "object-based". That means they take into account the existence of objects and program state. This differs from a value-oriented view, as it is common to (pure) functional languages and also is often taken for abstract data types. The value oriented view concentrates on values "as a whole" where operations have no side effects. This results in the typical "decompose and recompose" pattern, for example, when replacing an element of a list object:

```
L := L (1 .. N-1) & NEW_ELEM & L (N+1 .. COUNT (L));
```

Although purely functional abstract data types have nice mathematical properties, they seem inadequate for an object-based, state oriented language. The above notation is tedious and the introduced inefficiency (through value copying) is hard to eliminate. Therefore, the data types of our catalogue provide a model of structure objects that consist of element occurrences (or component objects), which can be manipulated as objects. The above list replacement procedure goes like

```
L (N) := NEW_ELEM;
```

Due to the capabilities of Ada, our notation is a little different

```
SET_ELEM (L, N, NEW_ELEM);
```

which does not affect the concept.

Although the object-based view is taken for all data types, the element occurrences of certain structures are "read-only". This is due to the fact, that for types like orders, the object's structure depends on the value of its elements.

Element occurrences are modeled by the type **INDEX** that will be introduced later.

The object-based view is restricted to making the element occurrences accessible. It does not introduce the notion of object identities. Equality for structure objects is the value equality, that means two lists are equal, if their corresponding element occurrences are equal. Another property that is not introduced through the object-based view is

## 5.1.2 Structure Sharing

The definition of our data types guarantees – by defining the structure type limited private – that no two structures share element occurrences. Structure sharing may lead to global side effects, that means the value of one structure may be changed by changing an element of another structure. This is in conflict with modular encapsulation and in fact is a common source of errors that are hard to trace.

Technically, structure sharing is often only used to implement operations that do not result in shared structures. Consider as an example the destructive append operation for lists, where one list is appended to another list and no longer used by itself. With a pointer implementation of linked lists, this can simply be done by linking the last element of one list to the first element of the list to be appended and then setting the variable of the appended list to empty.

```
L1 := L1 & L2;
L2 := EMPTY;
```

This procedure requires (intermediate) structure sharing, although at the end, no structures are really shared. Our catalogue provides operations that **MOVE** elements or structure parts from one structure to another. The append procedure is done in a single step

```
MOVE (TO => L1, FROM => L2);
```

which allows us to get the intermediate structure sharing under complete control of our operations and thereby avoids sharing that can be observed outside.

There may be situations, where structure sharing is nevertheless desirable. This may either be achieved by explicitly modeling the element values as access values, such that even two different occurrences of the same access value may share the same accessed object, or indices may be used to explicitly represent the element occurrences.

Finally, the data type stack may implement its structures by sharing, since it provides only a restricted access to the elements. The COPY operation may therefore be implemented by just copying the "anchor" of the structure and sharing the elements. This is another typical pattern for which explicit structure sharing is often demanded but which can be hidden within the data type's implementation.


## 5.1.3   Compact and Dispersed Representations


Besides the logical concepts of object and value, certain representational aspects (of storage layout) have motivated the design of our catalogue. Although these aspects are hidden within the implementation, we find it helpful to get an abstract understanding of these concepts in order to properly assess the (performance) behavior of several application patterns.

For this purpose, we distinguish two classes of value representations, namely *compact* and *dispersed*. A compact value is a value whose representation is stored in a single (Ada) object; a dispersed value is represented by an *anchor* and by separate *nodes*, that are stored in different objects. A type is called dispersed if it has dispersed values; otherwise it is called compact.

A typical example for a dispersed value is a linked list, whereas a tabular list (implemented by an array) is compact.

For compact values, the predefined operations of the (Ada) programming language, in particular assignment and implicit deallocation, can be used to implement the corresponding logical operations (COPY and DEALLOCATE) of the catalogue. For dispersed values, some extra actions must be performed, like copying the anchor and all the nodes, or deallocating all the nodes and then the anchor.

The property of being compact or dispersed is not only relevant for structure objects but even more for the elements. In case that both, the structure and its elements are compact, operations on the whole structure can be performed by a single programming language operation. If the structure is compact, but the elements are not, a deallocate operation, for example, still would have to iterate over all elements and deallocate them before deallocating the whole structure. The same procedure is necessary if the structure itself is dispersed, independent from the property of the elements. For allocation and deallocation see also section 5.3.1.4.

The fact that values may be dispersed motivates the introduction of the operations MOVE and TRANSFER. These operations behave like a composition of INSERT and COPY with REMOVE. Since the dispersed value is removed after being inserted or copied, it is a valid implementation (that prevents structure sharing) to insert or copy only the anchor of the dispersed value.

## 5.1.4   Recursive Composition

Several operations of the structure are based on operations of the element type. For example, the COPY operation on structures performs a COPY on the elements, a DEALLOCATE of the structure DEALLOCATEs the elements and a test, whether two structures are EQUAL tests for EQUAL elements. Section 5.4 will show how the element type's operations are made available to the structure operations.

Whenever we will talk about copying, transferring, deallocating or comparing elements, this always means the application of the COPY, TRANSFER, DEALLOCATE, or EQUAL operation that is provided for the element type.

In order to support the recursive application of type instantiations with data types from the catalogue – for example instantiating a list of integers which is then used as element type of a set (of lists of integers) – all data types provide all generic parameter operations that are required for an element type. All these operations have <> defaults, so they will be automatically used, provided they are visible at the place of the instantiation.

Therefore, and in general, it is advisable to write an Ada use clause for all instantiations of modules from the catalogue. Writing use clauses is not always useful. In cases, where a package implements an abstract object, it is often better to enforce the selected (object-oriented) notation OBJ.OP (...). This notation clarifies, to which module the operation belongs. This is not a problem for the catalogue operations, since they all have the structure to which they are applied as their first parameter, which relates them to the package where they are declared.

## 5.2  Types

The main types that each catalogue data type provides, are the structure type STRUCT and the index type INDEX. Values of type STRUCT represent composite values that are structured according to the characteristics of the data type. Index values are used to refer to elements within a structure. In addition, there may be types for INSERT_POSITIONs, REMOVE_POSITIONs, structure PARTs, and ITERATION_ORDERs.

The general operation classes on the types will be discussed in section 5.3. Operations for the construction of insert positions and parts are data type specific and are explained in the corresponding sections in chapter 6.

### 5.2.1  The Type STRUCT

A structure is a composition of elements. The universal type name STRUCT is offered by each data type as a name for the structure type. In addition, a more specific name, like LINKED_LIST or TREE, is offered as an alternative.

```
type STRUCT is limited private;
subtype <subtype-specific-Name> is STRUCT;
```

The fact that the structure type is declared limited private makes no predefined Ada operations available for values or objects of this type. In particular there are no predefined operations for assignment and equality. However, there are explicitly defined operations for structure types, that are used for assignment and comparison. All the operations will be discussed in section 5.3.

After having instantiated a data type package, objects of the structure type can be declared.

```
package STUDENT_SET_PACKAGE is new SETS (STUDENT);
STUDENT_SET : STUDENT_SET_PACKAGE.STRUCT;
```

or

```
STUDENT_SET : STUDENT_SET_PACKAGE.SET;
```

The first notation allows a simpler replacement of the selected data type, since the name STRUCT can be left unchanged. The data type package should be clear from the name of the instantiation, anyway. The notation without STUDENT_SET_PACKAGE as prefix should not be used, since in case of several instantiations of the same data type, the types defined by the different instantiations might not be distinguishable.

If the structure type is object_bounded (a variant that will be described in section 5.5.2), the structure type has a discriminant SIZE that denotes the maximum number of elements of a structure object:

```
type STRUCT (SIZE : NATURAL) is limited private;
```

This number must be provided as a constraint for the discriminant SIZE for objects of the structure type. The declaration

```
MY_STUDENTS : STUDENT_SET (100);
```

declares a set object that can contain a maximum of 100 elements.

## 5.2.2   The Type INDEX

The type INDEX is used to reference single elements of a structure value. The type INDEX is private, so that index values can be compared and assigned.

```
type INDEX is private;
```

Conceptually, each index (except NIL) is always relative to exactly one structure. In linked representations, the index will usually be a pointer to some node that represents the element in the structure; for tabular representations, the index is usually an integer number designating the position of the element in the table.

The index type has always a special value obtained by the function

```
    function NIL return INDEX;
```

which designates no element.

As long as a structure is not modified, the relationship between an index value and the designated element remains unchanged. For linked representations, a structure may even be modified and the remaining elements are still referred to by the same indices as before the modification. We call this property *index invariance*. Tabular representations are not index invariant. The user is responsible for the proper association of indices and structures.

All constructor or selector operations that are based on an index have the corresponding structure as an additional parameter, although in the linked case, the operation might not actually require the whole structure. Consider as an example the GET_ELEM operation:

```
    function GET_ELEM (S : in STRUCT;
                       I : in INDEX) return ELEM_TYPE;
```

It is a precondition of all such operations, that the index is in fact a proper index of the given structure.

The concept of indices is another example for the summary technique. It summarizes the concepts of node pointers and numeric array indices. This abstraction eliminates the numeric property of tabular list indices. However, the numeric position is an important concept of tabular lists. Again, the summary technique is used to provide the concept of 'numeric positions' that abstracts from the tabular and linked implementation. This is done by the operations INDEX_VAL, and INDEX_POS that convert a numeric position into an index and vice versa. These operations yield the identity for (non-diluted) tabular lists, whereas they require an O(n) effort in the linked case.

### 5.2.3   INSERT_POSITIONs and REMOVE_POSITIONs

Insert positions and remove positions specify the place at which an element shall be inserted or from which an element shall be removed. The types `INSERT_POSITION` and `REMOVE_POSITION` are provided for values that characterize such positions. Certain data types have no notion of insert positions (e.g. sets), or do not allow the user to explicitly specify an insert position (e.g. orders). An example for an insert position for a linear list is "after the element denoted by index I". For remove positions there is a special *nil position* that refers to no element; in all other cases, insert and remove positions are specified relative to a certain structure that must be provided in addition to the position as a parameter to the operation for which the position is given.

There are several reasons why we introduce such positions as an extra concept. First, they abstract from concrete indices to a certain degree. That makes the insert/remove operations independent from the concrete data type. Only the operations to construct the positions depend on the data type characteristics. In addition, this abstraction may save some writing. For example, when the first element of a list shall be removed, we need not write

        REMOVE (S, FIRST (S));

but simply

        REMOVE (S, FIRST);

That seems only a little advantage, but consider a list with a name like `THE_CURRENTLY_AVAILABLE_RESOURCES`!

Furthermore, the introduction of insert/remove positions presents a nice way to describe the restrictions imposed on specific data types like stacks or queues. These data types can be described as lists that provide only the appropriate operations to construct insert/remove positions. Conversely, if for a list only the characteristic subset of insert/remove positions is used, the list may be replaced by a (possibly more efficient) specific data type.

Finally, insert/remove positions can be used to increase efficiency for linked representations, by providing access to those nodes whose links have to be changed. Consider, for example, the remove position for a linear list "after the element denoted by I". In the case of a singly linked list, the index I can now be used to efficiently access the element whose link must be changed. This aspect will be further discussed with the corresponding insert and remove operations.


### 5.2.4   Structure PARTs

The private type `PART` characterizes a part of a structure. It is provided for lists, trees and orders. Parts are used to restrict the effect of certain structure operations to the given part of the structure. As for positions, the definition of a part depends on the data type.


### 5.2.5   The Type ITERATION_ORDER

The enumeration type `ITERATION_ORDER` is provided by data types that have an internal structure, like lists, trees and orders. It characterizes the order in which elements are visited by iteration operations.


# 5.3   Operations

This section gives an overview of the operations for structures and indices. There are many operations that are common to most data types. Some have particular parameters for the different data types. The general operational concepts will be explained in this section, whereas the specific details are left to the chapter 6. We use the square bracket notation

        ... [ data-type-dependent ] ...

to indicate that the part in brackets is only provided for specific data types.

The parameter names of all operation follow some common conventions. Where there is no doubt about the role of a parameter, parameters of type `STRUCT` are named S, E is used for parameters of type `ELEM_TYPE`, I for `INDEX`, `TO_POS` for `INSERT_POSITION`, `FROM_POS` for `REMOVE_POSITION` and `SUB` for `PART`.

We distinguish the following operation classes:


- Constructors

- Operations based on indices

- Access by position count

- Selectors

- Iterators

- Order dependent operations

- Hash function


These classes contain the following general operations, some of which offer different possible parameterizations.

Constructors:

```
CLEAR
INSERT, FIND_OR_INSERT
REMOVE, REMOVE_ALL, SLICE
MOVE, SWAP
COPY, TRANSFER
DEALLOCATE
```

Operations based on indices and position counts:

```
NIL
GET_ELEM, SET_ELEM, TRANSFER_ELEM
MODIFY_ELEM, MODIFY_ELEM_BY_POS
INDEX_VAL, INDEX_POS
```

Selectors:

```
COUNT
IS_EMPTY
FIND, SKIP
COUNT_ELEM
```

```
IS_ELEM
EQUAL, "="
FIRST, LAST
NEXT, PREVIOUS
```

Iterators:

```
APPLY, ITERATE, ITERATE_MOVE
REDUCE, UREDUCE, AREDUCE
FIND_PROPERTY, SKIP_PROPERTY, COUNT_PROPERTY
EXISTS, FORALL
APPLY_CORRESPONDING, ITERATE_CORRESPONDING, MODIFY_CORRESPONDING
```

Order dependent operations:

```
COMPARE, <, <=, >, >=
MAX, MIN
REMOVE_MAX, REMOVE_MIN
```

Hash function:

```
HASH_FUNCTION
```

The constructor and index based operations are visualized by figures. These general figures cannot illustrate specific aspects, like that for a set no elements occur more than once. Nevertheless, most concepts can be abstractly represented, like the concept of PARTs and INSERT_POSITIONs and REMOVE_POSITIONs. The figures represent the elements as positive numbers; the TRANSFER operation for the elements sets the source to 0. You may get a better picture of the performance characteristics, if you imagine the elements themselves as (possibly dispersed) structures, where the number indicates the element's COUNT. A ? indicates that the value at this location is undefined or irrelevant.

There are several data types, for which the ELEM_TYPE is split into a KEY_TYPE and an INFO_TYPE. The operations will first be introduces in terms of the ELEM_TYPE. The corresponding operations for the key/info data types will be specified at the end of the corresponding sections.

## 5.3.1   Constructors

Constructors and some forms of constructive iterators are the only operations that may change the "composition" of an object. For objects that have an internal structure, like lists or trees, the value of the structure object can in addition be modified by modifying the value of the elements (but preserving the structure) using operations based on indices or position counts.

### 5.3.1.1   Initialization and Clear

There are no predefined functions that yield a structure value as result. Thus, structure values are always associated to some Ada object, and the first operation that creates a structure value is the (static) declaration or the dynamic allocation of a structure object; the last operation that is performed with a structure object is its deallocation. Deallocation will be discussed as the last constructor operation.

After allocation, Ada initializes objects if their type implies any initial value. This is the case for all types from our catalogue. Structure types are mostly represented as records, and the components of these records have the appropriate initial values. The initial values for structures is always the empty structure. Therefore, if an object of some structure type is declared, its initial value can be assumed as empty. An explicit initialization for structures is not possible, since the structure type is limited.

After an object has been manipulated, the operation CLEAR can be used to reset it to the initial value.

```
procedure CLEAR (S : in out STRUCT);
```

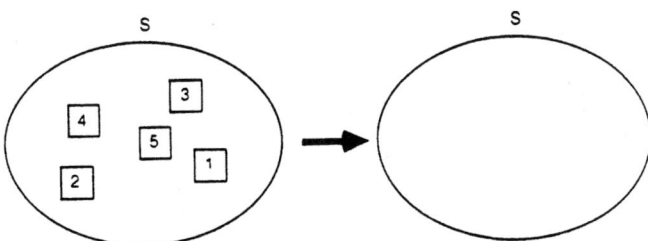

CLEAR (S) is equivalent to REMOVE (S, WHOLE_STRUCT). All elements that are currently in the structure are removed and thereby deallocated by using the deallocation procedure, if any, that is given as generic parameter. Space that is occupied for the storage of elements is released and can, for example, be reused by further insertions. The way in which storage space for elements is allocated and deallocated will be discussed in section 5.3.1.4.

## 5.3.1.2   Insertions, Removals and Moves

The construction primitives for structure objects are INSERT and REMOVE. The MOVE operation is a combination of both.

INSERT allows to add an element to a structure.  The operation works by copying the element value that is inserted.  Copying, as we will see later, copies all nodes of a dispersed element value, since there is no structure sharing.  We will discuss an alternative to copying the elements when we come to the MOVE operation.

There exist several (overloaded) definitions of INSERT. The most simple are

```
procedure INSERT (S      : in out STRUCT;
                  E      : in ELEM_TYPE
            [ ;TO_POS : in INSERT_POSITION [:= LAST]]);

procedure INSERT (S      : in out STRUCT;
                  E      : in ELEM_TYPE ;
            [ TO_POS : in INSERT_POSITION [:= LAST]; ]
                  I      : out INDEX);
```

which behave identical, except that the second in addition yields the index of the newly inserted element. They are provided for all data types. For lists and trees the insert position may be explicitly specified by the parameter TO_POS. For lists, the element is inserted at the end, if no explicit insert position is specified. For trees, there is no such default insert position. Note, that if no actual value is given for a parameter with a default, all subsequent parameters, for example the index I, must be associated using the named notation <formal> => <actual>.

Data types with an explicit insert position, like lists or trees, allow the insertion of a new element without specifying the element value itself.

```
procedure INSERT (S       : in out STRUCT;
                  TO_POS : in INSERT_POSITION [:= LAST];
                  I       : out INDEX);
```

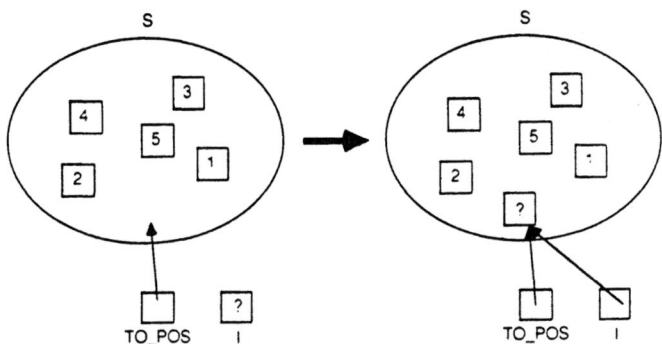

In this case the inserted value is the initial value, if any, which is provided for the element type, or otherwise undefined. The value may later be set by using the operations SET_ELEM or TRANSFER_ELEM.

Inserting a whole structure or a PART into another structure is done with

```
procedure INSERT (TO       : in out STRUCT;
                  FROM     : in STRUCT
                [ ;SUB    : in PART := WHOLE_STRUCT ]
                [ ;TO_POS : in INSERT_POSITION [:= LAST]]);
```

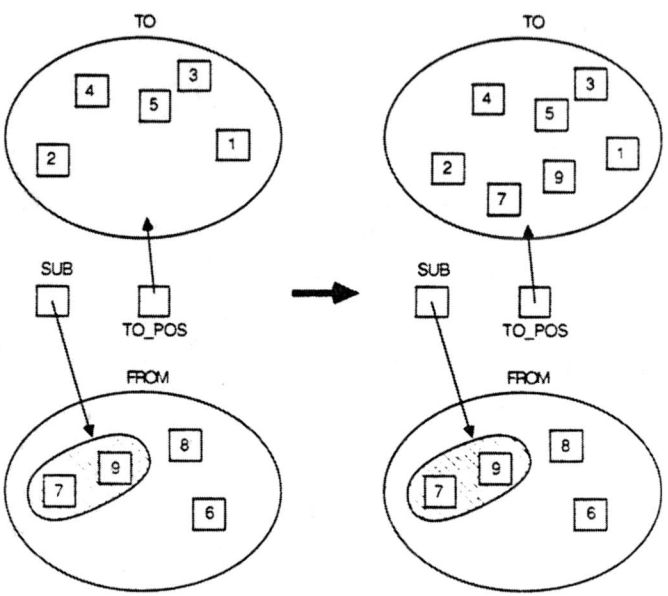

Since there is no structure sharing for our data types, element values are copied from the given part, that is defined by FROM and SUB, to the structure TO. The source structure FROM is left unchanged, which can be seen from the fact, that it is a parameter of mode in. Again, we will find an alternative with the MOVE operation.

The structure of the elements in the part is preserved by the insertion. A subtree, for example, that is inserted from a part given by FROM and SUB, will have the same tree structure in TO.

FIND_OR_INSERT is a combination of the operations FIND and INSERT.

```
procedure FIND_OR_INSERT (S       : in out STRUCT;
                          E       : in ELEM_TYPE;
                        [ TO_POS  : in INSERT_POSITION; ]
                          I       : out INDEX;
                          FOUND   : out BOOLEAN);
```

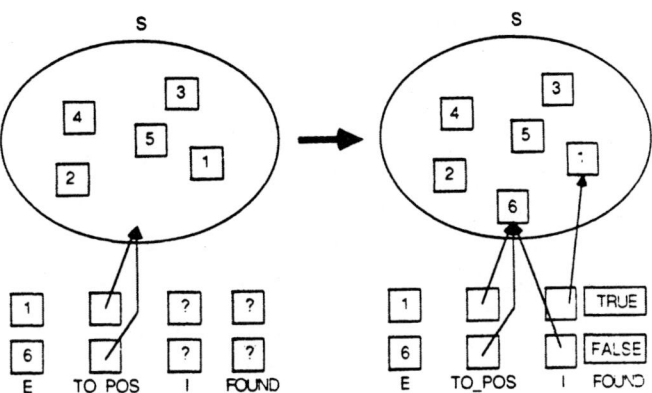

It looks for an occurrence of the given element value in the structure. If such an occurrence exists, it yields its index in the out parameter I, and FOUND is set to TRUE. Otherwise, the element is inserted (at the given position), I yields the new index and FOUND is set to FALSE.

The general way to remove an element is by denoting its position.

```
procedure REMOVE (S         : in out STRUCT;
                  FROM_POS : in REMOVE_POSITION);
```

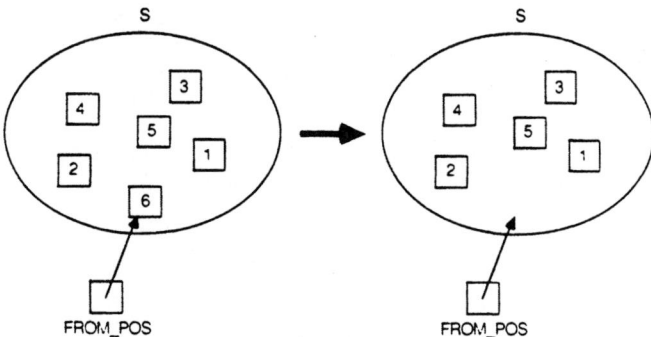

If FROM_POS indicates the nil position, nothing is done; otherwise the element at the indicated FROM_POS is removed from S. In the case of a dispersed structure, the space for the element node is deallocated. In case of a dispersed element type, the element value itself is also deallocated.

The operation

      **procedure REMOVE (S : in out STRUCT; SUB : in PART);**

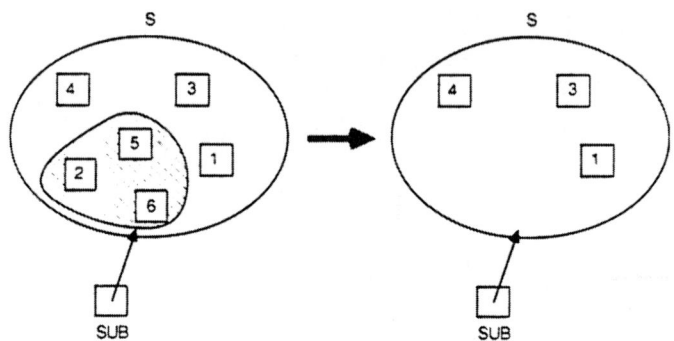

removes all elements from S that occur within the given part SUB. If SUB is the
**WHOLE_STRUCT**, S becomes empty.  The effect of this operation is the same as as
successive application of the element-wise **REMOVE** operation, however, the removal of
a complete part may be implemented more efficiently.

The operation

      **procedure REMOVE (S : in out STRUCT; E : in ELEM_TYPE);**

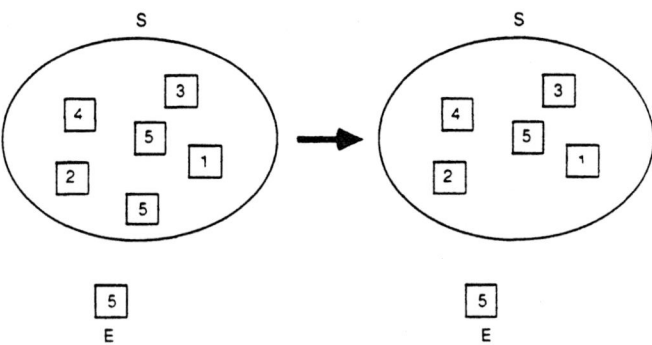

searches for some element with value E and, if there is one, removes it. If there is
no element with value E, the structure S remains unchanges. It is not defined, which
element is removed, if there is more than one element with the value E.

The operation

```
procedure REMOVE_ALL (S : in out STRUCT; E : in ELEM_TYPE);
```

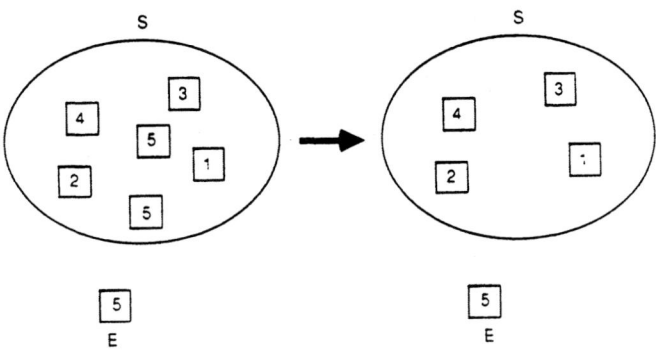

acts similar to REMOVE (S, E) but removes all elements – possibly none – with value E, instead of only one.

The above REMOVE operations remove the element from the structure and deallocate it. In several cases, however, the element shall be removed from the structure but ABSORBed by some other structure or variable. The GENERIC_REMOVE operation provides this possibility:

```
generic
    with procedure ABSORB (E : in out ELEM_TYPE);
procedure GENERIC_REMOVE (S        : in out STRUCT;
                          FROM_POS : in REMOVE_POSITION);
```

The ABSORB operation may, for example, MOVE the element into another structure (see the example at the end of section 5.3.5).

Slicing is a particular form of element removal, where those elements are removed that do not belong to a given part. The operation is only provided for types that have PARTs.

```
procedure SLICE (S : in out STRUCT; SUB : in PART);
```

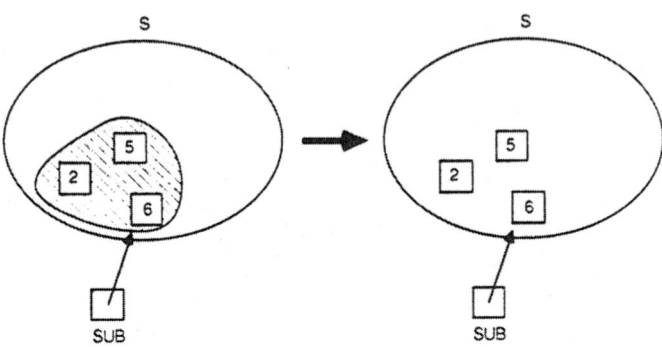

The **MOVE** operation moves one or more elements from some source to some destination, by removing them from the source. This property can be exploited in a way that element values are transferred rather than copied. Transferring a dispersed value means to only copy its anchor. Three basic cases are distinguished for the **MOVE** operation:

- move elements within one structure

- move elements between structures

- move elements from a variable to a structure or vice versa.

The first two cases allow the user to move a single element as well as a part (for the data types that have **PART**s).

The first case is only provided for structures with explicit insert positions, that means for lists and trees.

```
procedure MOVE (S        : in out STRUCT;
                FROM_POS : in REMOVE_POSITION;
                TO_POS   : in INSERT_POSITION [:= LAST]);

procedure MOVE (S      : in out STRUCT;
                SUB    : in PART;
                TO_POS : in INSERT_POSITION [:= LAST]);
```

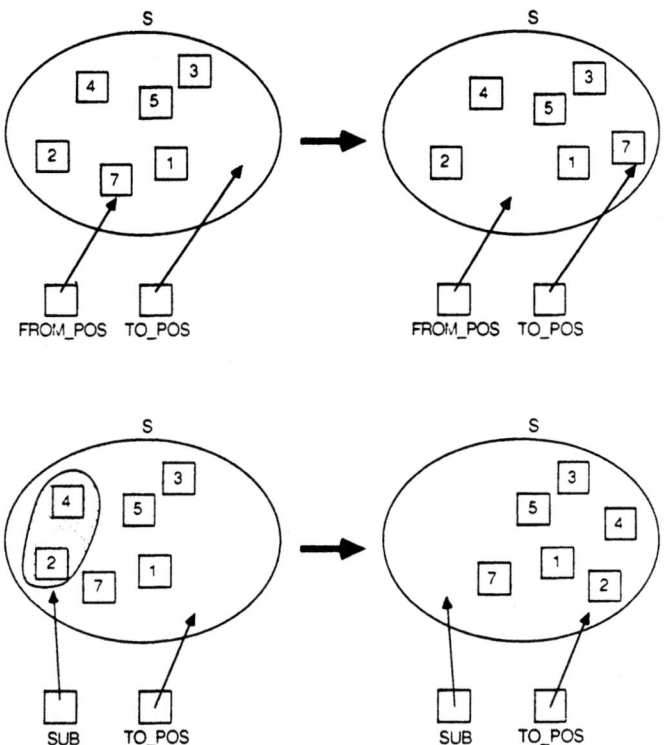

For linked structures, MOVE works by rearranging links, if this is possible (it is, for example, impossible for trees with node dependent sons). In the tabular case, the element is transferred.

For moving one or more elements between different structures, we provide the operations

```
procedure MOVE (TO       : in out STRUCT;
                FROM      : in out STRUCT;
                FROM_POS  : in REMOVE_POSITION
           [ ;TO_POS   : in INSERT_POSITION [:= LAST] ]);


procedure MOVE (TO       : in out STRUCT;
                FROM      : in out STRUCT
           [ ;SUB      : in PART := WHOLE_STRUCT ]
           [ ;TO_POS  : in INSERT_POSITION [:= LAST] ]);
```

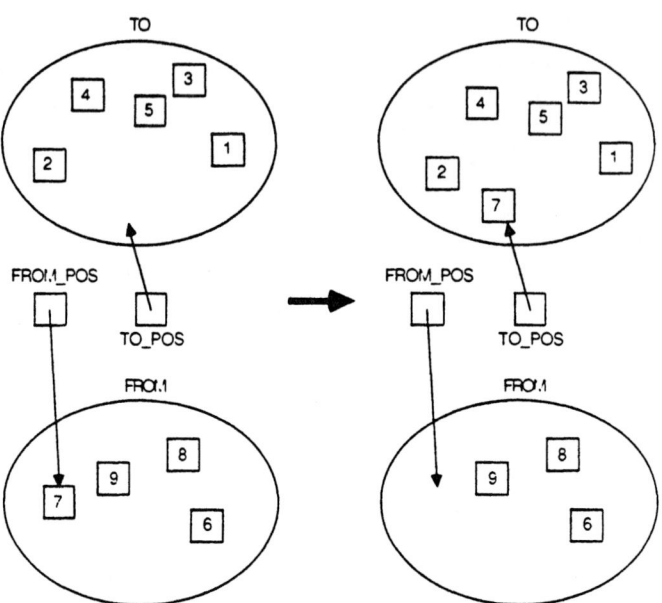

FROM_POS or SUB is a position or part within the structure FROM. TO_POS can only be given for lists and trees and is then relative to TO. The order of the parameters was chosen this way in order to make use of the default mechanism for TO_POS. In general, if an operation has a parameter TO_POS, it is always the last parameter (of mode in).

Moving elements across structures does never guarantee to preserve the index of the moved element, not even in the linked case. This is due to the object-bounded variant, that associates a collection of elements to each object and elements have to be moved from one collection to another in this case. Elements are transferred in this case and in the tabular cases; otherwise the links are rearranged.

Although the first MOVE operation seems to be a special case of the second one, we cannot write

```
MOVE (TO => S, FROM => S, ...);
```

because of illegal aliasing. Both structures TO and FROM are modified and it would make a difference, whether the parameters are passed by reference or by copy. This violates the Ada rules on parameter passing and makes the given construct erroneous.

For moving elements from or to a variable, the operations

```
procedure MOVE (TO        : in out STRUCT;
                FROM      : in out ELEM_TYPE
          [ ;TO_POS       : in INSERT_POSITION [:= LAST] ]);


procedure MOVE (TO        : in out ELEM_TYPE;
                FROM      : in out STRUCT;
                FROM_POS  : in REMOVE_POSITION);
```

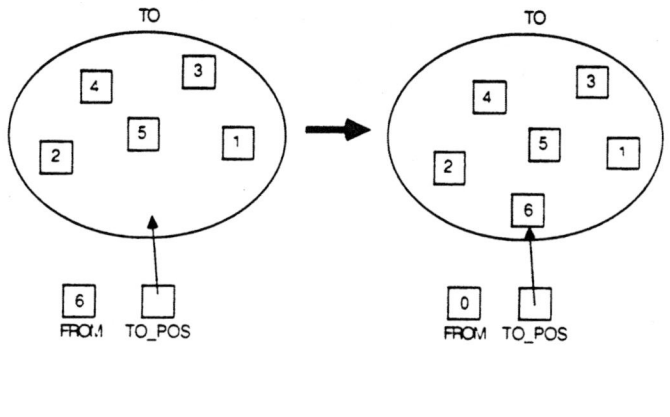

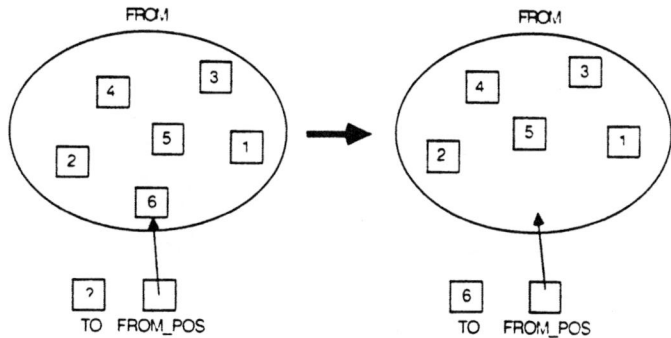

are used. Elements are inserted to or removed from the given structure and transferred from or to the given variable. This means if an element FROM is moved to a structure TO, the element is not available in FROM any more.

Swapping elements is some sort of "double MOVE", that can make use of the fact that to the position from which some element is (re)moved, another element is moved. In the linked case, swapping is done by link rearrangement, in the tabular case, elements are transferred.

```
procedure SWAP (S              : in out STRUCT;
                POS1, POS2 : in REMOVE_POSITION);
```

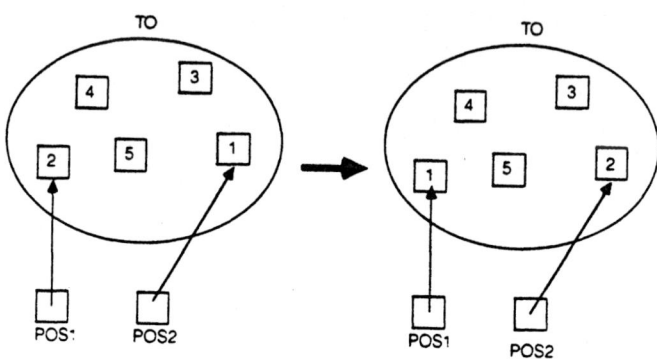

SWAP exchanges the elements at the given positions. It is available for all structures with explicit insert and remove positions.

To summarize the use of INSERT, REMOVE, and MOVE we suggest the classification in figure 5.1. It distinguishes the locations to or from which an element is inserted or removed, and whether COPY or TRANSFER is used.

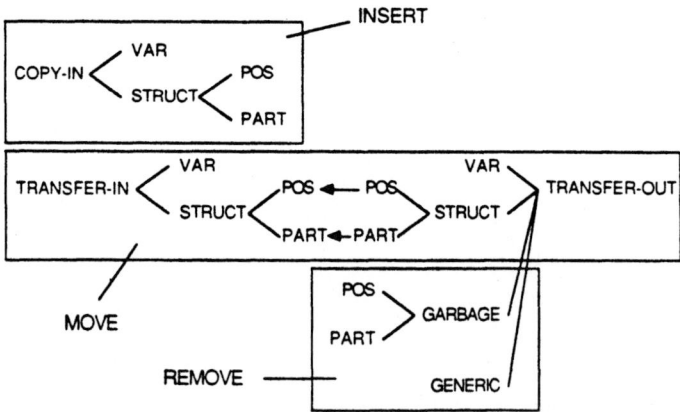

Figure 5.1: Insert, Remove, and Move

As in several other cases, the catalogue operations (like MOVE) combine more primitive operations (like transfer-in and transfer-out for structures), in order to exploit special situations. Although the semantics of MOVE can be explained in terms of transfer-in/out, MOVE can be implemented more efficiently, for example by unlinking the whole

**SUB**-part from one structure and linking it into the other one, thus avoiding the iterative **TRANSFER** of each element in the part.

For key/info data types the operations that were introduced in this section have the following profile:

```
procedure INSERT (S    : in out STRUCT;
                  K    : in KEY_TYPE;
                  INFO : in INFO_TYPE);

procedure INSERT (S    : in out STRUCT;
                  K    : in KEY_TYPE;
                  INFO : in INFO_TYPE;
                  I    : out INDEX);

procedure INSERT (S : in out STRUCT;
                  K : in KEY_TYPE;
                  I : out INDEX);

procedure FIND_OR_INSERT (S     : in out STRUCT;
                          K     : in KEY_TYPE;
                          I     : out INDEX;
                          FOUND : out BOOLEAN);

procedure REMOVE (S : in out STRUCT; K : in KEY_TYPE);

generic
   with procedure ABSORB (K    : in out KEY_TYPE;
                          INFO : in out INFO_TYPE);
procedure GENERIC_REMOVE (S        : in out STRUCT;
                          FROM_POS : in REMOVE_POSITION);

procedure MOVE (TO        : in out STRUCT;
                FROM_KEY  : in out KEY_TYPE;
                FROM_INFO : in out INFO_TYPE);

procedure MOVE (TO_KEY   : in out KEY_TYPE;
                TO_INFO  : in out INFO_TYPE;
                FROM     : in out STRUCT;
                FROM_POS : in REMOVE_POSITION);
```

### 5.3.1.3   Copy and Transfer

COPY and TRANSFER both assign a value from a given source to a given destination. Whereas COPY leaves the source unchanged, TRANSFER resets the source to its initial empty value. Note the different modes for the parameter FROM.

```
procedure COPY (TO   : in out STRUCT;
                FROM : in STRUCT;
                SUB  : in PART);
procedure COPY (TO   : in out STRUCT; FROM : in STRUCT);
```

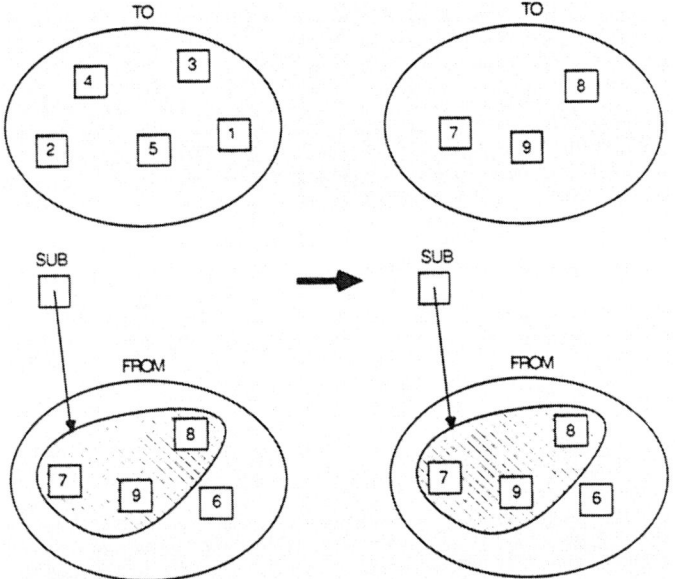

```
procedure TRANSFER (TO, FROM : in out STRUCT; SUB : in PART);
procedure TRANSFER (TO, FROM : in out STRUCT);
```

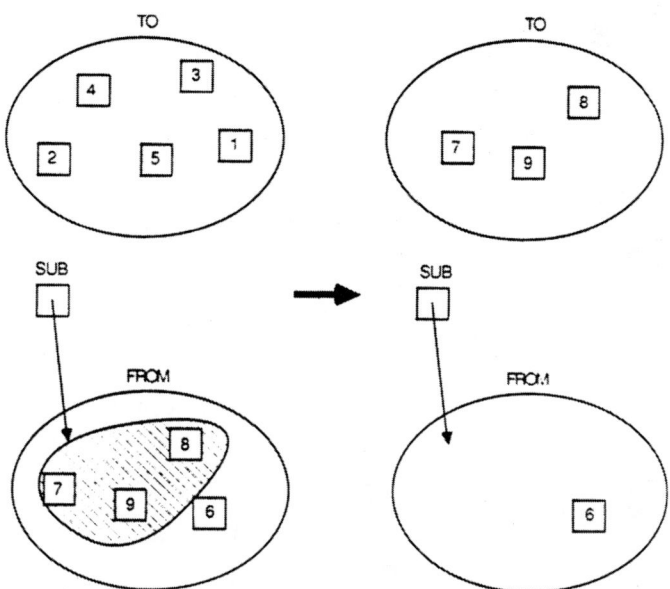

Both operations first **CLEAR** the destination **TO**. **COPY** then acts like **INSERT**, whereas **TRANSFER** behaves like **MOVE**. While **COPY** must in fact copy all element occurrences, **TRANSFER** need not transfer all element values but may rather copy the anchor or value of the complete structure, depending on whether the structure itself is dispersed or compact.

Both operations are duplicated instead of using **WHOLE_STRUCT** as a default for SUB, because the second form of **COPY** and **TRANSFER** is the same as for the generic procedure parameters for the element type. This allows the immediate use of these operations when the structure type is used as the element type of another catalogue data type.

### 5.3.1.4   Allocation and Deallocation

Allocation and deallocation operations determine the allocation and deallocation of storage space that is used for the structure and its elements. Implicit storage allocation and deallocation in Ada works on compact values or only on the anchors of dispersed values.

For the data types from our catalogue two questions arize: first, how is the storage
for structure values deallocated, if the structure values are dispersed, and second,
how is the storage of elements deallocated if elements are removed from a structure?
Deallocation of dispersed values is not automatically achieved by the programming
language's run-time system since the property of being compact or dispersed is not
immediately related to the language.

DEALLOCATE deallocates the storage that is occupied by nodes of a dispersed value;
for compact values DEALLOCATE does nothing. After the application to an object, the
object's value is undefined.

```
procedure DEALLOCATE (S : in out STRUCT);
```

For structure types the operation deallocates the storage occupied by any nodes of the
structure (if the structure type is dispersed) and it calls the DEALLOCATE operation
for all elements that are currently in the structure. This procedure may work recur-
sively, until all nodes that are somehow accessed by the structure value have been
deallocated. This mechanism does only work properly, because there is no structure
sharing. Otherwise, deallocation would be more complicated, since it would have to
consider multiple references to nodes, and could only deallocate a node if it is no
longer referenced.

For compact structures with a compact element type, storage is implicitly deallocated when the structure leaves its scope; otherwise the DEALLOCATE operation can be
applied to achieve this effect. For compact structures with a compact element type
the DEALLOCATE operation should be eliminated by an optimizing compiler, since it
does not perform any action (see also section 5.4.3). Therefore, even if a structure is
compact for a certain variant, it is advisable to deallocate the structure at the end of
its scope in order to avoid the dependency on the chosen variant.

DEALLOCATE must not be confused with CLEAR which does not only deallocate the
constituents of a structure but also resets it to its well-defined initial value. This
reset can have a significant additional cost, in particular in the case of object-bounded
structures. It is not required, if the object is to be immediately deallocated, and
therefore no longer used.

## 5.3.2 Operations Based on Indices

As opposed to constructor operations, which change the structure of an object, the operations based on indices may be used to manipulate the value of elements of an object by preserving its internal structure.

For all operations, the index parameter must denote some valid index of the given structure.

Although some data types, like sets, do not require an explicit notion of indices (i.e. element occurrences), this notion is provided for orthogonality. There are several operations that yield indices as a result, for example FIND_PROPERTY, which looks for an element with a certain property. The GET_ELEM operation is used in such cases to come from the index to the element value. The GET_ELEM operation is read-only. It yields the value of the element in the structure S at the index position I.

```
function GET_ELEM (S : in STRUCT;
                   I : in INDEX) return ELEM_TYPE;
```

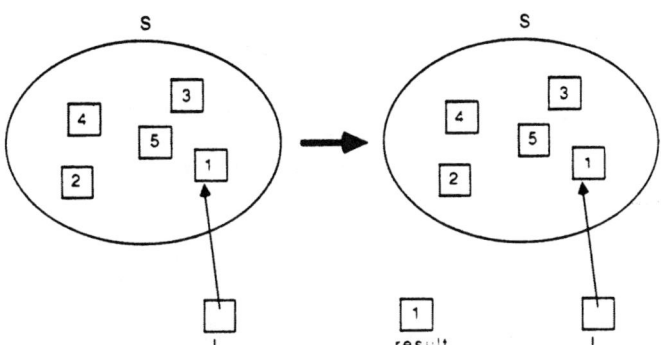

The following index based operations are only provided for data types with explicit insert positions, that means for lists and trees. For other types they might destroy the implicitly defined element structure.

SET_ELEM copies the element value from E to the element with index I in the structure S.

```
procedure SET_ELEM (S : in out STRUCT;
                    I : in INDEX;
                    E : in ELEM_TYPE);
```

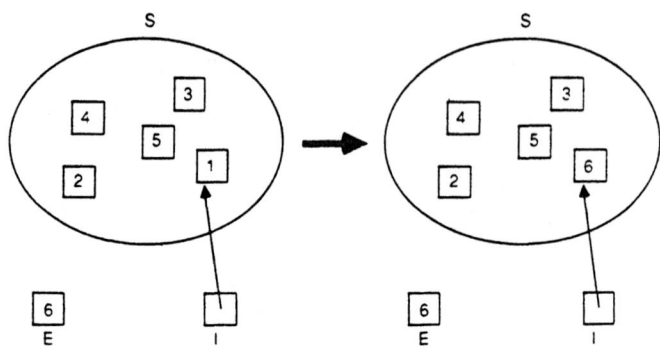

```
procedure TRANSFER_ELEM (TO     : in out ELEM_TYPE;
                         FROM   : in out STRUCT;
                         FROM_I : in INDEX);
procedure TRANSFER_ELEM (TO   : in out STRUCT;
                         FROM : in out ELEM_TYPE;
                         TO_I : in INDEX);
```

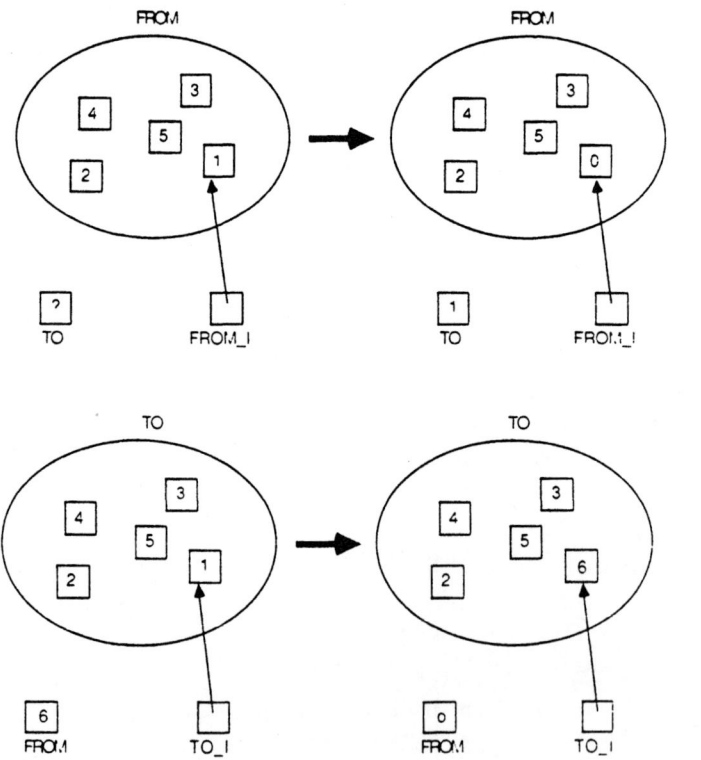

The **TRANSFER_ELEM** operations transfer an element value to or from a variable from or to an element in a structure, respectively. These operations are useful when **TRANSFER** is more efficient than **COPY**, in particular, for dispersed element types. Note the difference between **TRANSFER_ELEM** and **MOVE**. Both are based on the element type's **TRANSFER** operation, but **TRANSFER_ELEM** transfers the element to an already existing element within the structure, whereas **MOVE** creates a new element occurrence and then performs the transfer.

```
generic
    with procedure MODIFICATION (E : in out ELEM_TYPE);
procedure MODIFY_ELEM (S : in out STRUCT; I : in INDEX);
```

**MODIFY_ELEM** has the same effect as a sequence of **GET_ELEM**, **MODIFICATION** and **SET_ELEM**. However, **GET_ELEM** and **SET_ELEM** copy the element value, whereas the **MODIFICATION** operation may work "in situ". This is particularly useful for multi-level types, like lists of sets of something. As an example for **MODIFY_ELEM**, consider the increment of a given element:

```
package LIST_OPS is new LISTS (INTEGER);
L : LIST_OPS.STRUCT;
I : LIST_OPS.INDEX;

procedure INCREMENT_ELEM (E : in out INTEGER) is
begin
   E := E + 1;
end INCREMENT_ELEM;

procedure INCREMENT is new LIST_OPS.MODIFY_ELEM (INC_ELEM);

INCREMENT (L, I);
```

For key/info data types the operations that were introduced in this section have the following profile:

```
function GET_KEY  (S : in STRUCT; I : in INDEX) return KEY_TYPE;

function GET_INFO (S : in STRUCT;
                   I : in INDEX) return INFO_TYPE;
```

```
procedure SET_INFO (S    : in out STRUCT;
                     I    : in INDEX;
                     INFO : in INFO_TYPE);

procedure TRANSFER_INFO (TO     : in out INFO_TYPE;
                         FROM   : in out STRUCT;
                         FROM_I : in INDEX);

procedure TRANSFER_INFO (TO   : in out STRUCT;
                         FROM : in out INFO_TYPE;
                         TO_I : in INDEX);

generic
   with procedure MODIFICATION (INFO : in out INFO_TYPE);
procedure MODIFY_INFO (S : in out STRUCT; I : in INDEX);
```

These profiles allow the arbitrary modification of an element's info part, whereas the key part can only be read, but not modified.


## 5.3.3   Access by Position Count

For linear structures, like lists and orders, the elements can also be accessed by their position count. The first element has position count 1. The operations INDEX_POS and INDEX_VAL convert a numeric position into an index and vice versa. The operations are named in accordance with the Ada attributes POS and VAL. The positional operations GET/SET/TRANSFER_ELEM are overloaded with the index based operations; the generic operation is named MODIFY_ELEM_BY_POS since overloading for Ada generics is illegal.

The position based operations can be supported very efficiently for certain array representations of lists, where the array offset can be immediately computed from the position count. The operations are analogous to the operations based on indices; the operations except the GET_ELEM operations are defined only for data types with an explicit insert position.

```
function INDEX_VAL (S : in STRUCT;
                    P : in POSITIVE) return INDEX;
function INDEX_POS (S : in STRUCT;
                    I : in INDEX) return POSITIVE;
```

```
      function GET_ELEM (S : in STRUCT;
                         P : in POSITIVE) return ELEM_TYPE;


      procedure SET_ELEM (S : in out STRUCT;
                          P : in POSITIVE;
                          E : in ELEM_TYPE);


      procedure TRANSFER_ELEM (TO     : in out ELEM_TYPE;
                               FROM   : in out STRUCT;
                               FROM_P : in POSITIVE);


      procedure TRANSFER_ELEM (TO   : in out STRUCT;
                               FROM : in out ELEM_TYPE;
                               TO_P : in POSITIVE);


      generic
         with procedure MODIFICATION (E : in out ELEM_TYPE);
      procedure MODIFY_ELEM_BY_POS (S : in out STRUCT;
                                    P : in POSITIVE);
```

## 5.3.4   Selector Operations

Selectors operations neither modify the structure nor the element values of a structure
parameter. Several selector operations require the notion of equality of element values.
This notion is provided by the generic parameter EQUAL, if it is given or otherwise by
the predefined equality on the element type.

```
      function COUNT (S   : in STRUCT
                  [ ;SUB : in PART := WHOLE_STRUCT ]) return NATURAL;
```

COUNT yields the number of elements that are currently in (the part given by SUB of)
the structure S.

```
      function IS_EMPTY (S : in STRUCT) return BOOLEAN;
```

IS_EMPTY determines whether the structure S is empty, that means S has no elements,
that means its COUNT is 0.

```
function FIND (E    : in ELEM_TYPE;
              S    : in STRUCT
           [ ;SUB : in PART := WHOLE_STRUCT ]) return INDEX;

function SKIP (E    : in ELEM_TYPE;
              S    : in STRUCT
           [ ;SUB : in PART := WHOLE_STRUCT ]) return INDEX;
```

FIND looks for an element with value E in (the part given by SUB of) the structure S.
SKIP is only defined for lists and orders and finds the first occurrence that is not equal
to E. Both return the index of such an occurrence, if it exists; otherwise the index
value NIL is returned.  For lists and orders, the search is from the first to the last
element; for others data types it is undefined. If a particular search order is desired,
the more general iterators FIND_PROPERTY and SKIP_PROPERTY can be used.

```
function COUNT_ELEM (S    : in STRUCT;
                     E    : in ELEM_TYPE
                  [ ;SUB : in PART := WHOLE_STRUCT ])
                     return NATURAL;
```

COUNT_ELEM yields the number of occurrences of the element value E in (the part given
by SUB of) the structure S.

```
function IS_ELEM (S    : in STRUCT;
                  E    : in ELEM_TYPE;
                  SUB : in PART := WHOLE_STRUCT) return BOOLEAN;
```

IS_ELEM determines, whether the element value E occurs in (the part given by SUB
of) the structure S, that means whether FIND yields some index different from NIL.

```
function "=" (LEFT, RIGHT : in STRUCT) return BOOLEAN;
function EQUAL (LEFT, RIGHT : in STRUCT)
               return BOOLEAN renames "=";
```

"=" compares the two structures LEFT and RIGHT for (structural) equality. Note the
difference between structural equality and identity.  Two structures may be equal
even if they are not identical. Two structures are identical if they contain the same
occurrences of elements (since there is no structure sharing, either all or none occurrences of two structures are identical).  Element values are compared by using the
equality operation on the element type if it is given with the generic parameter EQUAL

or otherwise the predefined equality.

**EQUAL** is a synonym for "=". We have chosen it as the standard name for equality, since "=" can only be defined for limited types.

The operations FIRST, LAST, NEXT, and PREVIOUS are defined for linear structure, like lists, orders or stacks.

```
function FIRST (S : in STRUCT) return INDEX;

function FIRST (S : in STRUCT) return ELEM_TYPE;

function LAST (S : in STRUCT) return INDEX;

function LAST (S : in STRUCT) return ELEM_TYPE;

function NEXT (S        : in STRUCT;
               I        : in INDEX;
               CIRCULAR : in BOOLEAN := FALSE) return INDEX;

function PREVIOUS (S        : in STRUCT;
                   I        : in INDEX;
                   CIRCULAR : in BOOLEAN := FALSE) return INDEX;
```

FIRST and LAST yield the first and last index or element value. If the structure is empty, the result is NIL. NEXT and PREVIOUS allow to traverse the structure in both directions, where NEXT steps in the direction from first to last, and PREVIOUS in the opposite direction. If the CIRCULAR parameter is set to TRUE, the operations wrap around at the end or beginning of the structure; otherwise the result is NIL, if the end or beginning of the structure is reached.

For key/info data types the operations that were introduced in this section have the following profile:

```
function FIND (S : in STRUCT; K : in KEY_TYPE) return INDEX;
function FIND_INFO (S    : in STRUCT;
                    INFO : in INFO_TYPE) return INDEX;
```

```
function COUNT_KEY (S : in STRUCT
                    K : in KEY_TYPE) return NATURAL;
function COUNT_INFO (S    : in STRUCT;
                     INFO : in INFO_TYPE) return NATURAL;


function IS_KEY (S : in STRUCT; K : in KEY_TYPE) return BOOLEAN;
function IS_INFO (S    : in STRUCT;
                  INFO : in INFO_TYPE) return BOOLEAN;
```

## 5.3.5   Iterators

An iterator allows the application of some ACTION to all elements of a structure, one after the other. Due to two different underlying structures, like lists and trees, there are basically different iteration patterns, for example a linear one for lists:

```
I := FIRST (S);
while I /= NIL loop
   <iteration body>;
   I := NEXT (S, I);
end loop;
```

and a recursive one for trees:

```
procedure TREE_ITERATE (I : in INDEX) is
begin
   <iteration body>;
   for N in 1 .. NR_OF_SONS (S, I) loop
      TREE_ITERATE (SON (S, I, N));
   end loop;
end TREE_ITERATE;
TREE_ITERATE (ROOT (S));
```

Especially for higher level structures we want to abstract from the concrete iteration pattern and provide an iteration operation from which we just know that it enumerates each occurrence of the structure exactly once, without having to know its representation. This operation is provided by the generic iterators APPLY, ITERATE and ITERATE_MOVE.

```
generic
   with procedure ACTION (E : in out ELEM_TYPE) is NONE1;
   with function  SELECTION
                     (E : in ELEM_TYPE) return BOOLEAN is TRUE;
   with function  UNTIL
                     (S : in STRUCT;
                      I : in INDEX) return BOOLEAN is FALSE;
   with procedure ACTION_WITH_INDEX
                     (E : in ELEM_TYPE;
                      I : in INDEX) is NONE;
   with function  SELECTION_WITH_INDEX
                     (S : in STRUCT;
                      I : in INDEX) return BOOLEAN is TRUE;
procedure APPLY (S    : in out STRUCT
              [ ;SUB : in PART := WHOLE_STRUCT ]
              [ ;ORD : in ITERATION_ORDER := ... ]);


generic
   with procedure ACTION (E : in ELEM_TYPE) is NONE;
   with function  SELECTION
                     (E : in ELEM_TYPE) return BOOLEAN is TRUE;
   with function  UNTIL
                     (S : in STRUCT;
                      I : in INDEX) return BOOLEAN is FALSE;
   with procedure ACTION_WITH_INDEX
                     (E : in ELEM_TYPE;
                      I : in INDEX) is NONE;
   with function  SELECTION_WITH_INDEX
                     (S : in STRUCT;
                      I : in INDEX) return BOOLEAN is TRUE;
procedure ITERATE (S    : in STRUCT
                [ ;SUB : in PART := WHOLE_STRUCT ]
                [ ;ORD : in ITERATION_ORDER := ... ]);
```

```
generic
   with procedure ACTION (S : in out STRUCT; I : in INDEX);
   with function  SELECTION
                  (S : in STRUCT;
                   I : in INDEX) return BOOLEAN is TRUE;
   with function  UNTIL
                  (S : in STRUCT;
                   I : in INDEX) return BOOLEAN is FALSE;
procedure ITERATE_MOVE (S   : in STRUCT
                       [ ;SUB : in PART := WHOLE_STRUCT ]
                       [ ;ORD : in ITERATION_ORDER := ... ]);
```

The iteration principle is the same for the three iterators. It iterates over elements of the structure S and applies the ACTION to these elements. For structures that have PARTs, the iteration iterates only over the elements of the given part SUB. For types with an iteration order, like lists and trees, an iteration order can be specified, that determines in which order the elements of the structure are visited (for example, FROM_FIRST for lists or INFIX for binary trees). The type ITERATION_ORDER is different for each data type. It will be discussed in the corresponding sections of chapter 6.

Iteration may be selective, that means only elements for which SELECTION yields true are iterated over. UNTIL specifies a condition for iteration exit. Iteration is terminated when this predicate yields true. It is tested before each iteration step.

The default operations TRUE and FALSE for selection and termination make the operations iterate over all elements of the structure (part).

APPLY and INSERT provide the additional generic parameters ACTION_WITH_INDEX and SELECTION_WITH_INDEX. They are executed in the same way as ACTION and SELECTION and provide access to the index of the current element. This index must not be used to change the structure that is iterated over. Most of the higher level iterators of the catalogue, like FIND or MAX, make use of this facility in to return the index of an element with the sought property. These hooks are not needed for ITERATE_MOVE, since the ACTION and SELECTION operations themselves have the structure and the index of the current element as a parameter.

The difference between the three operations is the kind of ACTION that can be performed with the elements. APPLY can modify the element values of the structure S over which it iterates, since E is an in out parameter. ITERATE has only read access to the structure and the current element. APPLY and ITERATE both leave the internal structure unchanged; they do not insert or remove elements. `ITERATE_MOVE` allows the `ACTION` to remove the current element from the structure; `ACTION` may (but need not) completely remove the element denoted by the index `I` or moved it to another structure. These are the only structural changes that `ACTION` may perform.

The Ada mechanism for parameter modes enforces a proper use of iteration. `APPLY` and `ITERATE_MOVE` can only be used for structures for which write access is granted; they are not allowed for structure objects that are constants or in parameters.

As an example for the use of iterators, suppose we have some structure `PROJECTS` with elements that describe a project and we want to determine whether the sum of the budgets of all research projects is greater than a given `RESEARCH_BUDGET`. We implement this problem by selectively applying a `SUM_UP` operation to the appropriate elements of the `PROJECTS` structure, until the sum is greater than the given bound:

```
function RESEARCH_BUDGET_EXHAUSTED
            (PROJECTS         : in SET_OF_PROJECTS;
             RESEARCH_BUDGET : in INTEGER) return BOOLEAN is
   SUM : INTEGER := 0;

   procedure SUM_UP (P : in PROJECT) is
   begin
      SUM := SUM + P.BUDGET;
   end SUM_UP;

   function IS_RESEARCH_PROJECT (P : in PROJECT)
                                    return BOOLEAN is
   begin
      return P.DOMAIN = RESEARCH;
   end IS_RESEARCH_PROJECT;

   function EXHAUSTED (P : in PROJECT) return BOOLEAN is
   begin
      return SUM >= RESEARCH_BUDGET;
   end EXHAUSTED;

   procedure SUM_UP_ITERATION is
      new ITERATE (ACTION    => SUM_UP,
                   SELECTION => IS_RESEARCH_PROJECT,
                   UNTIL     => EXHAUSTED);
```

```
begin
  SUM_UP_ITERATION (S);
  return SUM >= RESEARCH_BUDGET;
end RESEARCH_BUDGET_EXHAUSTED;
```

Note that some subprograms that are parameters of **ITERATE** access global variables. This is a quite typical behavior in the case of iteration and there is nothing wrong with that. The iteration operations access and possibly modify global data in the same way as an ordinary loop would do. They may even be independent from their parameters, as it is the case for the **EXHAUSTED** function in our example. This, too, is quite a typical pattern.

We see that it takes some more effort to set up and to provide the procedures and functions required as generic actual parameters for **ITERATE**, than to write a usual while-loop. However, we gain the following advantages:

- As mentioned before, the general iteration scheme makes us independent from the representation of a structure. This is not only a question of adaptability to a new implementation choice but also a question of efficiency. Each underlying implementation may choose its most efficient iteration scheme, because the programmer refrained from overspecification.

- The three operations (application, selection and until) characterize three different aspects of an iteration. In an ordinary loop, these aspects are often mixed. We find it worthwhile to think in these terms and to make them explicit.

- The iteration operations guarantee termination of the iteration (provided the parameter operations terminate). This is perhaps the most significant benefit from using the iterators because the omission of some loop increment is a common error when programming with explicit loops.

- Finally, for more complicated selection and until predicates, we may be able to reuse these predicates in other iterations.

The **ITERATE_MOVE** operation is typically used to remove all elements from the structure that are selected by some property, or to move these elements to another structure, for example, in order to convert the structure. If the element type is dispersed, it may be worthwhile to iteratively **MOVE** the elements from one structure to the other. This requires the **ITERATE_MOVE** operation, since **APPLY** and **INSERT** must not remove any elements from the structure that is iterated over. A typical conversion is from unbounded to bounded structures at the end of a composition phase:

```
      package DYNAMIC is new LINKED_LISTS (ITEM);
      use DYNAMIC;
      DYNAMIC_ITEMS : DYNAMIC.STRUCT;

  begin -- composition
      ...
      INSERT (DYNAMIC_ITEMS, IT);
      ...
      declare
         package STATIC is new TABULAR_LISTS (ITEM);
         use STATIC;
         STATIC_ITEMS  : STATIC.STRUCT (COUNT (DYNAMIC_ITEMS));

         -- conversion
         procedure REMOVE_AT_INDEX_TO_STATIC
                         (S : in out DYNAMIC.STRUCT;
                          I : in DYNAMIC.INDEX) is

            procedure MOVE_TO_STATIC (IT : in out ITEM) is
            begin
               MOVE (TO => STATIC_ITEMS, FROM => IT);
            end MOVE_TO_STATIC;

            procedure REMOVE_TO_STATIC is
               new GENERIC_REMOVE (MOVE_TO_STATIC);

         begin
            REMOVE_TO_STATIC (S, AT_INDEX (I));
         end REMOVE_AT_INDEX_TO_STATIC;

         procedure DYNAMIC_TO_STATIC is
            new DYNAMIC.ITERATE_MOVE (REMOVE_AT_INDEX_TO_STATIC);

      begin -- analysis

         DYNAMIC_TO_STATIC (DYNAMIC_ITEMS);
         ...
         FIND (STATIC_ITEMS, IT);
         ...
      end;
```

Conversion from or to structures that have a key and a value work similarly.

For key/info data types the operations that were introduced in this section have a corresponding profile where the element type parameters

```
E : <mode> ELEM_TYPE;
```

are replaced by the two parameters

```
K    : <mode> KEY_TYPE;
INFO : <mode> INFO_TYPE;
```

with the same mode.


## 5.3.6   Reduction

Reduction is an often occurring iteration pattern, where a binary operation is successively applied to elements of the structure, for example, to calculate the sum of elements, or to find the maximum element.

```
generic
   with function OPERATION (LEFT, RIGHT : in ELEM_TYPE)
                           return ELEM_TYPE;
   with function SELECTION (E : in ELEM_TYPE)
                           return BOOLEAN is TRUE;
   with function UNTIL (E : in ELEM_TYPE)
                       return BOOLEAN is FALSE;
function REDUCE (S   : in STRUCT
             [ ;SUB : in PART ]
             [ ;ORD : in ITERATION_ORDER := DONT_CARE ])
                return ELEM_TYPE;
```

With respect to the parameters SELECTION, UNTIL, S, SUB and ORD, reduction behaves like the iteration operations discussed before. These parameters determine to which elements of the structure (and possibly in which order) the reduction is applied.

An instance of the function REDUCE, with an OPERATION op, applied to elements E_1, E_2, ..., E_n, yields the result E_1 op E_2 op ... op E_n.

Thus, we can calculate the sum of integer elements of a set with

```
function SUM is new INT_SET_OPS.REDUCE ("+");
...
INT_RESULT := SUM (INT_SET);
```

For data types that have no iteration order, reduction is applied in some unspecified order. To guarantee the independence of the reduction result from the chosen order, OPERATION must be commutative and associative.

REDUCE must not be applied to an empty structure (part) since no meaningful result can be returned in this case. This difficulty is removed with UREDUCE that allows the specification of a Unit of the element type.

UREDUCE is identical to REDUCE except for the additional generic parameter UNIT. A unit U for a given operation op is a value for which E op U = U op E = E. If UREDUCE is applied to an empty sequence of elements, it returns the unit as a result. The provided unit should always have the given unit property, so the reduction may add the unit to the given structure and then apply the usual REDUCE to the result, that is now guaranteed to be not empty.

```
generic
   with function OPERATION (LEFT, RIGHT : in ELEM_TYPE)
                              return ELEM_TYPE;
   with function UNIT return ELEM_TYPE;
   with function SELECTION (E : in ELEM_TYPE)
                              return BOOLEAN is TRUE;
   with function UNTIL (E : in ELEM_TYPE)
                          return BOOLEAN is FALSE;
function UREDUCE (S    : in STRUCT
                 [ ;SUB : in PART ]
                 [ ;ORD : in ITERATION_ORDER := DONT_CARE ])
                   return ELEM_TYPE;
```

For the sum, zero is the unit. So we would write:

```
function ZERO return INTEGER is begin return 0; end ZERO;
function SUM is new UREDUCE ("+", UNIT => ZERO);
```

REDUCE and UREDUCE apply an OPERATION where the operators LEFT and RIGHT and the function result are of the same type, namely the element type. Suppose that we want to calculate a floating point value by dividing 1.0 through all (selected) integers from the structure. Since the applied operation now takes a float and an integer value and returns a float, the REDUCE operations introduced so far cannot be used. The solution is the use of AREDUCE (where the A stands for asymmetric).

```
generic
    type RESULT_TYPE is limited private;
    with function OPERATION (LEFT  : in RESULT_TYPE;
                             RIGHT : in ELEM_TYPE)
                            return RESULT_TYPE;
    with function UNIT return RESULT_TYPE;
    with function SELECTION (E : in ELEM_TYPE)
                            return BOOLEAN is TRUE;
    with function UNTIL (E : in ELEM_TYPE)
                        return BOOLEAN is FALSE;
function AREDUCE (S   : in STRUCT
                 [ ;SUB : in PART ]
                 [ ;ORD : in ITERATION_ORDER := DONT_CARE ])
                 return RESULT_TYPE;
```

Different from UREDUCE, the operand LEFT and the result of OPERATION and the UNIT are of a type RESULT_TYPE, which must also be supplied as a generic parameter.

For our example, the unit is obviously 1.0. The division of a float by an integer is not predefined in Ada, so we have to define this operation ourselves.

```
function ONE return FLOAT is begin return 1.0; end ONE;
function "/" (LEFT : in FLOAT; RIGHT : in INTEGER)
            return FLOAT is
begin
    return LEFT / FLOAT (RIGHT);
end;

function RECIPROCAL_PRODUCT is
    new AREDUCE (RESULT_TYPE => FLOAT,
                 OPERATION   => "/",
                 UNIT        => ONE);
...
FLOAT_RESULT := RECIPROCAL_PRODUCT (INT_STRUCT);
```

We have chosen the UNIT as a function instead of a value since an in parameter does not work for a limited element or result type.

For key/info data types there are two classes of reduction operation; one class with the same names as the operation introduced in this section, where the parameters of type ELEM_TYPE are replaced by KEY_TYPE parameters, and one with the names [UA]REDUCE_INFO, where the parameters of type ELEM_TYPE are replaced by INFO_TYPE parameters.

## 5.3.7 Find, Skip and Count

The functions FIND_PROPERTY, SKIP_PROPERTY, and COUNT_PROPERTY are the generalized versions of the FIND, SKIP and COUNT operations that we already introduced.

In all cases, an index to some element with the given PROPERTY is returned. If no such element exists, the result is the index value NIL.

As before, parts and iteration orders may be specified for those structures which provide these notions.

```
generic
    with function PROPERTY (RIGHT : in ELEM_TYPE) return BOOLEAN;
function FIND_PROPERTY
            (S   : in STRUCT
        [ ;SUB : in PART ]
        [ ;ORD : in ITERATION_ORDER := DONT_CARE ])
            return INDEX;


generic
    with function PROPERTY (RIGHT : in ELEM_TYPE) return BOOLEAN;
function SKIP_PROPERTY
            (S   : in STRUCT
        [ ;SUB : in PART ]
        [ ;ORD : in ITERATION_ORDER := DONT_CARE ])
            return INDEX;
```

```
generic
   with function PROPERTY (RIGHT : in ELEM_TYPE) return BOOLEAN;
function COUNT_PROPERTY
               (S   : in STRUCT
            [ ;SUB : in PART ]
            [ ;ORD : in ITERATION_ORDER := DONT_CARE ])
               return NATURAL;
```

As an example we search for an employee who has no superior manager in the company.

```
function HAS_NO_MANAGER (E : in EMPLOYEE) return BOOLEAN is
begin
   return E.MANAGER = null;
end HAS_NO_MANAGER;

function A_DIRECTOR is new FIND_PROPERTY (HAS_NO_MANAGER);
...
D := A_DIRECTOR (EMPLOYEES);
```

For key/info data types the operations correspond to the ELEM_TYPE operations in the same way as for reduction. The INFO-operations are called FIND_INFO_PROPERTY, SKIP_INFO_PROPERTY, and COUNT_INFO_PROPERTY.


## 5.3.8   Existential and Universal Quantifiers

The existential and universal quantifiers EXIST and FORALL determine whether in a given structure an element with a given property exists or, respectively, whether all elements satisfy the PROPERTY. The usage is similar as for FIND_PROPERTY with the difference that the result is now boolean.

```
function HAS_A_DIRECTOR is new EXISTS (HAS_NO_MANAGER);

function ANARCHY is new FORALL (HAS_NO_MANAGER);
...
B := HAS_A_DIRECTOR (EMPLOYEES);

B := ANARCHY (EMPLOYEES);
```

For key/info data types the operations correspond to the ELEM_TYPE operations in the same way as for reduction. The INFO-operations are called EXISTS_INFO and FORALL_INFO.

## 5.3.9 Order Dependent Operations

Order dependent operations depend on an order relation over element values. For those data types that generally require an order relation for their implementation this order function is taken. For other data types, the order relation must be supplied as the generic parameter COMPARE of the generic package ORDER_OPERATIONS, in which all order dependent operations are included. The result type of COMPARE is the ternary enumeration type ORDER_RELATION, which is declared as

```
type ORDER_RELATION is (LESS, EQUAL, GREATER);
```

in the BUILDING_BLOCK_UTILITIES.

```
generic
    with function COMPARE (LEFT, RIGHT : in ELEM_TYPE)
                        return ORDER_RELATION is <>;
package ORDER_OPERATIONS is

    function COMPARE (LEFT, RIGHT : in STRUCT)
                    return ORDER_RELATION;

    function "<"  (LEFT, RIGHT : in STRUCT) return BOOLEAN;
    function "<=" (LEFT, RIGHT : in STRUCT) return BOOLEAN;
    function ">"  (LEFT, RIGHT : in STRUCT) return BOOLEAN;
    function ">=" (LEFT, RIGHT : in STRUCT) return BOOLEAN;

    function MAX (S : in STRUCT;
                [ ;SUB : in PART := WHOLE_STRUCT ]) return INDEX;
    function MAX (S : in STRUCT;
                [ ;SUB : in PART := WHOLE_STRUCT ])
                    return ELEM_TYPE;
```

```
      function MIN (S : in STRUCT;
                    [ ;SUB : in PART := WHOLE_STRUCT ]) return INDEX;
      function MIN (S : in STRUCT;
                    [ ;SUB : in PART := WHOLE_STRUCT ])
                      return ELEM_TYPE;

      procedure REMOVE_MAX (S : in out STRUCT;
                            [ ;SUB : in PART := WHOLE_STRUCT ]);
      procedure REMOVE_MIN (S : in out STRUCT;
                            [ ;SUB : in PART := WHOLE_STRUCT ]);
   end ORDER_OPERATIONS;
```

The operations COMPARE, "<", "<=", ">", and ">=" provide total ordering functions
on structure values. For lists, for example, the lexicographic ordering is such an order
relation. The subset relation on sets does not have this property. The order relations
defined by these order operations can be used when the structure type is used as
element type of another data type that requires a (total) ordering relation on its
elements.

MAX and MIN find the maximum or minimum element value or (one of its) occur-
rence(s). REMOVE_MAX and REMOVE_MIN remove a maximum or minimum element from
the given structure. If there are several occurrences of the minimum or maximum, an
arbitrary one is chosen.

As an example, we search for the employee with the maximum wage:

```
   function COMPARE_WAGES (LEFT, RIGHT : in EMPLOYEE)
                            return ORDER_RELATION is
   begin
      if    LEFT.WAGE < RIGHT.WAGE then return LESS;
      elsif LEFT.WAGE > RIGHT.WAGE then return GREATER;
      else                             return EQUAL;
      end if;
   end COMPARE_WAGES;

   package WAGE_ORDER is
      new SET_OF_EMPLOYEES.ORDER_OPERATIONS (COMPARE_WAGES);

   TOP_EMPLOYEE := WAGE_ORDER.MAX (EMPLOYEES);
```

We have chosen the COMPARE operation as the basis for comparison, instead of "<" or "<=", since COMPARE yields a ternary information in a single step, whereas two comparisons with "<" and EQUAL would be required otherwise. The ternary information is needed by the other comparison operations and in several other contexts. Although in our example, the effort is shifted into the COMPARE operation, this is not the general case. In particular, for composite values a single traversal of the structures is sufficient to determine the ternary result.

For a given "<" operation, the corresponding COMPARE operation can be obtained by instantiating the following generic operation from the BUILDING_BLOCK_UTILITIES.

```
generic
    type ELEM_TYPE is limited private;
    with function "<" (LEFT, RIGHT : in ELEM_TYPE)
                        return BOOLEAN is <>;
function COMPARISON (LEFT, RIGHT : in ELEM_TYPE)
                        return ORDER_RELATION;
```

The ORDER_OPERATIONS for key/info types have ELEM_TYPE replaced by KEY_TYPE. Two generic parameter operations must be specified for COMPARE, one for the KEY_TYPE and the INFO_TYPE.

## 5.3.10   Hash Operation

For the use of a structure type as element type of another structure that is implemented by hashing, the generic operation

```
generic
    with function HASH (E : in ELEM_TYPE) return INTEGER is <>;
function HASH_FUNCTION (S : in STRUCT) return INTEGER;
```

is provided. Its instantiation yields a hash function for the given structure type that can be used for the generic parameter operation HASH.

For key/info data types two generic parameter operations must be specified HASH, one for the KEY_TYPE and the INFO_TYPE.

# 5.4   Generic Parameters

In the simplest case of generic formal parameters there is just the element type that
is required.

```
generic
    type ELEM_TYPE is private;
package ADT is
```

An instantiation is then simply written as

```
package SET_OF_EMPLOYEES is new SET (EMPLOYEE);
```

ELEM_TYPE is the type of the elements of the data type. This type can be any non-
limited Ada type, either one that is predefined, like INTEGER, or any user defined type
including (constrained) array types or record types.

Depending on the chosen variant parameters there may be several other generic parameters. They will be outlined in the following sections. Which parameters exist in
which variants will be summarized later in the section on variant parameters.

Several parameters have default values or are specified using the Ada <> facility. They
need not be explicitly mentioned unless the implicitly chosen value shall be overridden.
Explicitly mentioned parameters should always be written in named notation, that
means by prefixing them with the name of the formal parameter. This can also be
done for the element type, but since the element type is always the first parameter it
is often convenient to use the positional notation.

In the simplest case, the element type must at least have the properties of a private
type, that means it must have predefined assignment and equality operations. In the
more general cases, any type may be used as the actual element type, a non limited
type as well as a limited type. In these cases, operations for equality, copy, transfer,
initialization and deallocation may have to be provided as actual generic parameters.
The following sections introduce these operations. Section 5.5.1 on variant parameters
explains, which of these operations must be provided for different classes of element
types.

## 5.4.1 Equal, Copy, and Transfer

EQUAL, COPY and TRANSFER on the element type are used by several operations on structures. For simple element types, the predefined equality and assignment operations are used.

```
generic
    type ELEM_TYPE is limited private;
    with function EQUAL (LEFT, RIGHT : in ELEM_TYPE)
                        return BOOLEAN is <>;
    with procedure COPY (TO   : in out ELEM_TYPE;
                        FROM : in ELEM_TYPE) is <>;
    with procedure TRANSFER (TO, FROM : in out ELEM_TYPE) is <>;
    ...
```

## 5.4.2 Initialization

For data types with an explicit insert position, like lists or trees, new elements can be inserted without specifying their value. This is helpful in case of element types that have a default value, in particular if these element types have an expensive copy operation; think, for example, of a tabular list. The major task of the initialization operation if to determine the space to be (initially) allocated for the element value. Since we assume that all elements must either be of fixed size or must be indirect, the initialization operation is only required for the case of indirect elements, including the case of variable elements, where the indirection is introduced within the data type itself. For the two cases, there are two different ways to specify the initialization. In the case of indirect and accessed elements, an initialization procedure is provided:

```
generic
    ...
    with procedure INITIALIZE (E : in out ELEM_TYPE) is <>;
```

In the case of variable-size elements, the initial discriminant value is specified:

```
generic
    ...
    INITIAL_ELEM : INTEGER := 0;
```

For simple elements, there is no explicit initialization; the element type may, however, have implicit initial values.


## 5.4.3   Deallocation

The generic parameter operation DEALLOCATE determines what happens when an element is removed from a structure.  It will in most cases result in a deallocation of the element value (if this is dispersed) and the UNCHECKED_DEALLOCATION of the designated element object.

```
generic
   ...
   with procedure DEALLOCATE (E : in out ELEM_TYPE) is <>;
```

For simple element types there is no deallocation; the value are assumed to be compact.


## 5.4.4   An Example

As an example for the definition and association of element operations, let us take access values that are used as elements; the equality shall be the equality of the designated element values: copying shall allocate a new dynamic object, whereas transfer shall just assign the pointer.  Finally, deallocation is implemented through Ada UNCHECKED_DEALLOCATION.

```
type REFERENCE is access OBJECT;

function EQUAL (LEFT, RIGHT : in REFERENCE) return BOOLEAN is
begin
   return LEFT.all = RIGHT.all;
end EQUAL;

procedure COPY (TO : in out REFERENCE; FROM : in REFERENCE) is
begin
   TO := new OBJECT'(FROM.all);
end COPY;
```

```
procedure TRANSFER (TO, FROM : in out REFERENCE) is
begin
   TO := FROM;
   FROM := null;
end TRANSFER;


procedure DEALLOCATE (E : in out REFERENCE) is
   procedure DEALLOC is
       new UNCHECKED_DEALLOCATION (OBJECT, REFERENCE);
begin
   DEALLOC (E);
end DEALLOCATE;


package REFERENCE_SET is new SET (REFERENCE);
```

All operations are passed implicitly (because of the <>).

The generic parameter operations have the same name and a corresponding signature
to the operations provided by the data type interfaces. That means that data types
can easily be combined.

```
package ENTITY_LIST is new LIST (ENTITY);
use ENTITY_LIST;
package SYMBOL_TABLE is new MAP (STRING, ENTITY_LIST.STRUCT);
   -- EQUAL, COPY, and TRANSFER from ENTITY_LIST
   -- are selected by <>
use SYMBOL_TABLE;
```

The use clause for ENTITY_LIST is necessary to make the <> feature work for the
instantiation of SYMBOL_TABLE.

These operations are particularly important for multi-level types, like sets of lists. In
this case the set operations, like INSERT or MOVE depend on the COPY and TRANSFER
operations of the element type. These operations may partly work in a recursive
manner: for a set of maps from strings to lists of integer, a copy applied to a set copies
the map elements which, in turn, leads to copying the lists. Again, the procedure for
deallocation works similar.

## 5.4.5   Key-Info Types

All considerations that were made for the element type so far, apply to key and info types as well. That means, all parameters that were mentioned so far exist for `KEY_TYPE` as well as `INFO_TYPE` instead of `ELEM_TYPE`.

## 5.4.6   Accessed Elements

Section 5.5.1 will introduce a variant that is based on a user defined access type that accesses the actual element type.

```
generic
    type ELEM_TYPE is limited private;
    type ELEM_ACCESS is access ELEM_TYPE;
    with procedure COPY (TO   : in out ELEM_ACCESS;
                         FROM : in ELEM_TYPE);
    ...
```

For this variant, the element type operation are partly given in terms of the access type. They will be outlined in section 5.5.1.

## 5.4.7   Bounded Collections

In the case of a bounded collection, the generic parameter `COLLECTION_SIZE` is used to specify the maximum sum of all elements that can be in structures of the newly instantiated type at a time. Note that the collection size is in fact in terms of the number of elements, not in terms of bits or bytes.

```
generic
    ...
    COLLECTION_SIZE : NATURAL;
```

# 5.5   Variant Parameters

Variant parameters control different aspects of the building blocks, like storage management, consistency checking, replacement of algorithms by data, properties of the element type and information hiding. Each variant parameter has a (mostly binary or ternary) set of possible values. By combining the choices for the different parameters we come to a tree of possible variants, where some branches are cut off due to restrictions on the combinations of certain parameter values. Figure 5.2 which mentions only a few of the possible parameters, may illustrate the exponential "explosion" through the combination of variant parameters.

Technically, the selection of a specific variant is done by a tool that takes the variant parameters and applies a macro processor to a parameterized building block, which summarizes all possible variants. This tool generates an Ada generic package whose name may be provided as a parameter or may be generated by the tool. The selected variant may be implemented using a certain variant of a lower level building block and so on. The variant selection tool is based on a description (similar to a Unix "makefile") which describes the dependencies between the variant parameters of the different levels. Some of these parameters can be derived from the parameters of the higher level variant others must be explicitly provided by the user of the tool. Names of lower level variants will usually be generated by the tool. The tool keeps track of already generated variants in order to use them for other variant generations.

The following sections introduce the general variant parameters and discuss their trade-offs.

## 5.5.1   Classes of Element Types

The different element type classes have already been mentioned when the generic parameters were discussed. The classes are distinguished mainly in order to simplify the use of the building blocks in simple and common cases but still to provide general solutions for the more complicated ones. The choice of the right variant is mainly determined by the element type.

| object_bounded | precondition check | simple_elements |
| | | indirect_elements |
| | | variable_size_elements |
| | | general_elements |
| | | accessed_elements |
| | constraint check | simple_elements |
| | | indirect_elements |
| | | variable_elements |
| | | general_elements |
| | | accessed_elements |
| | no_check | simple_elements |
| | | indirect_elements |
| | | variable_elements |
| | | general_elements |
| | | accessed_elements |
| collection_bounded | precondition check | simple_elements |
| | | indirect_elements |
| | | variable_elements |
| | | general_elements |
| | | accessed_elements |
| | constraint check | simple_elements |
| | | indirect_elements |
| | | variable_elements |
| | | general_elements |
| | | accessed_elements |
| | no_check | simple_elements |
| | | indirect_elements |
| | | variable_elements |
| | | general_elements |
| | | accessed_elements |
| unbounded | precondition check | simple_elements |
| | | indirect_elements |
| | | variable_elements |
| | | general_elements |
| | | accessed_elements |
| | constraint check | simple_elements |
| | | indirect_elements |
| | | variable_elements |
| | | general_elements |
| | | accessed_elements |
| | no_check | simple_elements |
| | | indirect_elements |
| | | variable_elements |
| | | general_elements |
| | | accessed_elements |

Figure 5.2: Combination of variant parameters

We distinguish five classes:

- `simple_elements`
- `indirect_elements`
- `general_elements`
- `variable_elements`
- `accessed_elements`
- `compact_elements`

We will now explain the six classes of element types and illustrate their usage.

### 5.5.1.1 Simple Elements

In the simplest case (`simple_elements`) the element type must be a private type other than an unconstrained array or record type. The predefined equality and assignment operations are taken for `EQUAL`, `COPY`, and `TRANSFER`. No other than implicit initializations take place. No deallocation is performed for elements; the element type is handled as if it were compact.

The generic parameter part looks as follows:

```
type ELEM_TYPE is private;
```

### 5.5.1.2 Indirect Elements

The catalogue data types allow the direct and indirect storage of element. In the direct case, the elements themselves are stored; in the indirect case, an access value (pointer) to the element is stored. Both variants provide the same signature: operations are always in terms of the element, not in terms of the access value.

There are two major reasons for using `indirect_elements`: improving the performance of the `TRANSFER` operation and handling unconstrained element types, in particular elements of variable size. For indirect elements, copying is implemented by deallocating the current target (if this is not `null`), and allocating a new one with the value of the source. Transfer is implemented by pointer assignment. Deallocation is Ada `UNCHECKED_DEALLOCATION` and initialization is done with the `null` access value.

For the indirect elements variant, the access type and the additional operations are defined within the data type package. The user must only provide the element type as in the simple case; the element type must not be limited. The generic parameter part is the same as in the simple case.

An instantiation example is

```
package SET_OF_STRINGS is new SET (STRING);
```

### 5.5.1.3   General Elements

In the `general_elements` case the following operations must be provided as generic parameters. The element type may be limited but must be no unconstrained array or record type.

The generic parameter part looks as follows:

```
type ELEM_TYPE is limited private;
with function EQUAL (LEFT, RIGHT : in ELEM_TYPE)
                     return BOOLEAN is <>;
with procedure COPY (TO   : in out ELEM_TYPE;
                     FROM : in ELEM_TYPE) is <>;
with procedure TRANSFER (TO, FROM : in out ELEM_TYPE) is <>;
with procedure DEALLOCATE (E : in out ELEM_TYPE) is <>;
```

The generic parameters have the same signature as the corresponding structure operations, which allows a hierarchical composition of structure types that makes use of the Ada `<>` facility. The general variant will be used in two cases; first, if the element type is in fact a limited type and the simple case is excluded for this reason; second, if the predefined operations for equality, assignment, or deallocation are not the intended ones.

The `BUILDING_BLOCK_UTILITIES` provide the generic package `ELEM_OPS` to define, for a given non-limited type, the operations that are needed as generic parameters of the

**general_elements** variant. This package may be instantiated for a given **ELEM_TYPE** to define the standard operations for this element type. Those operation that shall deviate from the standard behavior must then be explicitly redefined. Note that the operations from **ELEM_OPS** must be made visible by a use clause for the instantiated package, in order to be identified by the default <> mechanism.

### 5.5.1.4    Variable(-Size) Elements

The handling of elements of variable size is a particular case where the indirect element representation is used. An often occurring situation is that the size of the element type depends on an (integer) discriminant. This is the case for all our variable-size data types, like tabular lists. For this purpose a special variant is provided whose formal element type is discriminated. This variant creates an indirect element representation by making use of the given discriminant. The discriminant of the actual type may be of the type **INTEGER** itself or of some subtype, like **NATURAL** or **POSITIVE**. Besides the element type, the general element operations **EQUAL**, **COPY**, **TRANSFER**, and, in case that the element type is dispersed, **DEALLOCATE** must be provided. The initialization is given in terms of the initial discriminant value **INITIAL_ELEM**.

The generic parameter part looks as follows:

```
type ELEM_TYPE (D : INTEGER) is limited private;
with function EQUAL (LEFT, RIGHT : in ELEM_TYPE)
                    return BOOLEAN is <>;
with procedure COPY (TO   : in out ELEM_TYPE;
                     FROM : in ELEM_TYPE) is <>;
with procedure TRANSFER (TO, FROM : in out ELEM_TYPE) is <>;
with procedure DEALLOCATE (E : in out ELEM_TYPE) is <>;
INITIAL_ELEM : INTEGER := 0;
```

An instantiation example is

```
type VARIABLE_LENGTH_STRING (LENGTH : NATURAL) is
   record
      STR : STRING (1 .. LENGTH);
   end record;
package SET_OF_STRINGS is new SET (VARIABLE_LENGTH_STRING);
```

Element types with more than one discriminant or with discriminants of types other than **INTEGER** may be used as indirect elements as described in the previous section.

The major advantage of the special knowledge of the discriminant is, that the **COPY** operation will only deallocate the target value if its discriminant does not match the one of the source. If it does, the source value is immediately assigned to the already allocated target object.

## 5.5.1.5   Accessed Elements

The `accessed_elements` variant is used instead of `indirect_elements`, if the user already has an access type to the element type defined, and he wants to use this type to implement the indirection. For this variant, there are additional generic parameters denoting the access type and operations for this type:

```
type ELEM_TYPE is limited private;
with function EQUAL (LEFT, RIGHT : in ELEM_TYPE)
                    return BOOLEAN is <>;

type ELEM_ACCESS is access ELEM_TYPE;
with procedure COPY (TO   : in out ELEM_ACCESS;
                     FROM : in ELEM_TYPE) is <>;
with procedure COPY (TO   : in out ELEM_TYPE;
                     FROM : in ELEM_ACCESS) is <>;
with procedure TRANSFER (TO : in out ELEM_ACCESS;
                         FROM : in out ELEM_TYPE) is <>;
with procedure TRANSFER (TO : in out ELEM_TYPE;
                         FROM : in out ELEM_ACCESS) is <>;
with procedure INITIALIZE (A : in out ELEM_ACCESS) is <>;
with procedure DEALLOCATE (A : in out ELEM_ACCESS) is <>;
```

The **COPY** and **TRANSFER** operations determine what happens in case of a copy or transfer of an element value from or into a structure. For example, if the element type has a discriminant, the copy and transfer operations could check whether the discriminants of source and target are the same and, if they are different, deallocate the current element and allocate a new one with the right discriminant values.

The **BUILDING_BLOCK_UTILITIES** provide the generic package **ACCESS_OPS** to define, for a given element type and its general operations, an access type together with the operations that are needed as generic parameters of the `accessed_elements` variant.

The general operations for the element type may be defined with the generic package
`ELEM_OPS` from the `BUILDING_BLOCK_UTILITIES`.

### 5.5.1.6  Compact Elements

The `compact_elements` variant is a special case of `general_elements`, where the
element type is known to be compact. This may have an impact on the performance
of certain `REMOVE` and `DEALLOCATE` operations.

If a part of a structure (possibly the whole structure) is to be removed or deallocated
it is in general necessary to iterate over all elements of the part and deallocate them.
Even if the deallocation operation is `null` the iteration itself may take some significant,
but unnecessary time. This time may be saved if the element type is known to be
compact. In the `compact_elements` case, the `DEALLOCATE` operation must not be
given as generic parameter operation. All other parameters are the same as form
`general_elements`.

```
type ELEM_TYPE is limited private;
with function EQUAL (LEFT, RIGHT : in ELEM_TYPE)
                    return BOOLEAN is <>;
with procedure COPY (TO   : in out ELEM_TYPE;
                     FROM : in ELEM_TYPE) is <>;
with procedure TRANSFER (TO, FROM : in out ELEM_TYPE) is <>;
```

The choice of `compact_elements` is an optimization that may depend on the choice
of the element type's properties. It should therefore only be considered in the very
last phase of variant 'tuning'. The default `dispersed_elements` should be used in
doubt.

## 5.5.2  Collection Management

With respect to efficiency, the acceptance of higher level concepts is the better the
more exhaustive the well-known lower level patterns can be covered. This has been
a major concern in the design of higher programming languages, in particular in the
area of storage management. A (comprehensive) catalogue of data types must also
provide means that allow a wide coverage of storage allocation facilities. Efficient
storage management was one of the major concerns of our catalogue. The variant pa-

rameter for collection management determines one of the major choices; other variant
parameters like the one for the element type class and other generic parameters have
an impact on the storage management strategies, too.

Our catalogue distinguishes three patterns of space allocation for the occurrences of
elements in a structure. They differ in the granularity of allocated items, which ranges
from a single element over all values of a given structure to all values of all structures
of (an instance of) an abstract data type. Depending on the choice for this parameter
the total amount of elements may be restricted:

- In the `object_bounded` case, the space for all elements of a structure object is
  allocated when the object is declared. This is the time, when the maximum size
  of the structure must be determined. Elements are allocated within this space.
  If an element is removed, its space can only be reused for allocations within the
  same object. The space of all elements of an object is implicitly deallocated
  when the object itself is deallocated, that means when the scope of the object
  is left or when the object is deallocated from an access type collection.

- In the `collection_bounded` case, the space for all elements of all structures of
  a given type is allocated when the type is elaborated. This is the time, when
  the maximum size of the whole collection must be determined. There is no
  general upper bound for the size of a structure object except the size of the
  whole collection. Elements of a structure object are allocated in the space of
  the object's type. If an element is removed, its space can (only) be reused for
  allocations of elements of objects of the same type. The space of all elements of
  all structures is implicitly deallocated when the scope of the type is left.

- In the `unbounded CASE`, the space for an element is allocated when it is inserted
  and is deallocated when it is removed. There is no general upper bound for the
  size of a structure object except the maximum storage size. If an element is
  removed its space can be arbitrarily reused. There is no implicit deallocation
  of element space, if the implementation does not provide a garbage collection
  mechanism which is unlikely for a real time language like Ada).

In the first two cases, we can take advantage of the runtime stack management in
case of subprogram calls which deallocates structures and type collections "for free".
Figure 5.3 shall illustrate the three variants in the situation of a type declaration in
a subprogram and two nested subprogram calls that create objects of this type.

Summarizing the characteristics, a stricter bound implies a better implicit element
deallocation, a worse reuse of single element space and a greater average waste of

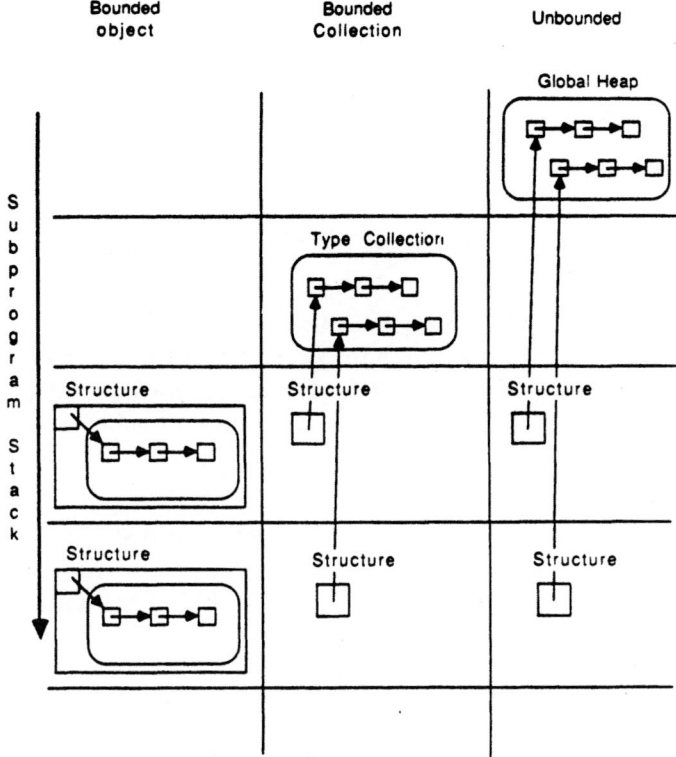

Figure 5.3: Variants for storage allocation

storage per structure object. With a virtual memory management, an access representation for the **unbounded** case may or may not cause more paging than an array representation, depending on whether element access is local with respect to the allocation time or local to the numeric positions. The right choice often depends on the language implementation. For the use of structures local to a subprogram, the quick implicit deallocation of the whole structure at the return from the subprogram is often superior to the slower explicit element deallocation if the sum of all structures existing at one time is small compared to all the structures created for the type.

The bounded variants should only be used, if the given upper bound is safe rather than a (rough) estimate. Such estimates can be extremely annoying (remember when the compiler told you about its 'stack overflow' or the command interpreter complained 'Arguments too long').

It is an often occurring pattern that structures are first built up and then used by read-only operations. A conversion from an unbounded to a bounded structure after the composition is complete is a considerable combination of the two variants.

## 5.5.3   Consistency Checking

The check of the consistent use of operations is an extremely helpful device, especially in the test phase of a system. It enables to localize the source of errors rather than their symptoms. Constraint checking does not come for free. Although recent methods achieve an average elimination of more than 90 per cent of Ada constraint checks, there still remain some. Besides that, the check of preconditions that are more complicated than simple equality or range checks, will be hard to eliminate automatically and will significantly contribute to the runtime.

For the data types of our catalogue there are two classes of checks:

- Ada constraint checks and
- checks of preconditions of the data type operations.

The satisfaction of the preconditions implies the satisfaction of Ada constraints (provided the catalogue is implemented correctly). Three variants are supported:

- With `precondition_check`, the precondition of each catalogue operation is explicitly checked whenever it is called. If a precondition is violated, the exception `ADT_USE_ERROR` (defined in the package `BUILDING_BLOCK_UTILITIES`) is raised.
- With `constraint_check`, Ada constraint checks are performed as usual and the usual exceptions (`CONSTRAINT_ERROR`, etc.) are raised if a check fails.
- With `no_check`, all kinds of Ada constraint checks are suppressed for the given data type. (Whether the compiler actually accepts the suppression depends on the implementation).

## 5.5.4   Algorithms vs. Data

For several operations there is a choice between executing the operation on demand or keeping a data-structure that represents the result of this operation. This data structure must then be updated by every operations that performs a relevant change on the structure. The best choice depends on the call profile of the operations: the more often an operation is called and the less often an operation is called that changes the value of this first operation, the better is the data representation of the first operation.

This mechanism can in general be applied to the `COUNT` operation which is implemented for every data type of the catalogue and which yields the number of elements that are currently in the structure. In the `counter` case, a counter is a component of the structure value that always holds the result of `COUNT`; it is incremented for each inserted element and decremented for each removed element. In the `no_counter` case, the number of elements is counted by iteration, each time the `COUNT` operation is called.

Further examples for this principle will be found for the specific data types; `PREVIOUS` and `LAST` are examples for linked lists.

## 5.5.5   Summary

To summarize, here are all general variant parameters with their possible values. The default comes first.

| | |
|---|---|
| Element type | `simple_elements, indirect_elements,` `variable_elements, general_elements,` `accessed_elements` |
| Dispersion | `compact_elements, dispersed_elements` |
| Collection management | `unbounded, object_bounded,` `collection_bounded` |
| Consistency checking | `precondition_check,` `constraint_check, no_check` |
| Algorithm vs. data | `no_counter, counter` |

# Chapter 6

# The Building Blocks

This chapter presents the specific data types of the catalogue, their different implementations and variants, their performance characteristics and their application.

Each section starts with a synopsis which roughly introduces the presented data type. Then we describe those operations that are specific for the data type and that have not already been described in chapter 5. After that we characterize the chosen implementations and give an overview of the provided specific and general variants. If the data type is represented using lower level data types, it is explained how these lower level types are used for representing the higher level.

# 6.1    Linked Collections

## 6.1.1    Synopsis

Linked collections are the basic data structure for linked lists and trees.  A linked collection allows the allocation of *nodes*, where a node consists of an element *value* of a given element type and a sequence of *links*; a link refers to a node. A reference to a node is called an *index*. There is a special index value *nil* that refers to no node. Nodes are not manipulable by themselves, but only through their indices.

The data type linked collections does not imply any structure, like a linear list structure, a tree structure, or a graph. It only knows about the number of links in an node. Depending on the chosen variant, this number is fixed or it is variable and must be determined for each node when it is allocated.

The reason for making linked collections a separate building block was to factor out different variants that have an impact on the performance of the higher level data types.

## 6.1.2    Types and Operations

```
procedure ALLOCATE (S      : in out STRUCT;
                   [ LINKS : in NATURAL; ]
                     I     : out INDEX);

procedure DEALLOCATE (S : in out STRUCT; I : in INDEX);
```

allocate and deallocate nodes.  The number of LINKS must only be given for a NODE_DEPENDENT_LINKS variant, which will be explained below.

```
function NR_OF_LINKS (S : in STRUCT;
                      I : in INDEX) return NATURAL;

function GET_LINK (S : in STRUCT;
                   I : in INDEX;
                   N : in POSITIVE) return INDEX;
```

```
procedure SET_LINK (S : in out STRUCT;
                    I : in INDEX;
                    N : in POSITIVE;
                    L : in INDEX);
```

If there is a fixed number of links per node, this is the result of NR_OF_LINKS; otherwise this operation returns the specific number of links of the given node. Links are denoted by their number, starting with 1. The parameter N of GET_LINK and SET_LINK denotes the number of the link; it must lie within the range 1 .. NR_OF_LINKS (S, I).

The usual index based operations GET/SET/TRANSFER/MODIFY_ELEM, are provided (see 5.3.2).

## 6.1.3 Implementation Overview

Linked collections may be implemented by access types or by arrays. In the first case, allocation and deallocation is done by the runtime system of the Ada programming language (using new and UNCHECKED_DEALLOCATION). The runtime system may, but need not supply a release mechanism for nodes thus returned to the system. It may therefore be necessary that the linked collections implement their own storage release mechanism, even in the case that access types are used. For a representation using arrays the release mechanism must in any case be provided explicitly. The array implementation represents indices by numeric indices of the array; allocation is done by selecting the next free index, or some index from the free list.

The access implementation has the (little) advantage that the address calculation is saved, which is needed for arrays. Moreover the runtime system may provide an elaborate garbage collection mechanism for access types, since it knows about all references to elements in the collection; this is not the case for the array implementation. Depending on whether the runtime system has the capability to allocate elements on a global collection with flexible size, the access implementation may be unbounded; array implementations are always bounded. For a bounded collection which is local to a subprogram, there is no difference between access types and array types with respect to the deallocation of the whole structure at the return from the subprogram, provided the runtime system places bounded access collections on the runtime stack. The deallocation is automatically achieved with the subprogram stack mechanism.

This discussion shows, that in the object/collection_bounded case an array implementation should be used, whereas the decision between array and access implementation is strongly implementation dependent in the **unbounded** case. This decision should not be left to the user by making it a variant parameter. It must be carefully considered when the catalogue is ported to some new implementation.

## 6.1.4   Specific Generic Parameters

In the case of a **fixed_links** variant, the number of links is given by the generic parameter when the linked collections are instantiated:

```
generic
    ...
    LINKS : POSITIVE;
```

## 6.1.5   Specific Variants

The choice between

```
    fixed_links, node_dependent_links
```

determines whether all nodes have the same fixed number of links or whether the number of links may be different for different nodes. In the first case, the number of links is determined by the generic parameter **LINKS**, when the data type is instantiated; in the second case the number of links is determined when an node is allocated and remains fixed from then on.

Node dependent links require an unbounded storage, since there is no upper bound for the number of links. Besides, a variant record for the node type can only be realized with the access implementation, since different nodes may have different sizes (discriminants). This implies that **node_dependent_links** may only be combined with **unbounded**.

## 6.1.6   General Variants

General variants are

```
simple_elements, indirect_elements, variable_elements,
    general_elements, accessed_elements, compact_elements
object_bounded, collection_bounded, unbounded
precondition_check, constraint_check, no_check
```

The data type linked collections is ultimately responsible for the implementation of the allocation management variants `object_bounded`, `collection_bounded` and `unbounded` for linked structures. Therefore, the decision for access or array types, that we mentioned above, may be crucial.

### 6.1.6.1  Combination of Variants

All combinations of the variants described above are possible except for the combinations

- of `node_dependent_links` with `object_bounded` or `collection_bounded`.

Figure 6.1 illustrates some of the possible variant combinations.

fixed links (1). object bounded

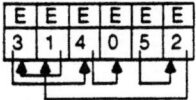

node dependent links. unbounded

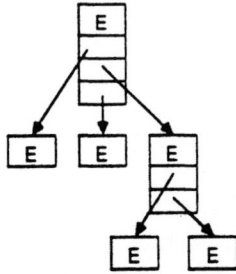

Figure 6.1: Some variants for linked collections

## 6.1.7    Representation of Linked Collections

Both the `object_bounded` and the `collection_bounded` variant are based on Ada
arrays. With the current implementation, the unbounded variant is based on Ada's
access types; with this variant, neither a `COLLECTION_SIZE` nor a `SIZE` discriminant
for a structure object needs to be specified; collection elements are allocated using a
**new** allocator from Ada.

# 6.2 Tabular Collections

## 6.2.1 Synopsis

Tabular collections are the basic data structure for tabular lists and trees. Like linked collections, a tabular collection consists of a sequence of *nodes*; a node is referred to by an *index*. A node may contain an element value or may be *invalid*. Invalid nodes may be indicated by special values or by flags. The linear sequence is represented by physical adjacency, either of the element values themselves or of *pointers* to the element values. This representation variant is hidden, but has an effect on the performance of several operations.

Like linked collections, tabular collections as a separate building block factor out different variants that affect the performance of higher level data types.

## 6.2.2 Types and Operations

The validity of a node can be checked and explicitly modified. Initially, the value and validity of a node is undefined. In the case of a special element value indicating that a node is invalid, these operations are based on generic parameter operations that must be provided for the element type (see 6.2.5).

```
function IS_VALID (S : in STRUCT; I : in INDEX) return BOOLEAN;

procedure VALIDATE (S : in out STRUCT; I : in INDEX);

procedure INVALIDATE (S : in out STRUCT; I : in INDEX);
```

The following three operations move element values from one node to another. Depending on the chosen variant, either the value itself or a pointer to the value is copied. The operations implicitly adjust the validity of the concerned nodes. If a transfer is from an invalid source, the target is invalidated.

```
procedure TRANSFER_ELEM (TO     : in out STRUCT;
                         FROM   : in out STRUCT;
                         FROM_I : in INDEX;
                         TO_I   : in INDEX);
```

```
procedure TRANSFER_ELEM (S      : in out STRUCT;
                         FROM_I : in INDEX;
                         TO_I   : in INDEX);

procedure SWAP (S : in out STRUCT; I1, I2 : in INDEX);
```

The usual index based operations GET/SET/TRANSFER/MODIFY_ELEM, are provided (see 5.3.2).


## 6.2.3   Implementation Overview

A tabular collection consists of one or more arrays of fixed length. Tabular collections are always object_bounded, that means the length is given as a constraint when a tabular collection object is declared.

There is one array that represents the linear sequencing of the elements in the collection. This array may either contain the element values themselves or pointers to the element values. In the second case, the element values are stored in a separate array of same length, but not necessarily in the same order as the corresponding pointers. This is an advantage, when the order of elements shall be changed, since not the elements themselves but rather the pointers must be copied. The greater the ratio between element size and pointer size the greater the advantage.

If there exist invalid nodes, these can either be marked by an invalid element value, that means a special element value that is not used otherwise, or by a flag. In the case of a flag, an additional bit-array is needed to store the flags. For a pointered variant, invalid nodes are always represented by using the nil pointer; therefore, the combination of pointered and invalid_value is not supported.


## 6.2.4   Specific Generic Parameters

In case of an invalid_value variant, a function that indicates the validity of an element value and a procedure that invalidates an element must be specified as actual generic parameters when the tabular collections are instantiated.

```
generic
   ...
   with function IS_VALID (E : in ELEM_TYPE)
                              return BOOLEAN is <>;
   with procedure INVALIDATE (E : in out ELEM_TYPE) is <>;
package TABULAR_COLLECTIONS
```

## 6.2.5  Specific Variants

The following variants are offered:

```
all_valid, invalid_flag, invalid_value
non_pointered, pointered
```

If all nodes are valid, neither a flag, nor an invalid element value is needed. The rest of the variants have already been described in the previous sections.

## 6.2.6  General Variants

General variants are

```
simple_elements, indirect_elements, variable_elements,
   general_elements, accessed_elements, compact_elements
precondition_check, constraint_check, no_check
```

Tabular collections are always `object_bounded`.

### 6.2.6.1  Combination of Variants

All combinations of the variants described above are possible, except for the combinations

- of `invalid_value` with `pointered`.

Figure 6.2 illustrates some of the possible variant combinations; white fields denote undefined values.

invalid-value (EI). non-pointered:

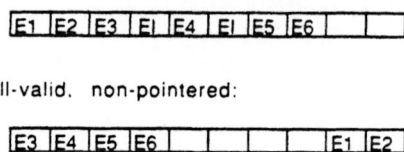

all-valid. non-pointered:

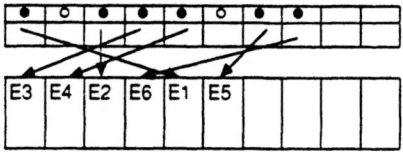

invalid-flag. pointered:

Figure 6.2: Some variants for tabular collections

# 6.3 Hash tables

## 6.3.1 Synopsis

Hash tables provide a particular implementation of an unordered collection of unique elements, which are divided into a key (of KEY_TYPE) and an info part (of INFO_TYPE). Hash tables allow a fast search for an element with a given key, which is mainly independent of the number of elements in the structure, by calculating the (array-) location of an element value from its key part.

The different hash table implementations differ mainly in the way how collisions, that means two different element values yielding the same position, are dealt with.

Hash tables are mainly used to implement other data types like sets and maps.

## 6.3.2 Types and Operations

A REMOVE_POSITION of a hash table is simply an INDEX; INSERT_POSITIONs cannot be specified, since elements are inserted according to their key part.

Hash tables provide

- the constructors CLEAR (see 5.3.1.1), FIND_OR_INSERT, GENERIC_REMOVE, and the MOVE operation from key and info variables into the structure (see 5.3.1.2),

- the operations based on indices GET_KEY, GET_INFO, SET_INFO, TRANSFER_INFO, MODIFY_INFO (see 5.3.2),

- the selectors COUNT, IS_EMPTY, FIND (see 5.3.4),

- and the iterators APPLY, ITERATE, ITERATE_MOVE (see 5.3.5).

As for all key/info data types, there is no way to modify the key part of an element in the hash table. The info parts, however, can be modified arbitrarily, using the operations based on indices. With some of the open addressing methods (ordered, Brents), constructor operations may change the correspondence between an index, and the element referenced by it. Therefore we specify the behavior of all hash tables as not index invariant; that means it is not allowed to keep an index that was obtained before performing a constructor operation, and to use it after this operation.

The characteristic property of hash tables is represented by the operations **FIND** and **FIND_OR_INSERT**, which have an average cost of $O(1)$, if the hash table size is chosen appropriately.

The set of operations is restricted to what is necessary to efficiently implement higher level operations. Fancy operations are not provided, since the data type is not intended for general use.


## 6.3.3   Implementation Overview


For lookup or insertion of elements, the given key is transformed by a hash function to an integer number. This number modulo the hash table size serves as insert position into the hash table. A suitable hash function should distribute all keys as even as possible over its range. Given such a hash function, and a proper ratio between the number of elements and the hash table size, there is a high probability that only one element maps to a particular position. Searching an element then only requires the computation of the hash function and an array access with the resulting position.

If several element values hash to the same position, which is called a *collision*, it becomes more complicated. There are several methods to resolve collisions that result in different hash table variants:


- Open addressing
  The collided element (for which the computed position is already in use) is stored in a different entry of the hash table, according to one of different methods.

- Hash chaining
  Collided elements are collected into a linked list; the list itself is stored in the hash table entry. The linked lists, also called chains, are either stored separately or in a part of the hash table. They may be unordered, sorted on the element values, or self-organizing to speed up searches.

- Hash buckets
  This method is similar to the second one. All elements hashing to the same position are kept in a bucket instead of a linked list. A bucket may be either an array in main memory, or a block of secondary storage.

Since hash buckets methods are mainly used for hashing on secondary storage we will not pursue them further.

## 6.3.4 Specific Generic Parameters

The instantiation of a hash table requires two specific parameters that specify the hash table size and the hash function that shall be used for the KEY_TYPE:

```
generic
   ...
   HASH_TABLE_SIZE : NATURAL;
   with function HASH (K : in KEY_TYPE) return INTEGER is <>;
package HASH_TABLES
```

## 6.3.5 Specific Variants

The primary selection is that of

open_addressing, hash_chaining

### 6.3.5.1 Open addressing

A hash table of fixed size (defined as an array of elements values) is used. For this reason, all open addressing variants are object_bounded and should only be selected if the maximum number of elements in the hash table is known in advance.

Initially, all entries of the hash table are empty. This can either be indicated by a particular key value, which is not needed by the user and which is passed as a generic parameter, or, if the user needs all values of the KEY_TYPE, a boolean array (of the same length as the hash table) serves to identify empty entries in the flag-diluted variant. These variants are distinguished by

empty_flag, empty_value

The `empty_flag` variant causes, in comparison to the `empty_value` variant, space
overhead, if the boolean array is not packed as a bit array, or some time overhead
to access the respective bit in the array. Therefore, it is recommended to use the
`empty_value` variant whenever possible.

Different variants for collision resolution are offered:

- `quadratic_probing`
  Quadratic probing adds 1, 4, 9, ... (modulo the hash table size) as increment
  to the original array position and probes the respective entries until it finds an
  empty one.

- `double_hashing`
  Double hashing uses a secondary hash function (which is to be passed as a
  generic parameter) to determine an increment. This is added (modulo the hash
  table size) repeatedly to the current position, until an empty entry is found.

- `ordered_hashing`
  Ordered hashing is a variant of double hashing. It places the elements into the
  hash table as if they had been inserted in increasing key sequence. This requires
  an order function on the key to be passed as a generic parameter. If there is a
  collision of an element to be inserted with another element having a greater key
  value, the new element is placed at its position, and a new entry for the greater
  element is searched for.
  Ordered hashing reduces the time for unsuccessful search such that it becomes
  equivalent to that of a successful search, with a small additional effort for an
  insert operation.

- `brents_open_hashing`
  Brent's open hashing is a variant of double hashing that minimizes the search
  time for a successful search, without reducing the search time for an unsuccessful
  search. Similar to ordered hashing, in case of a collision it also rearranges the
  positions of elements that are already in the hash table. This causes an increased
  effort for an insert operation.

Linear probing is not offered as a method for collision resolution, due to the clustering
of collided entries around the primary (i.e. non-collided) entries.

With open addressing methods, an element cannot simply be removed from a hash
table by resetting it to empty, since this could break a collision chain. Therefore
elements chains must either be shifted within the hash array, or an extra indicator

must be used for removed elements, which can be implemented by a flag or another special value. We call this way of representing removed elements *dilution*. So we have additional variants, namely

```
non_diluted, flag_diluted, value_diluted
```

Diluted entries can be reused when subsequent insertions lead to it. Diluted elements cause the search chains to become longer, which results in a certain performance degradation, together with the test of the dilution flag.

Summarizing, the open addressing variants are:

```
empty_flag, empty_value
non_diluted, value_diluted, flag_diluted
quadratic_probing, double_hashing,
    ordered_hashing, brents_open_hashing
```

### 6.3.5.2   Hash chaining

Only one variant of hash chaining methods is provided, which uses separate collision lists. Other variants like

- Coalesced hashing
- Coalesced hashing with cellar

do not seem to provide advantages over separate collision lists in an Ada environment.

The hash table itself contains only (the headers of) the separate collision lists, which contain the elements. A hash table is defined as a fixed size array of linked lists. A list contains all (collided) elements that map to the same hash table entry but no elements that map to other entries. If no element has yet been mapped to an entry, the list is empty. No special key value or flag-array is required as with the open addressing methods to indicate an empty entry. Also, removing of an element is very simple since it needs only to be removed from the list.

It should be noted that the hash table performance degenerates severely when the collision lists become longer because the search effort in the collision lists becomes then predominant. Instead of the O(1) time performance, we get with O(n/SIZE) a time performance linear to the ratio of the number of elements to the hash table size.

For hash chaining variants, only the **unbounded** and `collection_bounded` storage allocation variants are provided; the `object_bounded` case is best served with open addressing. Besides that, linked lists as we provide them, do not allow to implement object bounded hash tables in the sense, that the number of elements of a hash table are bounded. This is because one hash table consists of several lists, and either all lists (of all hash tables) can be bounded or a single list, but not an arbitrary set of lists.

## 6.3.6   General Variants

The general variants

```
simple_keys, indirect_keys, general_keys,
    variable_keys, accessed_keys, compact_keys
simple_infos, indirect_infos, general_infos,
    variable_infos, accessed_infos, compact_infos
object_bounded, collection_bounded, unbounded
precondition_check, constraint_check, no_check
counter, no_counter
```

are supported with characteristics as described in chapter 5.

## 6.3.7   Combination of Variants

All combinations of the variants described above are possible except for the combinations

- of `open_addressing` with `collection_bounded` or `unbounded`, and
- of `hash_chaining` with `object_bounded`.

Figure 6.3 illustrates some of the possible variant combinations; the identifiers **H***i* denote values that hash to position *i*.

open addressing. empty-flag. flag-diluted. quadratic probing

hash-chaining

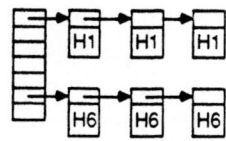

Figure 6.3: Some variants for hash tables

## 6.3.8   Representation of Hash tables

Open addressing hash tables are represented directly as arrays of the element type.
Hash tables with separate collision lists are represented as arrays of linked lists, with
a **single_link single_anchor circular** variant.

# 6.4   Lists, Linked Lists, Tabular Lists

## 6.4.1   Synopsis

Lists, linked lists and tabular lists implement linear sequences of *nodes* such that the sequencing of nodes can be freely manipulated by inserting or removing elements to or from arbitrary positions within the sequence. Each node of a list is accessible by means of an *index*.

Linked lists implement the *next/previous* relationship between nodes by explicitly storing links within the nodes. Nodes are allocated and deallocated on demand, so that existing nodes are not modified; once an element is inserted, its index remains the same until is is removed, we say linked lists are *index invariant*. Tabular lists express the *next/previous* relationship implicitly in form of physical adjacency. That means a tabular list stores all elements one after the other according to the next relationship. For tabular lists, inserting or removing a node may require the shifting of nodes, which results in the modification of the index of the shifted nodes; tabular lists are not *index invariant*. Lists abstract from the property of index invariance; they cannot be assumed to be index invariant so they can be implemented either by linked lists or by tabular lists.

As a consequence of not being index invariant, an index of a non-linked list must not be used any longer after the list structure has been modified by a constructor operation or a modifying iterator.

## 6.4.2   Types and Operations

Many of the list constructors and selectors allow a direct access to any position of the linear list structure.

**INSERT** and similar operations allow to insert a node or a sublist into a list at an arbitrary position, that is determined as a parameter of the **INSERT** operation. An **INSERT_POSITION** is defined relative to a given node, that is identified by its index, or as the first or last node.

```
type INSERT_POSITION is private;

function BEFORE  (I : in INDEX) return INSERT_POSITION;
function AFTER   (I : in INDEX) return INSERT_POSITION;
function FIRST      return INSERT_POSITION;
function LAST       return INSERT_POSITION;
function DONT_CARE return INSERT_POSITION;
```

The position **DONT_CARE** allows an element to be inserted at an arbitrary position; each list variant may freely choose this position to achieve the best insert efficiency; this is useful, when the list is used for implementing higher data types, like sets, where the sequencing is irrelevant. Figure 6.4 illustrates some possible cases; the identifiers in the nodes denote their indices.

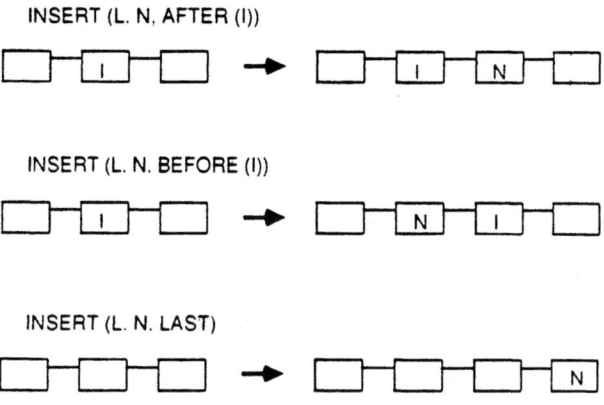

Figure 6.4: Insert positions for lists

Similarly to the **INSERT** operation, **REMOVE** and **MOVE** allow the removal of a node or a sublist from an arbitrary position of a list. A **REMOVE_POSITION**

```
type REMOVE_POSITION is private;

function AT_INDEX (I : in INDEX) return REMOVE_POSITION;
function AFTER    (I : in INDEX) return REMOVE_POSITION;
function FIRST       return REMOVE_POSITION;
function LAST        return REMOVE_POSITION;
```

is defined relative to a given node, that is identified by its index, or as the first or last node of the list. The position **AFTER (I)** refers to the node next to **I**; for singly linked lists, this allows an efficient removal, since the links in the node, that is previous to the removed node, have to be changed. Figure 6.5 illustrates some possible cases.

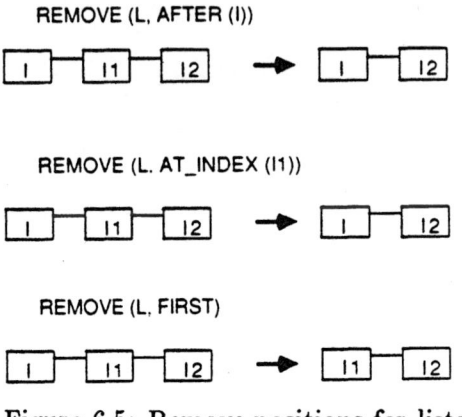

Figure 6.5: Remove positions for lists

## A PART

```
type PART is private;

function WHOLE_STRUCT return PART;
function SUBLIST (FROM     : in INDEX;
                  TO       : in INDEX := NIL;
                  CIRCULAR : in BOOLEAN := FALSE) return PART;
```

is defined either as the whole list by the parameterless function WHOLE_STRUCT, or as a SUBLIST of a list as follows: If CIRCULAR is false, either TO or FROM (or both) are nil, or TO must be some index that comes after FROM; if FROM is nil, the part starts with the first node, if TO is nil, the part extends to the last node, otherwise the part is the sublist extending from FROM to TO, inclusive. If CIRCULAR is true, TO and FROM may be any indices, including nil; if FROM is nil, the part starts with the first node, if TO is nil, the part extends over the whole list, possibly wrapping around at the end up to the node before FROM, otherwise the part extends from FROM, to TO, possibly wrapping around at the end of the list. Note that a PART can never be empty.

With the default setting, the part extends from the node FROM to the last node. Figure 6.6 illustrates the notion of list parts.

**The** possible iteration orders for lists are determined through

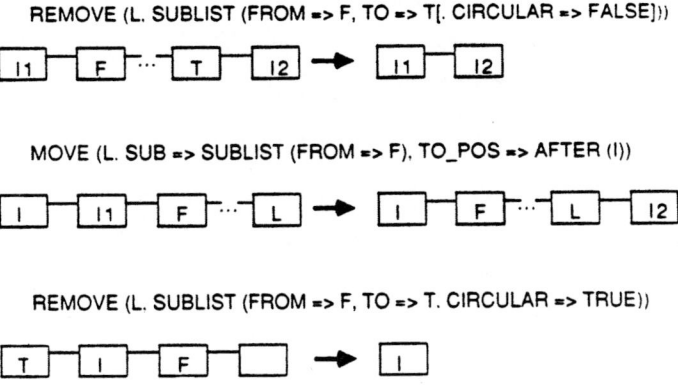

Figure 6.6: Parts of lists

```
type ITERATION_ORDER is (FROM_FIRST, FROM_LAST, DONT_CARE);
```

where **FROM_FIRST** lets iteration start from the first element and proceed towards the last, whereas **FROM_LAST** does just the opposite. With an iteration order **DONT_CARE** elements are enumerated in an arbitrary order that may be different (as efficient as possible) for different variants.

Lists provide

- the constructor operations CLEAR (see 5.3.1.1),
  INSERT, FIND_OR_INSERT, REMOVE, REMOVE_ALL, GENERIC_REMOVE,
  SLICE, MOVE, SWAP (see 5.3.1.2), COPY, TRANSFER (see 5.3.1.3), DEALLOCATE
  (see 5.3.1.4),

- the index based operations GET_ELEM, SET_ELEM, TRANSFER_ELEM, MODIFY_ELEM
  (see 5.3.2),

- the operations for access by position count INDEX_VAL, INDEX_POS,
  GET_ELEM, SET_ELEM, TRANSFER_ELEM, MODIFY_ELEM_BY_POS (see 5.3.3),

- the selector operations COUNT, IS_EMPTY, FIND, SKIP, COUNT_ELEM, IS_ELEM,
  "=", EQUAL, FIRST, LAST, NEXT, PREVIOUS (see 5.3.4),

- the iterators APPLY, ITERATE, ITERATE_MOVE (see 5.3.5),
  REDUCE, UREDUCE, AREDUCE (see 5.3.6),
  FIND_PROPERTY, SKIP_PROPERTY, COUNT_PROPERTY (see 5.3.7),
  EXISTS, FORALL (see 5.3.8),

- the order dependent operations COMPARE <, <=, >, >= MAX, MIN REMOVE_MAX, REMOVE_MIN (see 5.3.9),

- the hash function HASH_FUNCTION (see 5.3.10),

- and the list specific constructors SHIFT, INVERT (see 6.4.2.1), and

- iterators APPLY_CORRESPONDING, ITERATE_CORRESPONDING, MODIFY_CORRESPONDING (see 6.4.2.2), RUN, LONGEST_RUN, MAX_RUN (see 6.4.2.3), that will now be introduced.


## 6.4.2.1   SHIFT and INVERT

The constructors SHIFT and INVERT are available only for lists.

```
     procedure SHIFT (S : in out STRUCT; BY : in INTEGER);
```

SHIFT changes the numeric positions by circularly moving each element BY positions towards the end of the list, if BY is positive, or towards the beginning of the list, if BY is negative. That means, an element at position N is shifted to position (N + BY -1) mod COUNT (S) +1.

```
     procedure INVERT (S : in out STRUCT);
```

INVERT inverts the list, such that the old first node becomes the last, the second node becomes the last but one, and so on.


## 6.4.2.2   Double Iterations

Double iterators are provided for lists. They iterate simultaneously over two lists and perform the specified ACTION operation for corresponding elements LEFT and RIGHT. SELECTION and UNTIL behave as for single iterators. Three double iterators are distinguished by the parameter modes of their action operation. APPLY_CORRESPONDING may change both, ITERATE_CORRESPONDING none and MODIFY_CORRESPONDING just the LEFT, but not the RIGHT one. Double iteration is always performed from the first element towards the last.

If both lists or, respectively, list parts are of different lengths, iteration stops when the shorter list (part) is exhausted. The out parameter LENGTH indicates the relation between LEFT and RIGHT, where LESS means that LEFT is shorter that RIGHT.

```
generic
   with procedure ACTION
                    (LEFT    : in out ELEM_TYPE;
                     RIGHT   : in out ELEM_TYPE) is NONE1;

   with function  SELECTION
                    (LEFT, RIGHT : in ELEM_TYPE)
                     return BOOLEAN is TRUE;

   with function  UNTIL
                    (LEFT   : in STRUCT;
                     LEFT_I : in INDEX;
                     RIGHT  : in STRUCT;
                     RIGHT_I : in INDEX)
                     return BOOLEAN is FALSE;

   with procedure ACTION_WITH_INDEX
                    (LEFT    : in out ELEM_TYPE;
                     LEFT_I  : in INDEX;
                     RIGHT   : in out ELEM_TYPE;
                     RIGHT_I : in INDEX) is NONE1;

   with function  SELECTION_WITH_INDEX
                    (LEFT    : in STRUCT;
                     LEFT_I  : in INDEX;
                     RIGHT   : in STRUCT;
                     RIGHT_I : in INDEX)
                     return BOOLEAN is TRUE;

   procedure APPLY_CORRESPONDING
                    (LEFT      : in out STRUCT;
                     RIGHT     : in out STRUCT;
                     LEFT_SUB  : in PART := WHOLE_STRUCT;
                     RIGHT_SUB : in PART := WHOLE_STRUCT;
                     LENGTH    : out ORDER_RELATION);
```

```
generic
   with procedure ACTION
                     (LEFT     : in ELEM_TYPE;
                      RIGHT    : in ELEM_TYPE) is NONE;


   with function  SELECTION
                     (LEFT, RIGHT : in ELEM_TYPE)
                      return BOOLEAN is TRUE;


   with function  UNTIL
                     (LEFT     : in STRUCT;
                      LEFT_I  : in INDEX;
                      RIGHT    : in STRUCT;
                      RIGHT_I : in INDEX)
                      return BOOLEAN is FALSE;


   with procedure ACTION_WITH_INDEX
                     (LEFT     : in ELEM_TYPE;
                      LEFT_I  : in INDEX;
                      RIGHT    : in ELEM_TYPE;
                      RIGHT_I : in INDEX) is NONE;


   with function  SELECTION_WITH_INDEX
                     (LEFT     : in STRUCT;
                      LEFT_I  : in INDEX;
                      RIGHT    : in STRUCT;
                      RIGHT_I : in INDEX)
                      return BOOLEAN is TRUE;


procedure ITERATE_CORRESPONDING
              (LEFT      : in STRUCT;
               RIGHT     : in STRUCT;
               LEFT_SUB  : in PART := WHOLE_STRUCT;
               RIGHT_SUB : in PART := WHOLE_STRUCT;
               LENGTH    : out ORDER_RELATION);
```

```
generic
   with procedure ACTION
                    (LEFT    : in out ELEM_TYPE;
                     RIGHT   : in ELEM_TYPE) is NONE2;


   with function  SELECTION
                    (LEFT, RIGHT : in ELEM_TYPE)
                    return BOOLEAN is TRUE;


   with function  UNTIL
                    (LEFT    : in STRUCT;
                     LEFT_I  : in INDEX;
                     RIGHT   : in STRUCT;
                     RIGHT_I : in INDEX)
                    return BOOLEAN is FALSE;


   with procedure ACTION_WITH_INDEX
                    (LEFT    : in out ELEM_TYPE;
                     LEFT_I  : in INDEX;
                     RIGHT   : in ELEM_TYPE;
                     RIGHT_I : in INDEX) is NONE2;


   with function  SELECTION_WITH_INDEX
                    (LEFT    : in STRUCT;
                     LEFT_I  : in INDEX;
                     RIGHT   : in STRUCT;
                     RIGHT_I : in INDEX)
                    return BOOLEAN is TRUE;


procedure MODIFY_CORRESPONDING
                (LEFT      : in out STRUCT;
                 RIGHT     : in STRUCT;
                 LEFT_SUB  : in PART := WHOLE_STRUCT;
                 RIGHT_SUB : in PART := WHOLE_STRUCT;
                 LENGTH    : out ORDER_RELATION);
```

Double iteration is, for example, useful for vector operations. It is also the basis for the provided comparison operations.

### 6.4.2.3   Runs

A *run* is a sublist of equal elements. There are three operations that search for runs
with different properties. In all three cases, RUN_START refers to the first index of
the found run, if a run with the required property exists, otherwise this result is NIL
(in particular, if the structure or part is empty). RUN searches for some run of the
given element E with a minimum length of MIN_LENGTH; LONGEST_RUN searches for
the longest run of the given element E; MAX_RUN searches for the longest existing run,
regardless of the element value. The search is always from the first to the last element.
In both cases, RUN_LENGTH yields the length of the found run.

```
procedure RUN (S          : in STRUCT;
               E          : in ELEM_TYPE;
               MIN_LENGTH : in NATURAL;
               SUB        : in PART := WHOLE_STRUCT;
               RUN_START  : out INDEX);

procedure LONGEST_RUN (S          : in STRUCT;
                       E          : in ELEM_TYPE;
                       SUB        : in PART := WHOLE_STRUCT;
                       RUN_START  : out INDEX;
                       RUN_LENGTH : out NATURAL);

procedure MAX_RUN (S          : in STRUCT;
                   SUB        : in PART := WHOLE_STRUCT;
                   RUN_START  : out INDEX;
                   RUN_LENGTH : out NATURAL);
```

### 6.4.2.4   Examples

```
-- Addition for Vectors

package VECTOR_OPS is new LISTS (INTEGER);
use VECTOR_OPS;
subtype VECTOR is VECTOR_OPS.STRUCT;
```

```
procedure VECTOR_ADD (LEFT  : in out VECTOR;
                      RIGHT : in VECTOR) is

   LENGTH : ORDER_RELATION;
   procedure ADD (LEFT : in out INTEGER; RIGHT : in INTEGER) is
   begin
      LEFT := LEFT + RIGHT;
   end ADD;
   procedure V_ADD is new VECTOR_OPS.MODIFY_CORRESPONDING (ADD);

begin
   V_ADD (LEFT, RIGHT, LENGTH => LENGTH);
   if LENGTH /= EQUAL then
      raise CONSTRAINT_ERROR;
   end if;
end VECTOR_ADD;

-- Space allocation

package FREE_LIST_OPS is new LISTS (BOOLEAN);
use FREE_LIST_OPS;
subtype FREE_LIST is FREE_LIST_OPS.STRUCT;
subtype FREE_LIST_INDEX is FREE_LIST_OPS.INDEX;

function ALLOCATE (FREE_SPACE : in FREE_LIST;
                   SIZE       : in NATURAL)
                  return FREE_LIST_INDEX is
   START_INDEX : FREE_LIST_INDEX;

begin
   RUN (FREE_SPACE, E => TRUE,
        MIN_LENGTH => SIZE,
        RUN_START => START_INDEX);
   if START_INDEX = NIL then
      raise STORAGE_ERROR;
   else
      return START_INDEX;
   end if;
end ALLOCATE;
```

## 6.4.3   Implementation Overview

Linked lists are based on the abstract data type linked collections. Linked collections provide nodes, which consist of an element value and (for the implementation of linked lists) of one or two links to other nodes depending on whether both, the next and previous links, or only the next link are stored. Thus the element information is only accessible through the linked nodes; references to these nodes are used as **INDEX** into the list.

Linked collections implement nodes in different ways, either as array components or as access variables. Thus, linked collections abstract from the way in which nodes and links are implemented. They provide an index as a reference to an element (which is used from the linked list implementation) regardless on the way how the index is implemented.

The requirement for additional information associated with list structures, for example in double anchor lists or counted lists, makes it necessary to distinguish between a linked list and a reference to a node, whereas these are usually treated as synonyms.

Tabular lists are based on the data type tabular collections. Tabular collections provide an array of nodes that consist of an element value. The array index is used as index into the tabular list.

Linked lists are discussed intensively in computer science literature, for example in [9]. However, lists are discussed there on a rather low level, involving much implementation and data structure representation details. Tabular lists, though they are used intensively in systems programming, are rarely discussed and systematically dealt with in the literature, where mainly the linear and binary search algorithms are compared with each other. Explicit references to abstract data types similar to tabular lists can be found in [8] and [5].

Linked and tabular lists are prime examples for the usefulness of the separation of the representation of elements, which is realized by linked and tabular collections in different alternatives, and access discipline, which provides higher level operations that abstract from these alternatives, so the user need not worry about the lower level details.

## 6.4.4 List Specific Variants

Lists exhibit a wide variety of features. Most of them can be combined with each other.

The primary selection is that of

```
linked, tabular
```

Linked lists have the main advantage of a possibly unbounded size and a fast restructuring without shifting elements. The strengths of tabular lists are its constant time access to an element by its numeric position and its smaller storage size. The storage requirements, however, are often hard to assess. For a given number of elements, a linked list occupies more storage than a tabular one, due to the additional links that must be stored. However, the exact number of elements is often unknown and a tabular list must make worst case assumptions on the number of elements and thereby waste space.

All other variant alternatives and their combination are the same as for the linked or, respectively, tabular lists which will be described in the following sections.

## 6.4.5 General Variants of Lists

The general variants

```
simple_elements, indirect_elements, variable_elements,
    general_elements, accessed_elements, compact_elements
object_bounded, collection_bounded, unbounded
precondition_check, constraint_check, no_check
counter, no_counter
```

are supported with characteristics as described in section 5.5.

## 6.4.6   Combination of List Variants

All combinations of the variants described above are possible except for the combinations

- of `tabular` with `collection_bounded` or `unbounded`.

Linked and tabular lists may impose further specific restrictions on the combination of variant parameters.

## 6.4.7   Linked List Specific Variants

For linked lists the following variants are offered:

```
single_link, double_link, cached_link
linear, circular
single_anchor, double_anchor
```

### 6.4.7.1   Single vs. Double Link vs. Cached Link

For the `single_link` variant, a node contains a link to the next node. Lists with a `double_link` contain, in addition, a link to the previous node. This link to the previous node allows an efficient implementation of the **PREVIOUS** operation, and of all operations depending on it, like certain cases of insert and remove. For singly linked lists, these operations are also supported but may be quite inefficient since the list might have to be traversed from its first element (which is found through the list header), until the previous node is found.

In order to apply an operation to some node, the node must have been obtained as the result of some operation. In the single link case, nodes are only accessible via an anchor or via a next-link; in the latter case this means that before an operation is applied to some node, this node was obtained by a next operation applied to its previous node. A cache, which stores the previous/next pairs that are the parameters and results of a next operation, may facilitate a quick retrieval of the previous node for some given node. This is particularly helpful if a node was obtained by some iteration, for example `FIND`, in which case the user has no chance to store the previous node of the iteration result. The `cached_link` variant is thus a compromise between the space saving single link variant and the more time efficient double link variant.

### 6.4.7.2 Linear vs. Circular

For a linear variant, the next-link of the last node is `NIL`, and also the previous-link of the first node, for a doubly linked list. For the circular variant, the next and previous links wrap around to the beginning and, respectively, end of the list. This, however, does not affect the operations and their semantics. Both linear and circular operations options, which are selected by the boolean parameter `circular` in the respective operations, are offered by the linear and the circular variant as well.

To implement, for example, the (linear) next operation in the circular variant correctly, one uses the list (header), which is a parameter, to check, whether the node is the last node of the list; in this case the result has to be nil instead of the (circular) next link which is stored in this node and which points to the first element of the list. This additional test makes the linear operation options slightly more expensive with a circular variant. In the same way, additional tests make circular operation options slightly more expensive with linear variants.

Circular lists are of particular interest for operations on circular traversals, which start at some node 'wrapping around' at the end of the list.

For a circular list, the first node is always accessible as the circular next node of the last node. Therefore, a circular variant contains an anchor to the last node only.

### 6.4.7.3 Single vs. Double Anchor

A single anchor variant has in the list header only one pointer to the first node, or, respectively, in the case of a circular variant, one pointer to the last node.

The double anchor variant, where 'first' and 'last' pointer are present in the list header, makes inserting nodes at the end of a list efficient. The maintenance of the additional pointer to the last node requires more tests in insertions and deletions. This makes these operations slightly more expensive than those for single anchor lists.

For circular lists, only a single anchor variant is provided, where the anchor points to the last node of the list (since the first node can easily be reached from there, thus getting a fast access to both the first and last node).

## 6.4.8   General Variants of Linked Lists

The general variants

```
simple_elements, indirect_elements, variable_elements,
    general_elements, accessed_elements, compact_elements
object_bounded, collection_bounded, unbounded
precondition_check, constraint_check, no_check
counter, no_counter
```

are supported with characteristics as described in section 5.5.

## 6.4.9   Combination of Linked List Variants

All combinations of the variants described above are possible except for the combinations

* of `circular` with `double_anchor`.

Figure 6.7 illustrates some of the possible variant combinations.

## 6.4.10   Representation of Linked List by Linked Collections

Linked collections inherit the variant parameters that specify the element type, the storage management and checks of preconditions and constraints.

A fixed number of links is used (`fixed_links`) and the number of links, expressed by the generic parameter `links` is 1 for the `single_link` and `cached_link` and 2 for the `double_link` variant of linked lists.

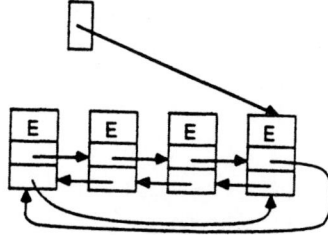

single link, linear, double anchor

double link, circular, single anchor

Figure 6.7: Some variants for linked lists

## 6.4.11  Tabular List Specific Variants

For tabular lists the following variants are offered:

```
non_diluted, flag_diluted, value_diluted
non_wrapped, wrapped
non_pointered, pointered
```

### 6.4.11.1  Non-diluted vs. Flag-diluted vs. Value-diluted

In a `non_diluted` variant, a sequence of nodes is implemented by a sequence of array elements. All array elements between the first and the last element correspond to nodes of the sequence. In a diluted variant, there may be array elements that do not correspond to valid nodes of the sequence, but to deleted nodes. Either a flag or a special element value, that is not used otherwise, serve to distinguish non-valid array elements. For the `flag_diluted` variant, an additional array of boolean flags with the same index range as the element array is set up. The flag indicates whether the array element is valid or not, that means whether it represents a node of the sequence or not. For the `value_diluted` variant, the particular element value is passed as a generic parameter.

As a consequence, a REMOVE operation requires a constant $O(1)$ effort for the diluted variant, since only the removed nodes (i.e. array elements) need to be set to invalid. A REMOVE operation for a non-diluted tabular list requires, however, shifting of the following or the preceding array elements to close the hole caused by the removal, thus requiring an $O(n)$ effort, proportional to the number of array elements.

Similar considerations apply for INSERT operations. In general, shifting is required for non-diluted variants to insert the new element between existing elements, which yields a proportional $O(n)$ effort. In the worst case, the same amount of shifting is required also for diluted variants if all array elements are valid. However, very often there may be invalid array elements near to the insertion position, which reduces the required shifting effort.

There is one big disadvantage of diluted variants with regard to access by position count operations. Since there may be holes in the array, there is no simple mapping from the logical position count to the physical array index. To get the n-th element, one must start from the first element and count for n valid array elements, which yields an $O(n)$ effort. In non-diluted variants, the position count can be directly mapped to the array index, such that access by position count is an operation with a constant $O(1)$ effort.

If the tabular list is not diluted, the number of elements can easily be computed from the position of the last (and, in case of a wrapped list, first) element; therefore we do not provide a variant for non-diluted, counted lists.

### 6.4.11.2   Non-wrapped vs. Wrapped

In a non_wrapped variant, the first valid array element represents the first node of the list. When a node is inserted into the list, the array elements subsequent to the insert position are always shifted upwards (i.e. in direction to higher indices), even if the new node is inserted before the first node. Usually, there is a free area at the high index positions of the array. There is an index in the header of the tabular list that points to the last valid array element, thus separating the used part of the array from the free area.

wrapped variants eliminate the shifting overhead for insertions at the front of the list. Instead of shifting the whole array upwards, a new array element is allocated below the old first valid element. As a consequence, an additional index is required in the list header, which points to the first element. In the case that there is no place below the old first element, i.e. it is the first element of the array, one wraps around and allocates the new element as the last array element (if that is free). The used area of the array can thus grow in two directions, upwards, and downwards wrapping around the end if required.

Wrapped variants are useful, in particular, to implement queues of a bounded size.

### 6.4.11.3 Non-pointered vs. Pointered

If the elements of the tabular list have a large size (for example 100 Bytes), and a larger number of array elements needs to be shifted with an INSERT or REMOVE operation (suppose 500), the shifting effort (in this case 50 KBytes), can get considerable, although tabular lists will be used primarily if the number of list elements is not too large, or there are not too many insertions and deletions.

This shifting overhead can be reduced by a pointered variant, if a list element size is large compared to the space required to store an index into an array, which is usually two or four Bytes. This is done by allocating all list elements in an array, at an arbitrary position, and leaving them at their respective position until the element is removed again. The sequence of the elements, i.e. the next/previous relation among them, is represented by a separate array of indices, where each index points into the array of list elements.

The effort saved by the pointered variant is proportional to the ratio of the list element size and the index size. The disadvantage of a pointered variant lies in its space overhead, which is proportional to the ratio of index size to list element size.

Pointered variants are recommended either if the element size is quite large (say at least five times the index size) and the list has some insertions between existing elements, or if the element size is smaller, but the number of insertions between existing elements is considerable. In particular, this may be the case with non-wrapped non-diluted variants.

The index array may in general be organized as discussed, that means wrapped or non_wrapped, and non_diluted, value_diluted, or flag_diluted. If, however, a tabular list is flag-diluted, the pointered variant has the additional advantage that no separate array of flags is required since a null value of the pointer can be used to indicate an invalid element; therefore we do not provide a variant for `value_diluted`, `pointered` tabular lists.

## 6.4.12    General Variants of Tabular Lists

The general variants

```
simple_elements, indirect_elements, variable_elements,
   general_elements, accessed_elements, compact_elements
precondition_check, constraint_check, no_check
counter, no_counter
```

are supported with characteristics as described in section 5.5.

No `collection_bounded` or unbounded variants are available since an array of fixed size must be allocated for a tabular list.

### 6.4.12.1    Combination of Tabular List Variants

All combinations of the variants described above are possible, except for the combinations

- of `value_diluted` with `pointered`, and
- of `counter` with `non_diluted`.

Figure 6.8 illustrates some of the possible variant combinations.

## 6.4.13    Representation of Tabular Lists by Tabular Collections

Tabular collections inherit the storage management variant `object_bounded` and the specific variants

```
non_pointered, pointered
```

non-wrapped, value-diluted (ED). non-pointered:

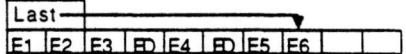

wrapped. non-diluted, non-pointered:

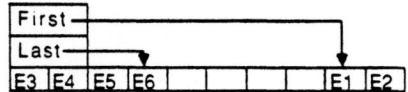

non-wrapped, flag-diluted, pointered:

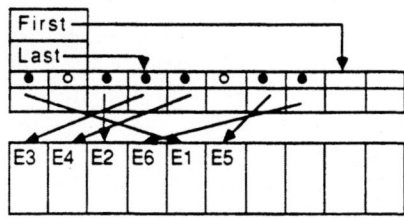

Figure 6.8: Some variants for tabular lists

The variants `non_diluted`, `flag_diluted` and `value_diluted` are represented by the respective variants `all_valid`, `invalid_flag` and `invalid_value`.

# 6.5   Stacks

## 6.5.1   Synopsis

Stacks are basically lists with a restricted set of insert and remove operations. The operations grant insert or remove access only to the first element of the structure. This restriction can nicely be expressed by restricting the concept of insert and remove positions. Furthermore there is no possibility to modify elements within the structure.

Due to these restrictions, stacks can easily be implemented by using structure sharing, which is more difficult (and not implemented) for all other data types. Note that structure sharing cannot be observed through the data type's interface, but only through performance observations.

## 6.5.2   Types and Operations

INSERT_POSITIONs, REMVOE_POSITIONs, and PARTs are taken from lists, but only FIRST is a valid INSERT_POSITION and REMOVE_POSITION for stacks. The only PART constructor is WHOLE_LIST. It is provided for uniformity with lists.

The ITERATION_ORDERs are the same as for lists, namely FROM_FIRST, FROM_LAST, and DONT_CARE.

Stacks provide

- the constructor operations CLEAR (see 5.3.1.1),
  INSERT, FIND_OR_INSERT, REMOVE, REMOVE_ALL, GENERIC_REMOVE,
  MOVE, (see 5.3.1.2 except those for PARTs),
  COPY, TRANSFER (see 5.3.1.3), DEALLOCATE (see 5.3.1.4),

- the index based operation GET_ELEM (see 5.3.2),

- the positional operations INDEX_VAL, INDEX_POS, GET_ELEM (see 5.3.3),

- the selector operations COUNT, IS_EMPTY, FIND, SKIP, COUNT_ELEM, IS_ELEM,
  "=", EQUAL, FIRST, LAST, NEXT, PREVIOUS (see 5.3.4),

- the iterators ITERATE, (see 5.3.5),
  REDUCE, UREDUCE, AREDUCE (see 5.3.6),
  FIND_PROPERTY, SKIP_PROPERTY, COUNT_PROPERTY (see 5.3.7),
  EXISTS, FORALL (see 5.3.8),

- the order dependent operations COMPARE <, <=, >, >= MAX, MIN REMOVE_MAX,
  REMOVE_MIN (see 5.3.9),

- the hash function HASH_FUNCTION (see 5.3.10),

- the list specific operations ITERATE_CORRESPONDING (see 6.4.2.2),
  RUN, LONGEST_RUN, MAX_RUN (see 6.4.2.3),

- and the stack specific operations PUSH, POP, TOP.

The stack specific operations are renamings of general list operations:

```
procedure PUSH (S : in out STRUCT; E : in ELEM_TYPE);
-- INSERT (S, E, FIRST);

procedure POP (S : in out STRUCT);
-- REMOVE (S, FIRST);

function TOP (S : in STRUCT) return ELEM_TYPE;
-- FIRST (S)
```

## 6.5.3   Implementation Overview

Stacks are implemented by linked or tabular lists. The restricted options for modifying a structure allow tabular implementations that must never shift elements. This is guaranteed by a preselection of appropriate variants of the underlying representation.

We have chosen to insert stack elements at position FIRST instead of LAST (which is the default insert position for lists), since iteration over stacks usually starts from the most recently inserted element. The chosen insert position allows iteration with single links in the linked case. We pay with a slight overhead in the tabular case, since a **wrapped** implementation must be chosen to avoid shifting. In addition, since single links are in the direction from the first to last, the shared implementation must add new elements to the front of the list.

A major advantage of the restricted operations is the possibility for a linked stack implementation to share structure parts among different structures. In the variant for **sharing**, the COPY operation is "lazy", that means is copies just the anchor but not the elements. Since the elements cannot be modified, the structure sharing has no observable effect. A reference count is required to properly deallocate the structures. Due to this overhead, structure **sharing** is optional.


## 6.5.4   Specific Variants

The variant parameters

```
sharing, no_sharing
linked, tabular
```

can be selected. The first controls whether structures shall be shared or not. The second specifies whether linked or tabular lists shall be chosen for the representation. Sharing can only be implemented with the **linked** variant.

Sharing has the additional cost of storing and maintaining a reference count. Therefore, the full advantage is only gained, if the element type together with the reference to the next element occupies significantly more space than the reference count.

The choice between the linked and the tabular variant mainly depends on whether the objects are bounded or not. In the **object_bounded** case, the tabular variant is in general superior.


## 6.5.5   General Variants

The general variants

```
simple_elements, indirect_elements, variable_elements,
    general_elements, accessed_elements, compact_elements
object_bounded, collection_bounded, unbounded
precondition_check, constraint_check, no_check
counter, no_counter
```

are supported with characteristics as described in section 5.5.

## 6.5.6  Combination of Variants

All combinations of the variants described above are possible, except for the combinations

- of `tabular` with `collection_bounded` or `unbounded`,
- of `sharing` with `tabular`, and
- of `sharing` with `object_bounded`.

`sharing` cannot be combined with `object_bounded`, since in the shared case there is no longer a single object representation to which the bound could apply.

Linked and tabular implementations may impose further specific restrictions on the combination of variant parameters.

## 6.5.7  Representation Specific Variants

### 6.5.7.1  Linked Stack Specific Variants

The linked stack specific variants are the same as for linked lists (see section 6.4.7):

```
single_link, double_link, cached_link
linear, circular
single_anchor, double_anchor
```

For the standard usage we suggest a `linear`, `single_link` and `single_anchor` implementation. A `double_link` implementation, together with `double_anchor` or `circular`, may be used to speed up the non-common stack traversal from last to first. The `cached_link` variant, which is mainly used to support the removal of elements that are the result of an iteration, has no obvious benefits for stacks.

### 6.5.7.2    Combination of Linked Stack Variants

The possible variant combinations in the linked case depend on the choice for `sharing`.
In case of no sharing, all variants are possible. In the shared case, the `double_link`
and `circular` variants are excluded, since there may be structures with different
fronts and shared tails.

Figure 6.9 illustrates the sharing of stacks; for non-shared variants see the list figure 6.7.

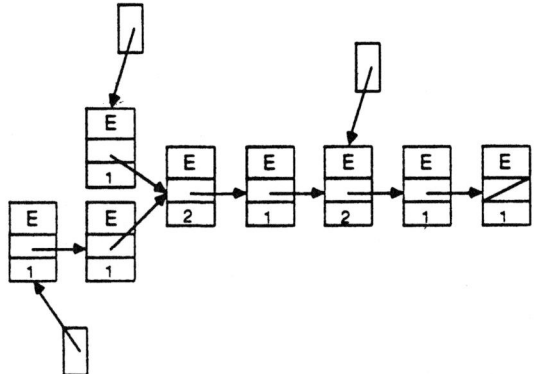

Figure 6.9: Structure sharing for stacks

### 6.5.7.3    Tabular Stack Specific Variants

The variant parameter

    non_pointered, pointered

can be selected; its effect is explained in section 6.4.11.3.

### 6.5.7.4    Combination of Tabular Stack Variants

The tabular stack specific variant for pointering may be combined freely with all other
variants for stacks. For an illustration of tabular variants see the list figure 6.8.

## 6.5.8 Representation of Stacks by Lists

The variant with **sharing** is immediately implemented on top of linked collections, since linked lists do not provide sharing. In case of no sharing, all selected variant parameters are inherited by the list implementation. For a tabular representation, the variant parameters **non_diluted** and **wrapped** are preselected (see section 6.4.11), since dilution cannot occur with the restricted **REMOVE_POSITION**s, and wrapping supports the efficient insertion at position **FIRST**.

# 6.6   Queues and Deques

## 6.6.1   Synopsis

Queues and deques (double ended queues) are basically lists with a restricted set of insert and remove operations. The operations grant insert or remove access only to the first or last element of the structure. This restriction can nicely be expressed by restricting the concept of insert and remove positions. Furthermore there is no possibility to modify elements within the structure.

A queue provides insert access to the first and remove access to the last element; a deque provides insert and remove access to both ends.

## 6.6.2   Types and Operations

INSERT_POSITIONs, REMVOE_POSITIONs, and PARTs are taken from lists, but only the following cases are permitted: both data types have the INSERT_POSITION FIRST and the REMOVE_POSITION LAST. Deques, in addition, have have the INSERT_POSITION LAST and the REMOVE_POSITION FIRST. The only PART constructor is WHOLE_LIST. It is provided for uniformity with lists.

The ITERATION_ORDERs are the same as for lists, namely FROM_FIRST, FROM_LAST, and DONT_CARE.

Queues and deques provide

- the constructor operations CLEAR (see 5.3.1.1),
  INSERT, FIND_OR_INSERT, REMOVE, REMOVE_ALL, GENERIC_REMOVE,
  MOVE, (see 5.3.1.2 except those for PARTs),
  COPY, TRANSFER (see 5.3.1.3), DEALLOCATE (see 5.3.1.4),

- the index based operation GET_ELEM (see 5.3.2),

- the positional operations INDEX_VAL, INDEX_POS, GET_ELEM (see 5.3.3),

- the selector operations COUNT, IS_EMPTY, FIND, SKIP, COUNT_ELEM, IS_ELEM,
  "=", EQUAL, FIRST, LAST, NEXT, PREVIOUS (see 5.3.4),

- the iterators ITERATE, (see 5.3.5),
  REDUCE, UREDUCE, AREDUCE (see 5.3.6),
  FIND_PROPERTY, SKIP_PROPERTY, COUNT_PROPERTY (see 5.3.7),
  EXISTS, FORALL (see 5.3.8),

- the order dependent operations COMPARE <, <=, >, >= MAX, MIN REMOVE_MAX,
  REMOVE_MIN (see 5.3.9),

- the hash function HASH_FUNCTION (see 5.3.10),

- the list specific operations ITERATE_CORRESPONDING (see 6.4.2.2),
  RUN, LONGEST_RUN, MAX_RUN (see 6.4.2.3).

### 6.6.3 Implementation Overview

Queues and deques are implemented by lists, which may be linked or tabular. The restricted options for modifying a structure allow tabular implementations that must never shift elements. This is guaranteed by a preselection of appropriate variants of the underlying representation.

All other implementation issues are discussed in section 6.4.3. No specific implementation techniques, like sharing for stacks, are used for queues and deques.

### 6.6.4 Specific Variants

The variant parameter

    linked, tabular

can be selected. It specifies whether linked or tabular lists shall be chosen for the representation. This choice mainly depends on whether the objects are bounded or not. In the object_bounded case, the tabular variant is in general superior.

### 6.6.5 General Variants

The general variants

```
simple_elements, indirect_elements, variable_elements,
    general_elements, accessed_elements, compact_elements
object_bounded, collection_bounded, unbounded
precondition_check, constraint_check, no_check
counter, no_counter
```

are supported with characteristics as described in section 5.5.


## 6.6.6   Combination of Variants

All combinations of the variants described above are possible, except for the combinations

- of `tabular` with `collection_bounded` or `unbounded`.

These are the same variants as for lists; for an illustration see figures 6.7 and 6.8.


## 6.6.7   Representation Specific Variants

The main purpose of providing queues and deques as data types in addition to lists, is the tailored selection of the specific variants for linked and tabular lists. Therefore, the variant parameters for the lists that are used for the representation, are mainly preselected for queues and deques. In the (unlikely) case that another variant combination seems more appropriate, linked or tabular lists can be used instead of queues or deques.

In the case of a linked representation, all variants are preselected as described in section 6.6.8.


### 6.6.7.1   Tabular Stack Specific Variants

In the tabular case, the variant parameter

`non_pointered, pointered`

can be selected; its effect is explained in section 6.4.11.3.

## 6.6.8   Representation of Queues and Deques by Lists

In the linked case, a `linear`, `double_link`, `double_anchor` list is used. In the tabular case, we use the `non_diluted`, `wrapped` variant. The reasons are the same as for stacks: dilution cannot occur with the restricted `REMOVE_POSITION`s, and wrapping supports the efficient insertion at position `FIRST`.

# 6.7    Trees, Linked Trees, Tabular Trees

## 6.7.1    Synopsis

Trees, linked trees and tabular trees have *nodes* that stand in a *father-son* relationship.
Each son has exactly one father, except for one element, called the *root*, which has
no father. The father-son relation ship is acyclic. The sons of a father are ordered,
such that each son appears at a certain position, where the first position is numbered
1. Not all son positions for a given father need to be occupied. A node of the tree is
referenced by an *index*.

Trees are primarily used to implement higher data types, in particular orders. The
exploitation of their structure for the representation of a data type's semantics is less
common that for lists, but still useful, for example for the representation of hierarchies.
Therefore, we have chosen to make trees primary data types that provide all general
operations.

Trees are implemented by linked trees or tabular trees. Tabular trees implement only
*binary trees*, that means trees where each node has at most two sons. For binary trees
there are some special operations, and therefore we distinguish binary and *n-ary trees*
as two different data types.

Linked trees implement flexible trees, where the number of sons is either fixed and
the same for all nodes, or where it can vary from node to node. Nodes can be
freely inserted at and removed from an arbitrary position in the tree. The father-son
relationship between nodes is expressed by *links* between nodes.

Tabular trees implement binary trees. Within this constraint, nodes can be freely
inserted at and removed from an arbitrary position in the tree. The father-son relationship between nodes is expressed by a numeric relationship between the indices of
an array in which the tree elements are stored.

As for lists, linked trees are index invariant while tabular trees are not. For details
refer to 6.4.1

## 6.7.2   Types and Operations

Many of the tree constructors and selectors allow a direct access to any position of
the tree structure.

INSERT and similar operations allow to insert a node or a subtree into a tree at an
arbitrary position that is determined as a parameter of the INSERT operation. An
INSERT_POSITION

```
type INSERT_POSITION is private;

function FATHER_OF (SON       : in INDEX;
                    NR_OF_SON : POSITIVE := 1)
                   return INSERT_POSITION;
function SON_OF (FATHER          : in INDEX;
                 NR_OF_SON       : POSITIVE;
                 NR_OF_GRANDSON  : NATURAL := 0)
                return INSERT_POSITION;
function ROOT (NR_OF_SON : NATURAL := 0) return INSERT_POSITION;
```

is defined relative to a given node (that is identified by its index), or as the root
node. This allows to insert new nodes between existing nodes (and not only as new
leaves of a tree). We distinguish two cases: inserting a node as FATHER_OF, or as
SON_OF a given node. When a node is inserted as father of some given node SON, this
son node becomes the son of the inserted node at position NR_OF_SON. When a node
becomes inserted as NR_OF_SON-th son of a given FATHER, the original NR_OF_SON-th
son becomes the NR_OF_GRANDSON-th son of the newly inserted node; if there is no son
with this number, that means if the new node is inserted as a leaf, NR_OF_GRANDSON
is 0. Finally, if the new node is inserted as ROOT, the original root becomes the
NR_OF_SON-th son of the newly inserted node; if there was no root before, that means
if the tree was empty, NR_OF_SON is 0. When a whole subtree is inserted, the insert
position must be determined as SON_OF some node or as ROOT, where in both cases
NR_OF_GRANDSON is 0. Figure 6.10 illustrates some possible cases; the identifiers in
the nodes denote their indices.

Similarly to INSERT, REMOVE and MOVE allow to remove a node from an arbitrary
remove position of a tree. A REMOVE_POSITION is defined relative to a given node
(that is identified by its index), or as the root node.

INSERT (TR, N. FATHER_OF (SON => S, NR_OF_SON => 2))

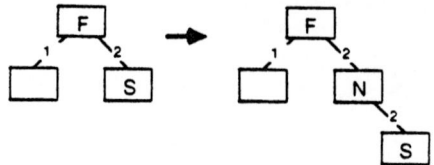

INSERT (TR, N, SON_OF (FATHER => F,
            NR_OF_SON => 2. NR_OF_GRANDSON => 1))

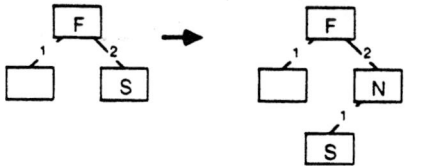

INSERT (TR. N. SON_OF (FATHER => S,
            NR_OF_SON => 1[. NR_OF_GRANDSON => 0]))

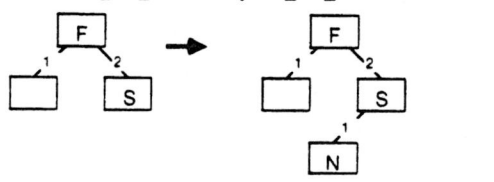

INSERT (TR. N. ROOT (NR_OF_SON => 1))

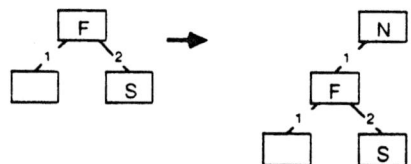

Figure 6.10: Insert positions for trees

```
type REMOVE_POSITION is private;

function AT_INDEX (I          : in INDEX;
                NR_OF_SON : in NATURAL := 0)
              return REMOVE_POSITION;
function SON_OF (FATHER          : in INDEX;
                NR_OF_SON       : POSITIVE;
                NR_OF_GRANDSON : NATURAL := 0)
              return REMOVE_POSITION;
function ROOT (NR_OF_SON : NATURAL := 0) return REMOVE_POSITION;
```

A node that shall be removed must at most have one son; the position of this son is given by **NR_OF_SON** for **AT_INDEX** and for **ROOT** and by **NR_OF_GRANDSON** for **SON_OF**; if the removed node has no son, this position is **0**. For singly linked lists, the **SON_OF** position allows an efficient removal, since the links in the node, that is the father of the removed node, have to be changed. Figure 6.11 illustrates some possible cases.

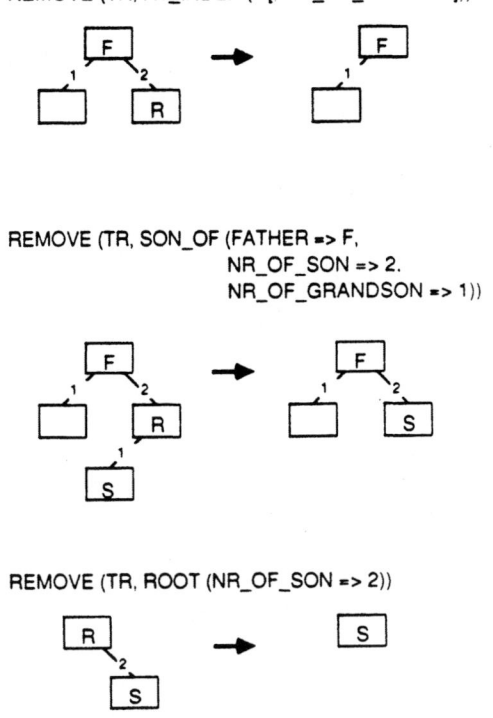

REMOVE (TR, AT_INDEX (R[. NR_OF_SON => 0]))

REMOVE (TR, SON_OF (FATHER => F,
NR_OF_SON => 2.
NR_OF_GRANDSON => 1))

REMOVE (TR, ROOT (NR_OF_SON => 2))

Figure 6.11: Remove positions for trees

## A PART

```
type PART is private;

function WHOLE_STRUCT return PART;
function SUBTREE (ROOT : in INDEX) return PART;
```

is defined either as the whole tree by the parameterless function **WHOLE_STRUCT**, or as a **SUBTREE** that is determined by its **ROOT** node. Figure 6.12 illustrates the notion of tree parts.

REMOVE (TR, SUBTREE (ROOT => R))

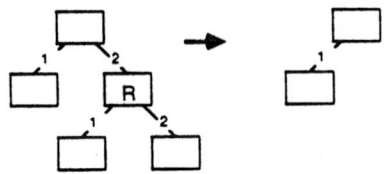

MOVE (TR.
        SUB => SUBTREE (ROOT => R),
        TO_POS => SON_OF (F, NR_OF_SON => 2))

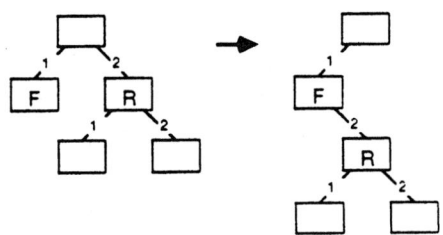

Figure 6.12:  Parts of trees

The possible iteration orders for trees are determined through

```
type ITERATION_ORDER is
     (PRE_ORDER, POST_ORDER, [IN_ORDER,] DONT_CARE);
```

where **IN_ORDER** iteration is only possible for binary trees. Figure 6.13 illustrates the different iteration orders.

Trees provide

- the constructor operations **CLEAR** (see 5.3.1.1),
  **INSERT, FIND_OR_INSERT, REMOVE, REMOVE_ALL, GENERIC_REMOVE, SLICE, MOVE,
  SWAP** (see 5.3.1.2), **COPY, TRANSFER** (see 5.3.1.3), **DEALLOCATE** (see 5.3.1.4),

- the index based operations **GET_ELEM, SET_ELEM, TRANSFER_ELEM, MODIFY_ELEM**
  (see 5.3.2),

PRE_ORDER

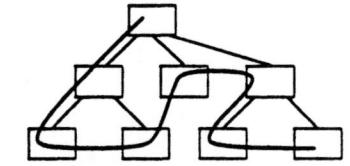

POST_ORDER

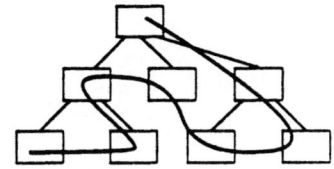

IN_ORDER

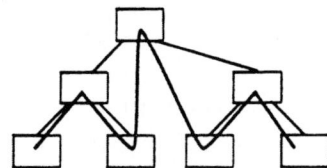

Figure 6.13: Iteration orders for trees

- the selector operations COUNT, IS_EMPTY, FIND, COUNT_ELEM, IS_ELEM, "=", EQUAL, (see 5.3.4),

- the iterators APPLY, ITERATE, ITERATE_MOVE (see 5.3.5),
  REDUCE, UREDUCE, AREDUCE (see 5.3.6),
  FIND_PROPERTY, COUNT_PROPERTY (see 5.3.7),
  EXISTS, FORALL (see 5.3.8),

- the order dependent operations COMPARE <, <=, >, >= MAX, MIN REMOVE_MAX, REMOVE_MIN (see 5.3.9),

- the hash function HASH_FUNCTION (see 5.3.10),

- and the tree specific constructors ROTATE (see 6.7.2.3),

- selectors ROOT, NR_OF_SONS, SON, FATHER, NR_OF_SON, FIND_FATHER, FIRST_VALID_SON, NEXT_VALID_SON (see 6.7.2.1), and

- iterators APPLY_TO_SONS, ITERATE_OVER_SONS (see 6.7.2.2), that will now be introduced.

The operations INSERT and FIND_OR_INSERT have an additional parameter SONS in
the variants for node_dependent_sons (see 6.7.8.1).  This parameter indicates the
number of sons of the node to be inserted, for example:

```
procedure INSERT (S       : in out STRUCT;
                  E        : in ELEM_TYPE;
                  SONS     : in NATURAL;
                  TO_POS   : in INSERT_POSITION);
```

### 6.7.2.1   Specific Selector Operations

In addition to the general selector operations defined in chapter 5.3.4, there are special
selectors that exploit the tree structure:

```
function ROOT (S : in STRUCT) return INDEX;

function ROOT (S : in STRUCT) return ELEM_TYPE;

function NR_OF_SONS (S : in STRUCT; I : in INDEX)
                return NATURAL;

function SON (S  : in STRUCT;
              I  : in INDEX;
              NR : in POSITIVE) return INDEX;

function FATHER (S : in STRUCT; I : in INDEX) return INDEX;

function NR_OF_SON (S        : in STRUCT
                    FATHER   : in INDEX;
                    SON      : in INDEX) return NATURAL;

procedure FIND_FATHER (S        : in STRUCT;
                       SON      : in INDEX;
                       FATHER   : out INDEX;
                       NR_OF_SON : out NATURAL);
```

```
procedure FIRST_VALID_SON (S          : in STRUCT;
                           FATHER     : in INDEX;
                           SON        : out INDEX;
                           NR_OF_SON  : out NATURAL);

procedure NEXT_VALID_SON (S          : in STRUCT;
                          FATHER     : in INDEX;
                          SON        : out INDEX;
                          NR_OF_SON  : in out NATURAL);
```

ROOT yields the root (index or value) of the given tree structure. NR_OF_SONS yields the maximum number of sons of the node denoted by I, which is not necessarily the actual number of sons of I, since not all son positions need to be occupied. SON yields the son with position NR. FATHER yields the father of the given node. For all the operations that yield the index of a node, this index is NIL, if no such node exists. NR_OF_SON finds out, which position the given SON has with respect to the given FATHER. FIND_FATHER is a combination of the operations FATHER and NR_OF_SON. For all these operations, numbering of sons starts with 1.

Finally, FIRST_VALID_SON and NEXT_VALID_SON allow to navigate over the (actually present) sons of a given father; if no (more) valid son is present, SON is set to NIL and NR_OF_SON gets 0; otherwise SON is set to first/next valid son and NR_OF_SON identifies its position. If NEXT_VALID_SON is called with NR_OF_SON being (initially) 0 this is equivalent to a call of FIRST_VALID_SON. An iteration over the sons of a node F could thus look as follows:

```
NR := 0;
loop
   NEXT_VALID_SON (TR, F, S, NR);
   exit when S = NIL;
   ... -- do something
end loop;
```

## 6.7.2.2  Specific Iterators

For this kind of iteration, there are also two special iterators for applying an operation to the sons of a given father I:

```
generic
   with procedure APPLICATION (S          : in out STRUCT;
                               FATHER,
                               SON        : in INDEX;
                               NR_OF_SON : in POSITIVE);

   with function SELECTION (E : in ELEM_TYPE)
                           return BOOLEAN is TRUE;
   with function UNTIL (E : in ELEM_TYPE)
                       return BOOLEAN is FALSE;
procedure APPLY_TO_SONS (S : in out STRUCT; I : in INDEX);

generic
   with procedure APPLICATION (S          : in STRUCT;
                               FATHER,
                               SON        : in INDEX;
                               NR_OF_SON : in POSITIVE);

   with function SELECTION (E : in ELEM_TYPE)
                           return BOOLEAN is TRUE;
   with function UNTIL (E : in ELEM_TYPE)
                       return BOOLEAN is FALSE;
procedure ITERATE_OVER_SONS (S : in STRUCT; I : in INDEX);
```

These iterators work analogous to the general iterators APPLY and ITERATE, except
for the parameters of the APPLICATION operation which denote the father and the son
to which the operation shall be applied, and the position of the son.

### 6.7.2.3   Rotation

For binary trees, there is a special constructor operation

```
procedure ROTATE (S   : in out STRUCT;
                  POS : in out REMOVE_POSITION);
```

which is primarily used for ordered trees.  The ROTATE operation "pulls up" the
node at the given position without changing the order of nodes "from left to right".
Figure 6.14 illustrates its behavior.

ROTATE (TR, AT_INDEX (R))

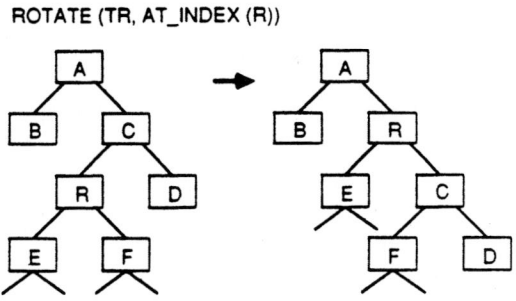

Figure 6.14: Rotate a tree

## 6.7.3  Implementation Overview

Linked trees are based on the abstract data type linked collections in the same way as lists are (see section 6.4.3). However, linked trees implement nodes with different numbers of links, that means with different maximum numbers of sons, whereas nodes of linked list always have one or two links.

Tabular trees store the tree elements into an array. The root is stored in the first array element, the first son (if any) of the node at position $n$ is stored at position $2*n$, and the second son at position $2*n + 1$. (Note that tabular trees do only implement binary trees). With this storage scheme, the father or son relationship is expressed by a numerical relationship between the array positions.

The advantage of tabular trees is that no space overhead to store the links to other tree nodes is required, since all links are replaced by the numerical relationship. The disadvantage is that all constructor operations, except for those concerning only leaf nodes, require the moving of all elements of the corresponding subtree in the array. Thus, the number of elements to be moved on an average is much smaller than for a tabular list; however, the logic of moving is more complicated than shifting.

The use of tabular trees is recommended, in particular, for the typical two-phase usage of data: in the first phase, the tree is constructed; after that, the construction is finished, and in the second phase, only operations are applied that do not modify the tree structure.

Tabular trees are based on the abstract data type tabular collections. Tabular collections provide an array of nodes that consist only of an element value. The array index is used as index in the tabular tree.

Like lists, trees are discussed intensively in computer science literature, for example in [9], but mostly on a low, implementation oriented level.


## 6.7.4   Specific Generic Parameters

The `fixed_sons` variant (see 6.7.8.1) of N-ary trees have the additional generic parameter

```
generic
   ...
   SONS: POSITIVE := 2;
package TREES
```

which determines the maximum number of sons of each node.


## 6.7.5   Tree Specific Variants

Similar to lists, trees exhibit a wide variety of features. Most of them can be combined with each other.

For binary trees, the primary selection is that of

```
linked, tabular
```

whereas n-ary trees can only be implemented as linked trees.

All other characteristics are the same as for the linked or, respectively, tabular trees. These characteristics include the possible further variant alternatives, their combination, and the performance. These characteristics will be described in the following sections.

Note that binary trees and n-ary trees do not make two variants, but are considered as two different data types. Nevertheless, we shall explain the characteristics of binary and n-ary trees together, assuming that binary trees are a special case of n-ary trees.

Special properties of the binary tree data type will be mentioned explicitly.

## 6.7.6   General Variants of Trees

The general variants

```
simple_elements, indirect_elements, variable_elements,
    general_elements, accessed_elements, compact_elements
object_bounded, collection_bounded, unbounded
precondition_check, constraint_check, no_check
counter, no_counter
```

are supported with characteristics as described in chapter 5.

## 6.7.7   Combination of Tree Variants

All combinations of the variants described above are possible except for the combinations

- of `tabular` with `collection_bounded` or `unbounded`.

Note that linked and tabular trees may impose further specific restrictions on the combination of variant parameters.

## 6.7.8   Linked Tree Specific Variants

The variants offered for linked trees are:

```
fixed_sons, node_dependent_sons, linked_sons
single_link, double_link, cached_link
```

### 6.7.8.1   Fixed Sons vs. Node Dependent Sons vs. Linked Sons

For the `fixed_sons` variant, each node has the same maximum number of sons. However, not each son position need actually be occupied. For example, leaves are nodes without sons. The maximum number of sons is in this case defined by the generic parameter SONS (see 6.7.4) when the building block is instantiated. This means that different instantiations are needed, if the user requires several `fixed_sons` trees with different numbers of sons.

Binary trees are always implemented using the `fixed_sons` variant.

For the `node_dependent_sons` variant, different nodes may have a different number of sons. The number of sons of one node, however, does not change throughout the lifetime of this node. It is determined by the parameter SONS of the INSERT operations. This parameter is only present for the node-dependent-sons variants.

Both the `fixed_sons` and the `node_dependent_sons` variant keep with each node an array of links to all of its sons. All of these links have the value NIL if no corresponding son exists. The `linked_sons` variant implements the father-son relationship by links between the father and its first (present) son and between "brothers", that means adjacent sons. Only the existing sons are represented by nodes, which makes it necessary that each node identifies its son position; sequencing of sons is done by increasing son positions. This representation efficiently implements trees where the ratio between the maximum son number and the number of sons, that are actually present, is relatively large. This may happen because the son positions are in fact sparsely filled, or because the maximum number of nodes is not yet known, when the father node is inserted.

For `node_dependent_sons`, different nodes may have different size. This variant can only be implemented together with an **unbounded** variant.

### 6.7.8.2   Single Link vs. Double Link vs. Cached Link

For the `single_link` variant, a node contains the links as described in the preceding section.

`double_link` variants contain, in addition, for each node a link to its father. The link to the father node allows an efficient implementation of the FATHER operation, and of all operations that require access to the father, like certain forms of insert and remove. For singly linked trees, these operations are also supported but are quite inefficient since the tree must be traversed from its root (which is found through the tree header), until the father node is found.

The `cached_link` variant works as described for linked lists in section 6.4.7.1. A cache stores the most recently accessed father son relationships and thus helps to efficiently retrieve the father of a node that has recently been reached via an explicit or implicit son operation.

## 6.7.9  General Variants of Linked Trees

The general variants

```
simple_elements, indirect_elements, variable_elements,
    general_elements, accessed_elements, compact_elements
object_bounded, collection_bounded, unbounded
precondition_check, constraint_check, no_check
counter, no_counter
```

are supported with characteristics as described in chapter 5.

## 6.7.10  Combination of Linked Tree Variants

All combinations of the variants described above are possible, except for the combinations

- of `node_dependent_sons` with `object_bounded` or `collection_bounded`.

Figure 6.15 illustrates some of the possible variant combinations.

single link, fixed sons (2)

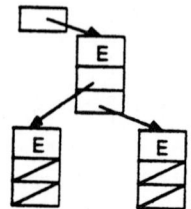

double link, node dependent sons

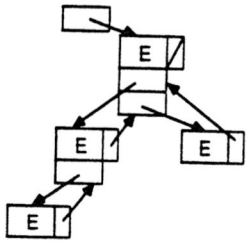

single link. linked sons

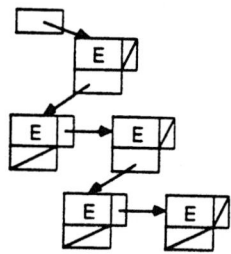

Figure 6.15: Some variants for linked trees

## 6.7.11   Representation of Linked Trees by Linked Collections

Linked collections inherit the variant parameters that control storage management (object_bounded, collection_bounded, unbounded) and checks of preconditions and constraints (precondition_check, constraint_check, no_check).

For the variants fixed_sons and linked_sons, a fixed number of links is used (fixed_links), whereas for node_dependent_sons, a node_dependent_links variant of linked collections is used.

# 6.7.12  Tabular Tree Specific Variants

Tabular trees exhibit only a few variants all of which can be combined with each other.

The following variants are offered:

```
invalid_flag, invalid_value
non_pointered, pointered
```

### 6.7.12.1  Invalid-flag vs. Invalid-value

While for tabular lists a single indicator for the last occupied array position was sufficient, the indication of unoccupied son positions for tabular trees is more complicated. For each son position (that means for both sons) it must be indicated, whether the son exists, or not. Similar to dilution of tabular arrays (see section 6.4.11), this can be done by a flag (`invalid_flag`) or by a special element value (`invalid_value`) that is no valid value for the given application.

There is a class of binary trees, called "complete" trees, for which the described tabular representation yields a compact range that is occupied by tree nodes. This range might be represented with a single indicator. However, it does not allow the representation of arbitrary tree structures and therefore we did not include it into our tabular tree variants.

### 6.7.12.2  Non-pointered vs. Pointered

This variant distinguishes, whether the actual element values or pointers to these values are stored in the array. In the second case, the effort for shifting element values may be reduces. The distinction is the very same as for tabular lists. For more details see section 6.4.11.

## 6.7.13    General Variants of Tabular Trees

The general variants

```
simple_elements, indirect_elements, variable_elements,
    general_elements, accessed_elements, compact_elements
precondition_check, constraint_check, no_check
counter, no_counter
```

are supported with characteristics as described in chapter 5.

No `collection_bounded` or unbounded variants are available since an array of fixed size must be allocated for a tabular tree.

### 6.7.13.1    Combination of Tabular Tree Variants

All combinations of the variants described above are possible, except for the combinations

- of `invalid_value` with `pointered`.

Figure 6.16 illustrates some of the possible variant combinations.

## 6.7.14    Representation of Tabular Trees by Tabular Collections

Tabular collections inherit the storage management variant `object_bounded` and the specific variants

```
non_pointered, pointered
invalid_flag, invalid_value
```

The Tree:

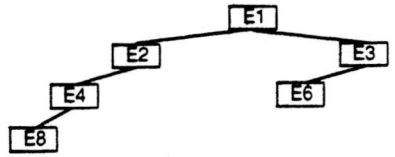

value-diluted (ED), non-pointered:

flag-diluted, pointered:

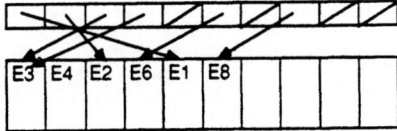

Figure 6.16: Some variants for tabular trees

# 6.8   Orders

## 6.8.1   Synopsis

Orders provide ordered collections of elements, where the order is defined by a relation on the element type that is given by a generic parameter.  Orders allow multiple occurrences of the same element value.

While the logical structure of orders is linear, orders may be represented by (linear) lists or by trees. The operations, that are defined for orders, exhibit only the logical linear structure; the representation is hidden.

There are two different data types for orders, namely orders with an ordinary element type, and orders whose elements are split into a key-part and an info-part. An order with an ordinary element type behaves like a key-info-order with this element type as KEY_TYPE and a void INFO_TYPE. There may be slight differences for parameter or type names that refer to the element type or the key type, respectively; for example, the element type is named ELEM_TYPE, and element type parameters are named E for some operations, while the key type is named KEY_TYPE and the corresponding parameters are named K; in addition, parameters of the INFO_TYPE are not present for the ordinary element data type. For details see the specifications in the appendix. For the remainder of this section, we will explain orders in terms of key-info-orders; the behavior of ordinary orders follows from the given equivalence.

The elements are ordered according to an ordering relation that must be provided as a generic function parameter

```
function COMPARE (LEFT, RIGHT: in KEY_TYPE)
                return ORDER_RELATION is <>;
```

with the package instantiation. If no actual generic parameter is provided, an appropriate COMPARE function that is visible at the point of the package instantiation is taken as a default. Note that the order relation is defined only on the key value.

## 6.8.2 Types and Operations

When an element is inserted into an order, its position is implicitly determined by its value and by the given ordering function. Therefore, there are no parameters that define an INSERT_POSITION.

PARTs and REMOVE_POSITIONs are defined as for lists (see section 6.4.2), except that a remove position cannot be defined as AFTER an index:

```
type PART is private;

function WHOLE_STRUCT return PART;
function SUBLIST (FROM     : in INDEX;
                  TO       : in INDEX := NIL;
                  CIRCULAR : in BOOLEAN := FALSE) return PART;


type REMOVE_POSITION is private;

function AT_INDEX (I : in INDEX) return REMOVE_POSITION;
function FIRST      return REMOVE_POSITION;
function LAST       return REMOVE_POSITION;
```

ITERATION_ORDERs are specified as for lists, namely from first to last, vice versa, or arbitrary.

Order constructor operations are not index invariant, that means it is not allowed to keep an index that was obtained before performing a constructor operation, and to use it after this operation.

Orders provide

- the constructor operations CLEAR (see 5.3.1.1),
  INSERT, FIND_OR_INSERT, REMOVE, REMOVE_ALL, GENERIC_REMOVE,
  SLICE, MOVE, (see 5.3.1.2),
  COPY, TRANSFER (see 5.3.1.3), DEALLOCATE (see 5.3.1.4),

- the index based operations GET_KEY, GET_INFO, SET_INFO, TRANSFER_INFO,
  MODIFY_INFO (see 5.3.2),

- the operations for access by position count `INDEX_VAL`, `INDEX_POS`, `GET_KEY`, `GET_INFO`, `SET_INFO`, `TRANSFER_INFO`, `MODIFY_INFO_BY_POS` (see 5.3.3),

- the selector operations `COUNT`, `IS_EMPTY`, `FIND`, `SKIP`, `COUNT_KEY`, `IS_KEY`, `FIND_INFO`, `SKIP_INFO`, `COUNT_INFO`, `IS_INFO`, `"="`, `EQUAL`, `FIRST`, `LAST`, `NEXT`, `PREVIOUS` (see 5.3.4),

- the iterators `APPLY` (only for key-info), `ITERATE`, `ITERATE_MOVE` (see 5.3.5), `REDUCE`, `UREDUCE`, `AREDUCE`, `REDUCE_INFO`, `UREDUCE_INFO`, `AREDUCE_INFO` (see 5.3.6), `FIND_PROPERTY`, `SKIP_PROPERTY`, `COUNT_PROPERTY`, `FIND_INFO_PROPERTY`, `SKIP_INFO_PROPERTY`, `COUNT_INFO_PROPERTY` (see 5.3.7), `EXISTS`, `FORALL`, `EXISTS_INFO`, `FORALL_INFO` (see 5.3.8),

- the order dependent operations `COMPARE` `<`, `<=`, `>`, `>=` `MAX`, `MIN` `REMOVE_MAX`, `REMOVE_MIN` (see 5.3.9), and

- the hash function `HASH_FUNCTION` (see 5.3.10).

There are no further, order specific operations.

## 6.8.3   Implementation Overview

Orders are implemented either on the abstract data type Lists or Trees. All different List variants are done in a way such that the order relationship among items is represented by the next/previous relation as defined on Lists. Whereas for Trees, the order relationship is represented differently in Ordered trees and in Heaps. Thus, the abstract data type Orders abstracts from the way in which the order relationship is represented.

Orders as such are not discussed in computer science literature, though nearly all of the different variants, which we offer, have been discussed in different places.

## 6.8.4   Specific Generic Parameters

Orders must be instantiated with a comparison function `COMPARE` that defines a total ordering relation on the key or element type.

```
generic
   ...
   with function COMPARE (LEFT, RIGHT : in ELEM_TYPE)
                         return ORDER_RELATION is <>;
package ORDERS
```

If only the ordering relation "<" is available, a comparison function can be instantiated from the generic function

```
generic
   type ELEM_TYPE is limited private;
   with function "<" (LEFT, RIGHT : in ELEM_TYPE)
                      return BOOLEAN is <>;
function COMPARISON (LEFT, RIGHT : in ELEM_TYPE)
                     return ORDER_RELATION;
```

from the BUILDING_BLOCK_UTILITIES like this:

```
function COMPARE is new COMPARISON (ET);
```

## 6.8.5   Specific Variants

The primary selection is that of a LIST or a TREE variant. All other characteristics are the same as for lists or trees.

## 6.8.6   General Variants

The general variants

```
simple_elements, indirect_elements, variable_elements,
   general_elements, accessed_elements, compact_elements
object_bounded, collection_bounded, unbounded
precondition_check, constraint_check, no_check
counter, no_counter
```

are supported with characteristics as described in chapter 5.

## 6.8.7   Combination of Variants

All combinations of the variants described above are possible.

## 6.8.8   Representation Specific Variants

### 6.8.8.1   Ordered List Specific Variants

In all list variants, the linear structure of nodes represents the order relation.

The choice between a linked list variant and a tabular list variant strongly depends on whether the list is `object_bounded` or not. If it is not `object_bounded`, only the linked variant is applicable; otherwise, the tabular variant is mostly superior for the following reasons:

- Tabular lists provide much faster `FIND` and `IS_ELEMENT` selector operations (O(log n) versus O(n)), based on the possibility of binary search, whereas the other selectors have about the same efficiency in both cases.

- The insert operation requires always to search for the insert position, based on the given key value. This is again O(log n) versus O(n). Once, the insert position is found, there are O(n) items to be shifted with a tabular list versus a constant O(1) effort with the linked list. If the key and info values are long, the shifting effort can be reduced by using a pointered tabular list. However, the absolute efforts for shifting in tabular lists and searching in linked lists, which are both O(n), are hard to compare.

- For the remove operation with a given key value the rationale is similar. For the remove operation with a given index, a non diluted tabular list has a shifting overhead in comparison to the linked list. This overhead is eliminated by selection of a diluted tabular list which, however, makes searching slightly more expensive.

Depending on the selection for linked or tabular representation, either the variant choices for linked lists or for tabular lists are offered.

For linked list variants, the choices are:

```
single_link, double_link, cached_link
linear, circular
single_anchor, double_anchor
```

The `double_anchor` and the `single_anchor circular` variants allow fast access of order O(1) to the largest key. The `double_link` variant allows to access a smaller element from the larger element efficiently, as for example with the `PREVIOUS` operation. If this kind of access is not required, but only an efficient `REMOVE` operation for an index that was found by iteration, the `cached_link` variant allows this without the overhead of an additional link per element.

For tabular list variants, the choices are:

```
non_diluted, flag_diluted, value_diluted
non_wrapped, wrapped
non_pointered, pointered
```

The `flag/value_diluted` variants allow an efficient `REMOVE` operation of order O(1). The `wrapped` variant is advantageous if the insertion order is mainly from the larger to smaller element values and, in particular, if the elements to be inserted are sorted in this order. The `pointered` variant should be selected, if the element size and/or info size are large, to minimize the required shifting overhead.

### 6.8.8.2 Combination of Ordered List Variants

All combinations of the variants described above are possible except for the combination

- of `circular` with `double_anchor`,

- of `pointered` with `value_diluted`,

- of `non_diluted` with `counter`, and

- of `tabular` with `collection_bounded` or `unbounded`.

Figure 6.17 illustrates some of the possible variant combinations.

tabular list, wrapped, non-pointered, non-diluted:

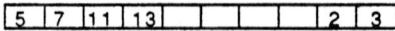

linked list, single link, linear, single anchor

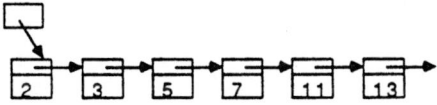

Figure 6.17: Some variants for ordered lists

### 6.8.8.3   Ordered Tree Specific Variants

Only binary trees are used to implement orders, since they have the smallest search effort considering the number of element-wise comparisons required.

Sorted trees show a good logarithmic O(log n) time performance in searching for an element, inserting an element according to its value, removing an element, finding the smallest or largest element, and finding the next smaller or larger element from a given element.

The only operation with a linear performance is access by position count (finding the n-th element), since this requires element-wise stepping through the tree in a in-order traversal. By adding to each node a `subtree_counter` that gives the number of nodes in its left subtree, this operation can also be done with O(log n) performance. A small overhead to maintain the counters is added to constructor operations, but they keep their O(log n) performance.

Another variant of ordered trees is characterized by how the path length from the root to a leaf is controlled. **unbalanced** trees have no special control mechanism, and lead to an O(n) vs. O(log n) performance in the degenerated case. **avl**-trees or **balanced** trees allow to guarantee a better worst-case behavior than unbalanced trees. However, there is an additional effort for insertion and removal of nodes.

As for lists, the tree variants may use a linked or a tabular representation.

Summarizing, the additional choices for a tree variant are:

```
subtree_counter, no_subtree_counter
avl, balanced, unbalanced
linked, tabular
```

For a linked tree, there remains the choice between

```
single_link, double_link, cached_link
```

while for tabular trees the open choices are

```
invalid_flag, invalid_value
non_pointered, pointered
```

### 6.8.8.4   Combination of Ordered Tree Variants

All combinations of the variants described above are possible except for the combination

- of `circular` with `double_anchor`,
- of `pointered` with `invalid_value`,
- of `tabular` with `collection_bounded` or `unbounded`.

Figure 6.17 illustrates some of the possible variant combinations.

## 6.8.9   Representation of Orders by Lists and Trees

All selected variant parameters are inherited.

AVL, linked, single link, subtree-sounter

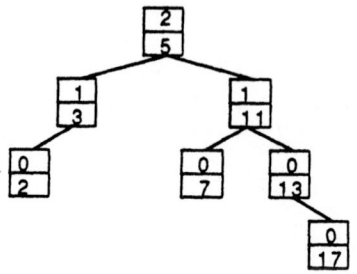

Balanced, tabular, object bounded (7), non-pointered.
no-subtree-sounter

| 7 | 5 | 11 | 2 | 3 | 13 | 17 |

Figure 6.18: Some variants for ordered trees

# 6.9 Sets and Maps

## 6.9.1 Synopsis

Sets and maps provide unordered collections of unique elements.

Maps differ from sets in having the elements further structured into a KEY and an INFO part, where only the keys need to be unique. This difference is similar to the difference of ordinary orders and key-info orders. Similar to the description of these two data types we shall explain only the operations of maps; the corresponding operations for sets follow from the equivalence of a set and a map with a void INFO part. The different names for types, operation or parameters, for example, ELEM_TYPE for sets and KEY_TYPE for maps, is the same as for orders. It may be looked up in detail in the appendix.

Sets and maps are implemented either by orders, lists, hash tables, or by arrays.

## 6.9.2 Types and Operations

Since the position of an element in the set or map is without significance, the constructor operations do not provide for explicit INSERT_POSITIONs. A REMOVE_POSITION is specified by an index. There is no notion of PARTs.

Since sets and maps do not have an inherent structure, no specific ITERATION_ORDERs can be specified.

Sets and maps are not index invariant, that means it is not allowed to keep an index that was obtained before performing a constructor operation, and to use it after this operation.

Sets and maps provide

- the constructor operations CLEAR (see 5.3.1.1),
  INSERT, FIND_OR_INSERT, REMOVE, REMOVE_ALL, GENERIC_REMOVE,
  MOVE, (see 5.3.1.2), COPY, TRANSFER (see 5.3.1.3), DEALLOCATE (see 5.3.1.4),

- the index based operations `GET_KEY, GET_INFO, SET_INFO, TRANSFER_INFO, MODIFY_INFO` (see 5.3.2),

- the selector operations `COUNT, IS_EMPTY, FIND, COUNT_KEY, IS_KEY, FIND_INFO, COUNT_INFO, IS_INFO, "=", EQUAL,` (see 5.3.4),

- the iterators `APPLY` (only for maps) `ITERATE, ITERATE_MOVE` (see 5.3.5), `REDUCE, UREDUCE, AREDUCE, REDUCE_INFO, UREDUCE_INFO, AREDUCE_INFO` (see 5.3.6), `FIND_PROPERTY, COUNT_PROPERTY, FIND_INFO_PROPERTY, COUNT_INFO_PROPERTY` (see 5.3.7), `EXISTS, FORALL, EXISTS_INFO, FORALL_INFO` (see 5.3.8),

- the order dependent operations `COMPARE <, <=, >, >= MAX, MIN REMOVE_MAX, REMOVE_MIN` (see 5.3.9),

- the hash function `HASH_FUNCTION` (see 5.3.10), and

- the set and map specific operations `UNION, INTERSECTION, DIFFERENCE, SUBSET, PROPER_SUBSET, SUPERSET,` and `PROPER_SUPERSET` (see 6.9.2.1), that will now be described.


### 6.9.2.1   Specific Operations

Sets and maps provide the following specific operations:

```
procedure UNION (LEFT : in out STRUCT; RIGHT : in STRUCT);
procedure INTERSECTION (LEFT  : in out STRUCT;
                        RIGHT : in STRUCT);
procedure DIFFERENCE (LEFT : in out STRUCT; RIGHT : in STRUCT);

function SUBSET (LEFT, RIGHT : in STRUCT) return BOOLEAN;
function PROPER_SUBSET (LEFT, RIGHT : in STRUCT) return BOOLEAN;
function SUPERSET (LEFT, RIGHT : in STRUCT) return BOOLEAN;
function PROPER_SUPERSET (LEFT, RIGHT : in STRUCT)
                        return BOOLEAN;
```

`UNION, INTERSECTION,` and `DIFFERENCE` have two sets or maps as operands, which are passed in as `LEFT` and `RIGHT` parameter. The `LEFT` parameter is used to return the result of the operation, that means the initial operand value is modified. For sets, these operations have the common mathematical meaning. For maps, the meaning of the operations is obtained by considering a map as a set of key-info-pairs. The result must again be a proper map; in particular, for the union of two maps there must be no key, for which the two maps have different info values.

SUBSET, PROPER_SUBSET, SUPERSET, and PROPER_SUPERSET have two sets or maps as operands and a BOOLEAN result. They check, if LEFT is a subset, proper subset, superset or proper superset of RIGHT. A is a subset/superset of B, if A is a subset/superset of B, but A is not equal to B. Again, the semantics for maps is obtained by considering the set of key-info-pairs.

## 6.9.3  Implementation Overview

Sets and maps are implemented on the abstract data types orders, lists, hash tables, or arrays.

The best time and space performance has the array implementation, which is applicable only if the key type is a discrete type. The info part is then stored in an array where the key type is used as index type. Therefore, for practical use it is not sufficient that the key type is discrete, but also has "reasonable" bounds such that an array with these index bounds can be allocated. For sets, the info part consists only of a bit, that indicates, whether the element is present or not.

Hash implementations do generally provide the second best time performance characteristics, but require a suitable hash function on the key that must be passed as a generic parameter.

Order implementations require an ordering relation on the key values that must be passed as a generic parameter. The keys are ordered according to this relation, and can for this reason be efficiently searched for.

If neither a hash function nor an ordering relation are available, the elements are put in an (unordered) list.

## 6.9.4    Specific Generic Parameters

Depending on the chosen variant, sets and maps have the same specific generic parameters as their representing building blocks. This means, for a representation by an order, we have (see 6.8.4)

```
generic
    ...
    with function COMPARE (LEFT, RIGHT : in ELEM_TYPE)
                            return ORDER_RELATION is <>;
package MAPS
```

and for a hash table representation (see 6.3.4

```
generic
    ...
    HASH_TABLE_SIZE : NATURAL;
    with function HASH (K : in KEY_TYPE) return INTEGER is <>;
package MAPS
```

## 6.9.5    Specific Variants

The primary selection is that of an order, a hash table, a list or an array variant. For an order variant, there is a further choice between a list and a tree variant.

## 6.9.6    General Variants

The general variants

```
simple_elements, indirect_elements, variable_elements,
    general_elements, accessed_elements, compact_elements
object_bounded, collection_bounded, unbounded
precondition_check, constraint_check, no_check
counter, no_counter
```

are supported with characteristics as described in chapter 5.

## 6.9.7 Combination of Variants

All combinations of the variants described above are possible.

## 6.9.8 Representation Specific Variants

### 6.9.8.1 Order-by-List Specific Variants

In all list variants of an order, the elements are ordered according to the given order relation. The representation is chosen such that each key or element occurs at most once. This is achieved by implementing the **INSERT** operation for sets and maps by using the **FIND_OR_INSERT** operation of orders.

Most of the variant choices, which exist for linked lists or for tabular lists, are preselected for the following reason: First, most constructor operations (with the exception of **REMOVE** and similar operations), and almost all selector operations need to search for the given element. Second, all set specific operations, like **INTERSECTION** step element-wise, in the order sequence, through all elements of both sets or maps.

With a linked list, searching is also done by stepping through all elements, until the position of the given element in the list is found. As a consequence, the performance of most constructor and selector operations is linear $(O(n))$. The performance of all set operations is also linear, since one can step simultaneously through both sets or maps. **double_link** variants would not provide any performance improvement, so they are not offered as a choice. Only the selection between the **single_link** variant and the **cached_link** variant is possible and should be considered, depending on whether **REMOVE** and similar operations are frequent. The link structure is **circular**, so it is easily possible to compare a given element value with the minimum and the maximum. As a consequence, only a **single_anchor** variant is provided.

Summarizing, the linked list variants are:

```
single_link, cached_link
circular
single_anchor
```

With a tabular list, searching is faster by using binary search than for linked lists. Set operations are performed by stepping element-wise through both sets or maps. However, for UNION, INTERSECTION, and DIFFERENCE, set operations start from the last elements, and the new last element of the LEFT set is put in a distance of COUNT (RIGHT) to the old last element. In this way, each element needs to be moved at most once, so we get an O(n) time performance for the number of moves.

As a consequence, the order of the time performance of all operations for tabular lists is superior to or, at least, as good as that of linked lists.

For a tabular list variant, all variants may be selected freely:

```
non_diluted, flag_diluted, value_diluted
non-wrapped, wrapped
non-pointered, pointered
```

The flag/value_diluted variants has some advantage because they allows an efficient REMOVE operation of order O(1), and since no access by position count operations are possible, where their performance is worse than that of a non_diluted variant. However, if there are no or only few removals, the non_diluted variant should be preferred.

The wrapped variant shows advantages if the insertions are mainly near the beginning of the list. The pointered variant should be selected, if the element length is large, to minimize the shifting overhead required.

## 6.9.8.2   Order-by-Tree Specific Variants

Sorted trees offer for most constructor and selector operations (as discussed above) a logarithmic time performance, whereas they have a linear time performance for the set specific operations.

The possible general variants for ordered trees include unbalanced and avl, but not balanced, since a balanced tree does not allow an efficient insertion or removal of arbitrary elements. For set and map implementation, ordered trees have no_subtree_counter. The remaining choices are:

```
unbalanced, avl
linked, tabular
```

The linked tree variant allows the additional choice between

```
single_link, cached_link
```

whereas the tabular variant offers

```
invalid_flag, invalid_value
non_pointered, pointered
```

### 6.9.8.3   Hash-Table Specific Variants

For a representation of a map (or set) by a hash table, the key (or element) is used as the key of the hash table, and the info component of the hash table is the info part of the map (or void).

For hash tables the primary variants are

```
open_addressing, hash_chaining.
```

For the open addressing variant the following additional choices are possible:

```
empty_value, empty_flag
value_diluted, flag_diluted
quadratic_probing, double_hashing,
    ordered_hashing, brents_open_hashing
```

If the set or map are `object_bounded`, only the the open addressing variant can be selected. For `collection_bounded` or unbounded sets or maps, both, hash chaining and open addressing are possible choices.

### 6.9.8.4   List Specific Variants

The (non ordered) list variant should only be chosen, if no ordering relation is given for the key or element type. All the constructor and selector operations requiring an implicit search show a linear time performance, since they need to step element-wise through the set or map.

The set specific operations show an even worse, quadratic time performance, since for one element of one set or map, all elements of the other set or map must be searched element-wise.

In particular, **INSERT** and similar operations show a linear performance (due to the search required) though the insertion itself can be made at an arbitrary position. For a linked list, a self-organizing behavior is obtained by inserting an element at the first position and by moving an element after having been accessed to the first position as well.

Due to these characteristics, a tabular list and a linked list show a similar time performance behavior, if the **flag/value_diluted** tabular list variant is used to prevent the shifting overhead with **REMOVE** and similar operations.

Most of the variant choices, which exist for linked lists or for tabular lists, are preselected.

For a linked list, **double_link**, **circular** or **double_anchor** variants would not provide any performance improvement, so they are not offered as a choice. Only the choice between the **single_link** and **cached_link** variant is possible and should be considered, if **REMOVE** and similar operations are frequent.

Summarizing, the linked list variants are:

```
single_link, cached_link
linear
single_anchor
```

With a tabular list, a **non_wrapped** variant is preselected because insertions are done at arbitrary (free) positions. Since elements remain at their position, once inserted, the **pointered** variant would not have any advantage and is excluded.

The following tabular list variants are possible:

```
non_diluted, flag_diluted, value_diluted
non_wrapped
non_pointered
```

The **flag/value_diluted** variants show some advantage because they allow an efficient **REMOVE** operation of order $O(1)$, and since no access by position count operations are possible, where their performance is worse than that of a **non_diluted** variant. However, for a set or map with no or very few removals of elements, a **non_diluted** variant may still be preferable.

### 6.9.8.5 Array Specific Variants

An array variant is applicable only to maps or sets, for which the keys (or elements) are of a discrete type. This discrete type is passed as a generic parameter

```
type ELEM_TYPE is (<>);
```

The discrete type is used as index range of an array. This array contains the info part of the map values or, for a set, a bit that indicates whether the value is an element of the set or not.

The number of elements is bounded by the given domain. Whether there is another bound (with respect to objects or collections) is irrelevant. Therefore, the choice of the variant **unbounded**, **collection_bounded**, **object_bounded** has no impact on the array representation.

Operations like **INSERT**, **REMOVE**, **FIND**, and **IS_ELEMENT** are very efficient of order $O(1)$, since each of them requires only one array access. Set specific operations need to visit each element, thus yielding a linear $O(n)$ time performance.

## 6.9.9 Representation of Sets and Maps

Orders, lists and hash tables inherit all required variant parameters.

# 6.10   Bags

## 6.10.1   Synopsis

Bags provide unordered collections, where elements may occur more than once. The operations for bags are the same as for sets, with the only difference that the semantics of the operations is extended to include the multiplicity of bag elements.

There are two generally different ways to implement bags.

- Each occurrence of a multiple element is kept separately in the collection (which is implemented either by an order or by a list).

- Each element is kept once in the collection, together with an element count that indicates the multiplicity of the element. Thus, we get a map from the element type to a positive number.

## 6.10.2   Types and Operations

As for sets and maps, bags do not have the notions of INSERT_POSITIONs, PARTs, or ITERATION_ORDERs; a REMOVE_POSITION is specified by an index.

Bags are not index invariant, that means it is not allowed to keep an index that was obtained before performing a constructor operation, and to use it after this operation.

- the constructor operations CLEAR (see 5.3.1.1),
  INSERT, FIND_OR_INSERT, REMOVE, REMOVE_ALL, GENERIC_REMOVE,
  MOVE, (see 5.3.1.2), COPY, TRANSFER (see 5.3.1.3), DEALLOCATE (see 5.3.1.4),

- the index based operations GET_ELEM, (see 5.3.2), (see 5.3.3),

- the selector operations COUNT, IS_EMPTY, FIND, COUNT_ELEM, IS_ELEM, "=",
  EQUAL, (see 5.3.4),

- the iterators ITERATE, ITERATE_MOVE (see 5.3.5),
  REDUCE, UREDUCE, AREDUCE (see 5.3.6),
  FIND_PROPERTY, COUNT_PROPERTY (see 5.3.7),
  EXISTS, FORALL (see 5.3.8),

- the order dependent operations COMPARE <, <=, >, >= MAX, MIN REMOVE_MAX, REMOVE_MIN (see 5.3.9),

- the hash function HASH_FUNCTION (see 5.3.10), and

- the bag specific operations SUBSET, PROPER_SUBSET, SUPERSET, and PROPER_SUPERSET.

The SUBSET and SUPERSET operations on bags are similar to the corresponding operations on sets, except that the number of element values is considered. For example, a bag B1 is a SUBSET of B2, if for each element E than occurs n times in B1, E occurs at least n times in B2.

## 6.10.3   Implementation Overview

There are two principally different ways to implement bags.

- Multiple elements are kept multiple times in the collection, either in an Order or in a List.

- Each element is kept once in the collection, together with an element count that indicates the multiplicity of the element. Thus, we get a map from the element type to a positive number. Different Map implementations are used, including the special Map implementation for discrete element types. It uses an array of natural numbers, which has the element type as an array index, to yield the multiplicity (including zero) of an element.

The array implementation, which is applicable only to bags with a discrete element type, has the best space performance and the best constant $O(1)$ time performance. It is obtained as the array implementation of a Map. It uses an array of natural numbers as Map range to indicate the multiplicity (including zero) of the corresponding element in the Bag.

Hash implementations of Maps do generally **provide** the second best time performance characteristics, but require a suitable hash function on the element values to be defined and passed as a generic parameter.

Order implementations (both of Maps and with multiple elements) require an order relationship on the element values to be defined and passed as a generic parameter. The elements are ordered according to this relation, and can for this reason be efficiently searched for.

If neither a hash function nor an order relationship are available, the elements are put in a (unordered) List (both as a Map implementation and with multiple elements).

## 6.10.4   Specific Generic Parameters

Depending on the chosen variant, sets and maps have the same specific generic parameters as their representing building blocks. This means, for a representation by an order, we have (see 6.8.4)

```
generic
   ...
   with function COMPARE (LEFT, RIGHT : in ELEM_TYPE)
                         return ORDER_RELATION is <>;
package MAPS
```

and for a hash table representation (see 6.3.4

```
generic
   ...
   HASH_TABLE_SIZE : NATURAL;
   with function HASH (K : in KEY_TYPE) return INTEGER is <>;
package MAPS
```

## 6.10.5   Specific Variants

The primary selection is between an order, an (unordered) list, and a map implementation.

The implementation should only be based on an unordered list, if there is no ordering relation available for the given element type. For an order variant, there is again the choice of a list or a tree variant.

The different variants of an order variant have exactly the same characteristics as those of a set variant by an order (see 6.9.5).

The variants of a Multiple List variant have a characteristics different from the corresponding Set variants and are described in the following.

For a map variant, the same variants as for maps are available with the same characteristics (see 6.9.5).

## 6.10.6   General Variants

The general variants

```
simple_elements, indirect_elements, variable_elements,
    general_elements, accessed_elements, compact_elements
object_bounded, collection_bounded, unbounded
precondition_check, constraint_check, no_check
counter, no_counter
```

are supported with characteristics as described in chapter 5.

## 6.10.7   Combination of Variants

All combinations of the variants described above are possible.

## 6.10.8   Representation Specific Variants

For order and list representations, the same variants are available with the same characteristics as for orders and lists that represent sets or maps (see section 6.9.8). For map representations, all map variants are available (see section 6.9.5).

## 6.10.9   Representation of Bags

All variant parameters, that are required by the implementation data types order, list, or map, are inherited. In addition, maps are instantiated with POSITIVE as INFO_TYPE.

# Chapter 7

# Technical Issues

This chapter presents some technical aspects that were considered for the actual implementation of our catalogue of building blocks. The first section introduces the facilities that allow the selection of variants of a given building block; the second section discusses some Ada design decisions that we have taken; finally, the third section outlines some deficiencies and open problems.

## 7.1 Selection of Building Block Variants

The number of different variant combinations for a single building block may exceed 1.000, so it is certainly impossible to separately maintain the different variants (without considering serious restrictions of the possible combinations). Although Ada allows the parameterization of modules by its concept of generic units, the effect of variant parameters can often not be modeled with generic parameters. As an example, consider the parameter CONSTRAINT_CHECK, on which it depends whether the pragma "suppress" appears or not; the existence of a declaration or pragma, however, cannot depend on an Ada generic parameter.

Since Ada does not offer a concept to implement (certain) variant parameters, and since maintenance requires to combine all variants in a single file, we use a macro language (the C preprocessor language "cpp") to distinguish the variants.

The macro mechanism has its advantages and drawbacks. An advantage is that the code is selected statically, that means at compile-time; so there is no run-time overhead to distinguish the variants. As a drawback, there is no code-sharing for different variants and the user has to go through the variant selection mechanism each time he needs a new variant, instead of just writing different instantiations of the same module. Besides that, the use of variant parameters is more error-prone than the use of a (strongly checked) language concept; misspelling of variant parameters, for example, are hard to detect.

Since the variant parameterization is independent from the programming language anyway, we developed a little interactive tool that asks the variant parameters from the user. The tool is controlled by a description of the variant parameters and their dependencies. Not all combinations of variant parameters are possible; the tool permits only the allowed combinations. The result of applying the tool is a setting of macro parameters which is used to run the macro processor cpp. Thus a consistent setting of the macro variables is guaranteed.

Figure 7.1 shows the procedure how building block variants are selected and the resulting Ada packages are instantiated.


# 7.2   Ada Design Decisions

This section shall discuss alternatives that were considered for the realization of our data type catalogue and shall motivate the taken decisions from the language point of view.

For the first major choice, there is no definite motive: why did we chose Ada? In fact, during the development of the building blocks we sometimes wished we had chosen a language like C++. Currently we are implementing similar building blocks in C++ and we experience how much simpler some problems could be solved in Ada.

The strong checking in Ada, from which the ordinary user certainly benefits, was often an obstacle to a simpler implementation. An example is the restriction that pointers may only refer to dynamically allocated objects. This is of course helpful in order to avoid dangling references, however, we could have encapsulated the use of these references in a way that they were save. Now that we have overcome all these problems we can benefit from the static Ada checking facilities, like for in/out parameters or limited types, not to speak of type checking and overloading resolution.

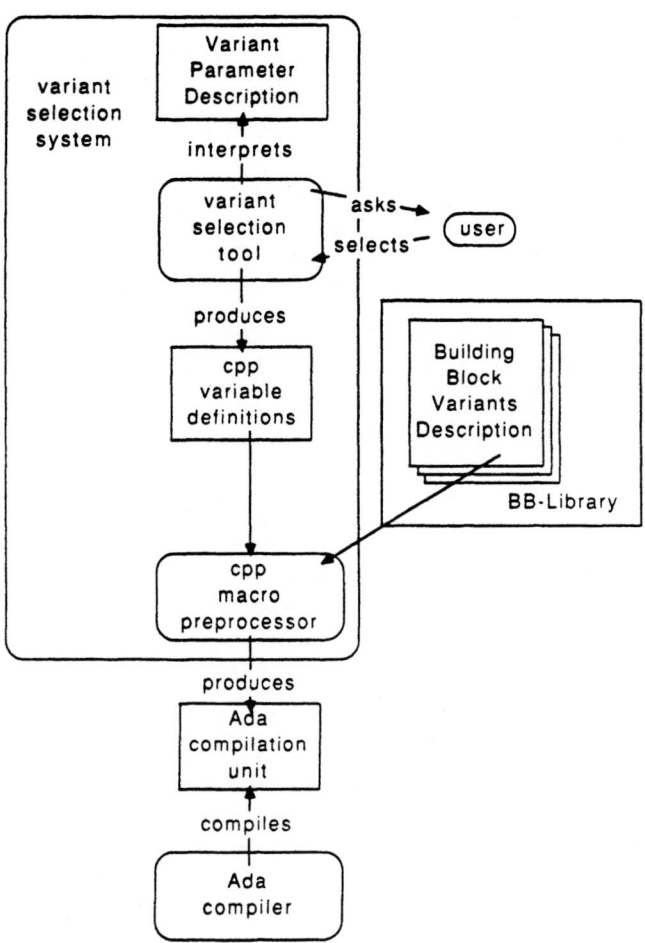

Figure 7.1: A System for the Selection of Building Block Variants

For the selection of main storage data structures as they are implemented in our catalogue, it is sometimes necessary to have an understanding of the storage management
of the language's run-time system. Notions like "run-time stack" or "global heap" influence the thinking about the impacts of variant choices. Ideally, these considerations
should be left to the compiler, because he has more knowledge about the machine and
about his own choices which are the basis for a proper judgement. However, today's
compilers seem to be not smart enough to leave such choices for them, so the user
must decide at least to a certain degree. Languages with a strongly restricted access
to storage structures, like Lisp or Prolog, were therefore excluded. Again on the first
glance, C++ offers a closer access to physical storage than Ada does. Its constructor

and destructor capabilities are conceptually adequate for what we were seeking. On the other hand, C++ has no statically declared objects of dynamic size, like dynamic arrays, but rather allocates such objects on the heap, where deallocation is not for free. The Ada facilities of statically declared dynamic-sized objects (controlled by discriminants) which can be stored on the run-time stack proved valuable. Unfortunately, the characteristics of different variants may strongly depend on the compiler strategies, for example, whether collections for access types are allocated locally or globally, or whether record and array parameters are passed by reference or by copy.

The structure of our catalogue is a hierarchy of building blocks, where higher level data types partially inherit operations from lower level ones. An object oriented language seems appropriate to model this situation. Ada is no proper object oriented language with classes and inheritance; the use of derived types is no real substitute. However, generic packages provide an excellent composition facility in our context. Instantiation implies a little more writing for the implementation of the "inherited" operations. However, we do not expect a strong dynamic evolution of the catalogue, and therefore object orientation seems not as promising as it is in rapidly evolving systems. Generics are also used to implement polymorphic types. It is argued that with the object oriented paradigm polymorphism is no longer an issue; we are not (yet) able to judge the applicability of this statement in our context.

Besides all these arguments, Ada simply offers a lot of details, like aggregates, arbitrarily nested scopes, and a library concept that made life easier. In the following sections we shall discuss special issues where we made use of particular Ada capabilities and we try to assess their usefulness. These issues are

- dispersion of structure object,

- composition of abstract types, and

- storage management

## 7.2.1   Dispersion of Structures Objects

Structures are values, whose storage representation may be dispersed over several separate Ada objects, like the anchor and the nodes of a linked list. The predefined Ada assignment works on single objects, so, for (the anchor of) a structure, it would copy only the anchor and not all the nodes of the list. If now after such an assignment two objects contain anchors to the same list of nodes, and the first object is used as (in out) parameter of a structure modifying operation, this operation has a side-effect on the second object. This side-effect may be the same as it is for the first object or it may even make the second object inconsistent, if the operation implies a modification of the anchor.

The consequences of such side-effects are in general undesired and often lead to errors that are hard to track. Therefore, we decided to disallow any form of (conceptual) structure sharing. In order to enforce this rule we must prohibit

- the immediate manipulation of elements without considering the context of some structure object, and
- the copying of structure anchors without copying the elements of the structure.

These restrictions must not induce a loss of efficiency. They shall, in particular, not imply that elements can only be "moved" by copying.

The first requirement is achieved by the design of the operations of the data type interface: all operations that manipulate a structure have this structure as an (in out) parameter. There is no structure modifying operation that has a parameter of type **INDEX** without a corresponding **STRUCT** parameter that must designate the structure to which the **INDEX** belongs. For example, an element, or a collection of elements may be moved from one structure to another, using the operation

```
procedure MOVE (TO       : in out STRUCT;
                FROM      : in out STRUCT;
                FROM_POS : in      REMOVE_POSITION;
                TO_POS    : in      INSERT_POSITION);
```

but there is no way to move an element to another structure without removing it from the structure to which it currently belongs. With this interface the explicit manipulation of "nodes" can be excluded. A problem that occurs in the case of aliasing will be discussed below.

The second requirement is achieved by making the structure type limited. This implies that the basic Ada operation that assigns just the anchor (without copying the nodes) is not available through the interface of the data type. There is, however, an interface operation **TRANSFER**, that transfers a structure from one object to another by just copying the anchor. The source object is cleared after the execution of **TRANSFER**, so there is no multiple access to structure parts.

Whereas the interface controls the explicit operations, implicit assignments occur when structures are passed as parameters. Multiple access from different objects to the same structure can thus occur in the case of parameter aliasing, for example, when the above MOVE operation is called with the same structure for TO and FROM. Ada does not explicitly forbid aliasing, but due to the rule that requires that parameter passing by copy and by reference must be equivalent, most Ada programs that involve aliasing are erroneous. Unfortunately, this property is not required to be checked by the compiler and most compilers don't even try to check for illegal aliasing. Erroneous aliasing makes it necessary to provide certain operations in two forms, one that works on two different structures and one that works only on a single structure. For our MOVE operations, the case that an element is moved within the same structure requires an extra MOVE operation

```
procedure MOVE (S        : in out STRUCT;
                FROM_POS : in     REMOVE_POSITION;
                TO_POS   : in     INSERT_POSITION);
```

not only for convenience, but because the call

```
MOVE (TO => S, FROM => S, ...)
```

would be erroneous.

## 7.2.2  Composition of Data Types

First of all, we had to choose whether our building blocks should model types or objects. We took the choice for types for several reasons: types are more general, since an object can always be built from a type. But what is more important is the possibility of combining types. The instances of a building block are now packages that declare types and these types can themselves be used as element types, that means as generic actual type parameters of other building blocks.

Hierarchical composition of generic packages introduces a duality between generic formal parameters and the operations provided by the package interface: operations that are (possibly) required as generic parameters (like hash functions) should be provided by each data type in the catalogue; conversely, the capabilities of a data type should be exhausted by accepting them as generic parameters, like COPY, TRANSFER or DEALLOCATE operations.

The data types from the catalogue, like lists or sets, and simple types, like integers or characters, have major differences in their operations. The catalogue types are limited, that means they have explicit COPY and TRANSFER operations; they generally have explicit DEALLOCATE operations (to release their elements) and have a variant (object_bounded) where the structure type has a discriminant. Whereas for the catalogue types certain operations are automatically provided, it would be inconvenient for simple types to explicitly provide similar operations. Therefore, we distinguish those variants for the element type, which require the specific operations (and have the appropriate <>-defaults) and expect the element type to have a discriminant, from those which expect a simple type and assume the predefined or basic Ada operations, like assignment.

## 7.2.3   Storage Management

Although Ada is a high level programming language that abstracts from storage layout details, we assume certain common characteristics with respect to the storage management strategies of the Ada runtime system and we expect an Ada compiler to exploit certain properties that we describe in the following. The efficient allocation and deallocation of objects and their elements was a major concern in the design of the data types in our catalogue.

Each element of a structure object requires a certain amount of space. The overall effort that is required for space allocation and deallocation and the total space consumption depends on the time and place where storage for these elements is allocated. Ada offers access types for the dynamic creation of objects. An access type provides a so-called collection; objects are allocated within the context of a collection; they may be explicitly deallocated (UNCHECKED_DEALLOCATION) or are implicitly deallocated when the whole collection is deallocated.

As described in chapter 5, we distinguish between the object-wise, the collection-wise, and the global allocation of space. For object-/collection-wise allocation, all elements of the object/collection can be deallocated in a single operation, when the corresponding object/collection is deallocated. The more global an element is allocated, the earlier can the space of an (explicitly) removed and deallocated element be reused, but the more heterogeneous may the reused spaces be. The trade-off between time-efficiency through implicit deallocation and space-efficiency through early release is, however, not the only criterion.

Since Ada does not have destructor operations, like C++, which are implicitly called for an object at the end of its scope, globally allocated elements of some object must either be removed by an explicit DEALLOCATE of the object at the end of its lifetime, or they will exist forever (unless the system provides for garbage collection, which is unlikely for a real-time language like Ada). If in the case of object-wise allocation, the elements are subcomponents (in the Ada sense) of the object they are implicitly deallocated together with the object without the necessity of explicitly DEALLOCATEing the object. Moreover, statically declared objects and collections that are stored on the runtime stack are implicitly deallocated when the runtime stack is popped.

# 7.3   Deficiencies and Open Problems

Ada was a superb choice for expressing consistency constraints, that guarantee the proper use of the abstract data types and their operations. We have learned a lot about the concepts required, like the right parameterization and choice of types. However, the concrete notation of these concepts is sometimes clumsy and then ruins the general applicability.

The major notational deficiency comes with generic operations, like ITERATE or MODIFY. The general application pattern of these operations requires the following three steps:

1. A "body" procedure with a given parameter profile must be written; only seldom can existing operations be used.

2. The generic operation is instantiated.

3. The instantiated operations is called (mostly only once).

This notation is particularly awkward for the manipulation of "multi-level" type instances, like maps from strings to stacks of descriptors (a typical symbol table structure). Consider such a map and assume we want to push a descriptor on top of the stack that is associated to a given symbol. In terms of our value semantics this means changing the map structure. This is enforced by the operation's signature, since the result of a map application cannot be used in a push operation, since the latter one alters its argument, and so the argument must be a variable. In order to alter this map info part, we must use the generic MODIFY_INFO operation:

```
procedure PUSH_DESCR (M     : in out STRING_STACK_MAP;
                      SYMB  : in STRING;
                      DESCR : in DESCRIPTOR) is


    procedure MODIFICATION (ST : in out STACK) is
    begin
        PUSH (ST, DESCR);
    end MODIFICATION;

    procedure MAP_PUSH is
        new STRING_STACK_MAPS.MODIFY_INFO (MODIFICATION);
begin
    MAP_PUSH (M, FIND (M, SYMB));
end PUSH_DESCR;
```

This notation seems a little awkward, although it is conceptually clear. We would prefer a notation like

```
procedure PUSH_DESCR (M     : in out STRING_STACK_MAP;
                      SYMB  : in STRING;
                      DESCR : in DESCRIPTOR) is
begin
    for ST : STACK := M at FIND (M, SYMB) do
        PUSH (ST, DESCR);
    end do;
end PUSH_DESCR;
```

A similar notation would be helpful for iterations, which also require a generic construct like the one above. The suggested notation might easily be handled by a transformational Ada preprocessor.

A second problem with generics, besides the clumsy notation, are the effort that must be spent at compile-time as well as at run-time. Most available compilers handle generic units by copying the source (that means the appropriate intermediate representation) and generating separate code for each instantiation. The method takes compile time and does not share code. This is particularly awkward in our case, since a lot of operations are provided which are possibly not entirely needed. An interpretative solution to generic parameters, as taken by at least one Ada system that the authors know of, avoids both problems and has apparently no significant impacts on efficiency.

We just mentioned the potential problem, that mostly only selective use is made of the comprehensive set of building block operations. We decided, not to split the building blocks into different modules, implementing different operation classes, since the user should not have to worry about where to find the operations he needs, and because of other, performance related problems. So what is required from an Ada system is a selective binding of the operation code that is actually required; again, we know of a single system with these capabilities, whereas most systems perform binding on a package level.

Selective linkage is one of the optimization techniques that are desirable, if not necessary, for a sensible (re-)use of data types from a catalogue. Another crucial technique is inline inclusion of operations together with constant propagation and folding. This is due to the fact that the interfaces are written in a functional style in order to allow a wide range of different implementation variants. Many functions, however, consist of a single expression or statement. In contrast to the techniques mentioned before, inline inclusion and constant propagation is a more conventional technique and is found in most Ada systems.

Finally, object-oriented features that are missing in Ada, like classes and inheritance, would have facilitated a more flexible design of additional operations that work on structures. With the current building block design in Ada, each instance of a building block yields a new type, that is not convertible to a similar type, not even to a type that results from another instantiation of the same building block. Since Ada is strongly types, each operation that is newly defined for a structure type must have this structure type as a parameter and is then not applicable to any other structure type. This situation can be relaxed with the definition of generic operations, that get the structure type and the required operations as generic parameters (using the <> feature). Operations for specific structure types can then be instantiated from this generic operation. This example illustrates that Ada generics can simulate some of the object oriented concepts. Again, the notation is anything but elegant.

# Chapter 8

# Case Study: A File Compression System

The goal of this case study is to demonstrate the use of the building blocks and, in particular, the choice of variants, in a realistic context.

## 8.1 The Overall Task

The task to be solved is the compression of text files with the goal of space saving archival. The idea is to find the most often occurring words in the file(s) and replace them by a code (consisting of an escape character followed by a one character code) in order to save space. The words that are coded are also stored in a file. Further files can be compressed according to this given code (which is not necessarily the optimum for the new files). Of course, compressed files can be re-installed which means they have to be decompressed.

Although reuse in the fields of user interfaces or file IO is certainly essential for a high software engineering productivity, our major concern is on the reuse of data-structures. Therefore, we concentrate on the implementation of the involved data types and the algorithms for the determination of the word-code mapping and for compression and decompression. We do not care about the way in which the user has to call the tools and how he provides the file names, which might be done through parameters on the input line or interactively through a menu; file handling will also not be spelled out in detail.

The design approach that we follow in this case study is mainly top-down. The refinement steps are not or only little influenced by the possibility of reuse. However, once the decision for a refinement is taken, reusable building blocks are considered as potential solutions. Further decisions concentrate on the selection of the appropriate variants of the used data types.

# 8.2   Search for Reusable Building Blocks (Phase 1)

The first step is to consider if one of the tasks given in the problem description can be implemented more or less directly reusing some of the building blocks in our library. (We would certainly find some Unix facility that lets us solve the problem right away, but then this chapter would be finished and we would not have made our point.) From the task descriptions it is easily to be seen that none of the reusable abstract data types from our catalogue does fit. Therefore, we begin the top-down design as usual (that means without considering reuse). After we have completed the first design step and got a decomposition into smaller tasks, we will have to repeat the current step and look if reusable building blocks from our library can be used to implement some of the smaller tasks.

# 8.3   Functional Decomposition (Phase 1)

Our first design step is the functional decomposition of the task and data.

Analyzing the sample text files consists of

- reading in each text file and isolating the words

- collecting the words and increasing the word frequency count

- when all sample text files are processed: select the words to be coded and put them in a file, for use by compression/decompression

Together with refining the task, we need to refine the data, which are text files and words. Words are sequences of characters. How a text file is split into words is not further discussed. Several methods are possible, for example, the attempt to identify word prefixes or suffixes and to split them from the word in order to obtain a greater multiplicity.

Compressing consists of

- reading in the word-code file and build an in-core structure for word look-up
- reading in each text file and isolating the words
- looking up if the current word is coded; if so, replace it
- writing out the compressed file.

Decompression performs similar steps but with different data. the compressed files logically consist of a sequence of items that have to be isolated, where an item is either a word or a code. The steps are

- reading in the word-code file and build an in-core structure for code look-up
- reading in each item file and isolating the words and codes
- test if the current item is a code; if so, replace it
- writing out the decompressed file.

## 8.4   Modular Decomposition

From the functional decomposition we derive the modular decomposition of our design following the principles of encapsulation and of functional and data abstraction.

Devices and data structures are prime candidates for encapsulation. The only devices in our example system are files. There are three data structures, one used for the word-frequency count, another one for the code or, respectively word lookup, and the structure used to store the the word-code pairs in a file.

When we encapsulate the devices and data items, we make them accessible by operations. We need to define the operations, so it is the question which operations are required. The answer is that exactly those operations are required that are described in the functional decomposition to be performed on the data structures. For example, two operations are described on the code-word lookup structure, namely building up the structure, and doing the lookup in the structure.

The following modules are defined as the result of encapsulation:

## 8.4.1   Words, Codes and Items

As an abstraction of the concrete representation of words as strings and codes as two byte characters, we consider WORDs as an abstract (private) type. This allows us to apply our system not only to text files but to arbitrary binary files as well, provided a given isolation operation.

For text compression, code items might be represented by an escape character followed by a one character code. In this case the escape character itself must be escaped, so there remain 255 codes that can be used for coding words. Independent of their file representation, codes are denoted by positive numbers ranging from 1 to NR_OF_CODES (which in this case would be 255).

ITEMs are the disjoint union of words and codes.

The operations that isolate words or items from a given file depend on the word's representation and therefore are nested in the unit that describes this representation. The packages WORD_FILE, ITEM_FILE, and CODED_WORD_FILE provide the required I/O operations. The distinction of compressed and uncompressed files is left to the implementation and not further discussed in this example. It might be implemented by a distinct file suffix or by an extra directory for compressed files. However, it is required, that this distinction is in fact implemented by the module, so that a word file and an item file are physically distinct even if they have the same name.

The GET operations perform the isolation of words and items. How the isolation is performed is irrelevant for the rest of the system. However, the compression factor may be increased by a sophisticated isolation technique, for example by isolating the root prefix of a word.

Finally, the operation that computes the WORD_SCORE depending on the word's frequency belongs in this unit. The word score is a measure for the overall space saving in the case that the given word would be coded. Since the representation of words and codes is hidden in this unit – in particular their representation within the files – this is the right place, where the space saving can be determined.

```
package WORDS_CODES_ITEMS is

   -- Basic Types
   -- ===========

   type WORD is private;

   NR_OF_CODES constant := 255; -- must be > 0
   type CODE is new POSITIVE range 1 .. NR_OF_CODES;

   type ITEM is private;
   -- disjoint union of WORD and CODE

   function MAKE_ITEM (W : WORD) return ITEM;
   function MAKE_ITEM (C : CODE) return ITEM;

   function IS_WORD  (I : ITEM) return BOOLEAN;
   function IS_CODE  (I : ITEM) return BOOLEAN;

   function WORD_OF  (I : ITEM) return WORD;
   function CODE_OF  (I : ITEM) return CODE;

   -- File Handling
   -- =============

   type FILE_MODE is (IN_FILE, OUT_FILE);

   package WORD_FILE is
      procedure OPEN (MODE : in FILE_MODE; NAME : in STRING);
      function  GET return WORD;
      procedure PUT (W : in WORD);
      function  END_OF_FILE return BOOLEAN;
      procedure CLOSE;
   end WORD_FILE;
```

```
   package ITEM_FILE is
      procedure OPEN (MODE : in FILE_MODE; NAME : in STRING);
      function  GET return ITEM;
      procedure PUT (C : in ITEM);
      function  END_OF_FILE return BOOLEAN;
      procedure CLOSE;
   end ITEM_FILE;

   package CODED_WORD_FILE is
      procedure OPEN (MODE : in FILE_MODE; NAME : in STRING);
      function  GET return WORD;
      procedure PUT (W : in WORD);
      function  END_OF_FILE return BOOLEAN;
      procedure CLOSE;
   end CODED_WORD_FILE;

   -- Word Score
   -- ==========

   function WORD_SCORE (W         : in WORD;
                        FREQUENCY : POSITIVE) return INTEGER;

   -- Standard Operations for Words
   -- =============================

   function "<" (LEFT, RIGHT : WIRD) return BOOLEAN;
   function HASH (W : WIRD) return INTEGER;

 private
   type WORD is new STRING;

   type ITEM is new STRING; -- ESC & CODE for word codes
 end WORDS_CODES_ITEMS;
```

## 8.4.2  The Word-Frequency Collection

is used for sampling the input files that shall be compressed. It encapsulates as a data structure the collection of words and corresponding frequencies. The unit implements the steps that have been worked out in the functional decomposition. The SAMPLE procedure implements the sampling of the files. We assume the existence of a package **STRING_SET_OPS** that implements sets of strings, for example by the instantiation

```
package STRING_SET_OPS is new INDIRECT_SETS (STRING);
```

where **INDIRECT_SETS** is a variant of SETS with indirect elements.

```
package WORD_FREQUENCY_COLLECTION is

    procedure GET_WORDS (WORD_FILE_NAME : STRING);

    procedure FIND_HIGH_SCORES;

    procedure PUT_CODED_WORDS (CODED_WORD_FILE_NAME : STRING);

end WORD_FREQUENCY_COLLECTION;

with WORD_FREQUENCY_COLLECTION;
with STRING_SET_OPS; use  STRING_SET_OPS;
procedure SAMPLE (WORD_FILE_NAMES     : STRING_SET;
                  CODED_WORD_FILE_NAME : STRING) is

    package WFM renames WORD_FREQUENCY_MAP;

    procedure GET_ALL_WORDS is
        new STRING_SETS.ITERATE (WFM.GET_WORDS);

begin

    GET_ALL_WORDS (WORD_FILE_NAMES);
    WFM.FIND_HIGH_SCORES;
    WFM.PUT_CODED_WORDS (CODED_WORD_FILE_NAME);

end SAMPLE;
```

## 8.4.3  The Word-Code Map

is used to implement the actual compression. It encapsulates the mapping from the (coded) words to their codes.

```
with WORDS_CODES_ITEMS;
use  WORDS_CODES_ITEMS;
package WORD_CODE_MAP is

   procedure INITIALIZE (CODED_WORD_FILE_NAME : STRING);
   -- get word code mapping from CODED_WORD_FILE

   function MAKE_ITEM (W : WORD) return ITEM;
   -- return the code of the word, if any,
   -- or the word itself otherwise.

end WORD_CODE_MAP;

with WORDS_CODES_ITEMS, WORD_CODE_MAP, STRING_SET_OPS;
use  WORDS_CODES_ITEMS, STRING_SET_OPS;
procedure COMPRESS (WORD_FILE_NAMES       : STRING_SET;
                    CODED_WORD_FILE_NAME : STRING) is
   package WCM renames WORD_CODE_MAP;
   procedure COMPRESS_FILE (FILE_NAME : STRING) is
   begin
      WORD_FILE.OPEN (IN_FILE, FILE_NAME);
      ITEM_FILE.OPEN (OUT_FILE, FILE_NAME);
      while not WORD_FILE.END_OF_FILE loop
         ITEM_FILE.PUT (WCM.MAKE_ITEM (WORD_FILE.GET));
      end loop;
      WORD_FILE.CLOSE;
      ITEM_FILE.CLOSE;
   end COMPRESS_FILE;
   procedure COMPRESS_ALL_WORDS is
      new BBS.STRING_SETS.ITERATE (COMPRESS_FILE);
begin
   WCM.INITIALIZE (CODED_WORD_FILE_NAME);
   COMPRESS_ALL_WORDS (WORD_FILE_NAMES);
end COMPRESS;
```

## 8.4.4   The Code-Word Map

is used to implement the decompression. It encapsulates the mapping from codes to
words.

```
with WORDS_CODES_ITEMS;
use  WORDS_CODES_ITEMS;
package CODE_WORD_MAP is

    procedure INITIALIZE (CODED_WORD_FILE_NAME : STRING);
    -- get word code mapping from CODED_WORD_FILE

    function MAKE_WORD (I : ITEM) return WORD;
    -- if I is a code, return the corresponding word,
    -- otherwise return the word I

end CODE_WORD_MAP;

with WORDS_CODES_ITEMS, CODE_WORD_MAP, STRING_SET_OPS;
use  WORDS_CODES_ITEMS, STRING_SET_OPS;
procedure DECOMPRESS (ITEM_FILE_NAMES      : STRING_SET;
                      CODED_WORD_FILE_NAME : STRING) is
    package CWM renames CODE_WORD_MAP;
    procedure DECOMPRESS_FILE (FILE_NAME : STRING) is
    begin
        ITEM_FILE.OPEN (IN_FILE, FILE_NAME);
        WORD_FILE.OPEN (OUT_FILE, FILE_NAME);
        while not ITEM_FILE.END_OF_FILE loop
            WORD_FILE.PUT (CWM.MAKE_WORD (ITEM_FILE.GET));
        end loop;
        ITEM_FILE.CLOSE;
        WORD_FILE.CLOSE;
    end DECOMPRESS_FILE;
    procedure DECOMPRESS_ALL_WORDS is
        new STRING_SETS.ITERATE (DECOMPRESS_FILE);
begin
    CWM.INITIALIZE (CODED_WORD_FILE_NAME);
    DECOMPRESS_ALL_WORDS (ITEM_FILE_NAMES);
end DECOMPRESS;
```

# 8.5   Search for Reusable Building Blocks (Phase 2)

Our objective is to reuse building blocks to implement the modules, which we have got as a result of the modular decomposition. When searching through the reusable library there are three cases:

1. We may find a building block that implements directly the functions required from a module. This is the best case which will, probably, not happen very frequently.

   In this case, we can use the specification of the building block directly as the specification of our module. We need to check if one of the different available implementations of this building block matches our performance requirements. If so we take this implementation and all work on this module is finished.

   If no implementation matches our performance requirements we need to determine if there exists a suitable implementation alternative. If the requirements were not realistic none such alternative will exist and the requirements need to be changed.

   In the case that an alternative implementation exists it must be evaluated if the benefits gained by the superior performance for our application outweight the cost required to do the additional implementation.

2. We may find a building block that implements functions similar to those required from a module. If we want to use this building block directly for the designed module, we need to change the design.

   For example, we might find a building block that isolates the words of a given line of text. However, our word isolation module was designed to have a complete text as input. To use the building block we have to modify the current design. This can be done, for example, by providing a function that isolates the lines from a given text, and passes them to the word isolation building block.

   After the design modification, we can use the specification of the building block directly as the specification of our module. All subsequent considerations are the same as in the 1.

3. We may find a building block that provides functions that can be used to implement a module.

   In this case, the building block will not replace the module. The module specification needs to be defined first, possibly influenced to some extent from the building block specification.

Let us now look at the modules, into which we have structured our application, which of these cases apply.

## 8.5.1    Words, Codes and Items

There is no such building block in our catalogue. However, isolating words is a frequently used function in text processing; we would expect to find such a function in a text processing library. As we have already discussed, there might be a need to adapt our module design to the functions that the reusable building blocks provide.

## 8.5.2    The Word-Frequency Collection

In order to find the (at most 255) words with the highest scores, we must determine for each word its frequency, that means the number of occurrences of this word in the given set of files. The words considered are determined by the file splitting operation WORD_FILE.GET. The adequate data structure for collecting items and then determining their frequencies is a MAP from WORDs to the number of their occurrences. Using a list would be an overspecification, since sequencing is irrelevant; using a set would be insufficient, since the number of occurrences of elements in the structure is relevant. Bags also seem to be appropriate on the first glance. However, after we have inserted all words in the frequency collection we must iterate over all words to find the high scores. This iteration should be applied to each word only once. A bag iteration would be apply the action to each word as often as it occurs in the structure.

For the map structure we must choose an indirect variant, because the element type WORD might be (and in fact is) an unconstrained type.

Once we have constructed the map of all occurring words, we must find the words with the highest scores. We need no more than 255 words, so we only have to consider at most 255 "high-scores". A structure that is ORDERed with respect to the word scores seems appropriate; the structure can be object-bounded to 255 elements. This structure is constructed by iterating over all occurring words, inserting the word, if the structure is not full with "better" words, possibly deleting the worst word, if the structure is full. Since we have an ordering relation and a hash operation defined for words, the map might be implemented by a (search) tree or a hash table. This decision depends on whether there is a good estimate for the number of words in the given files. If such an estimate exists, the hash table representation should be used, otherwise, the tree variant might be superior. For a very large, but unknown number of words it might even be sensible to first step through the files and count the words, which gives an upper bound for the number of different words that can then be used to determine the hash table size.

Finally, we must decide how to represent the ordered structure. If we would take words as the element type, we would have to use an indirect variant. However, we already have a "reference" to the words we want to store, namely the index in the map, over which we iterate. The actual word can be retrieved via this index. In general it is not advisable to use structure indices other than in a very local context; the structure might be modified which would invalidate the indices. We think that our context is local enough for the reasonable use of indices. Thus our ordered structure has a simple element type. A little disadvantage of this variant compared to the indirect-elements variant is that the operations on the structure are now in terms of the map indices instead of words. However, there is only one reading access to the ordered structure in `PUT_CODED_WORD`, so the extra effort seems reasonable.

Summarizing, for the map structure, we need a variant with the characteristics

```
unbounded
indirect_elements
no_counter
```

Finally, the order variant should be

```
object_bounded
simple_elements
counter
tree
```

Let us define the module's data structures and algorithms in detail.

```
with WORD_FREQUENCY_MAPS, WORD_SCORE_ORDERS;
with WORDS_CODES_ITEMS; use WORDS_CODES_ITEMS;
package body WORD_FREQUENCY_COLLECTION is

    -- Word Frequency Map
    -- ==================

    package WORD_FREQUENCY_MAP_OPS is
       new WORD_FREQUENCY_MAPS (KEY_TYPE  => WORD,
                                INFO_TYPE => POSITIVE);
    use WORD_FREQUENCY_MAP_OPS;

    WORD_FREQUENCY_MAP : WORD_FREQUENCY_MAP_OPS.STRUCT;
```

```
-- Word Score Order
-- ================

type WORD_SCORE is record
   INDEX : WORD_FREQUENCY_MAP_OPS.INDEX;
   SCORE : INTEGER;
end record;

function "<" (LEFT, RIGHT : WORD_SCORE) return BOOLEAN;

package WORD_SCORE_ORDER_OPS is
   new WORD_SCORE_ORDERS (WORD_SCORE);
use WORD_SCORE_ORDER_OPS;

HIGH_SCORES : WORD_SCORE_ORDER_OPS.STRUCT;

function "<" (LEFT, RIGHT : WORD_SCORE) return BOOLEAN is
begin
   return LEFT.SCORE < RIGHT.SCORE;
end "<";

-- Interface Operations
-- ====================

procedure GET_WORDS (WORD_FILE_NAME : STRING) is
   WORD_EXISTS : BOOLEAN;
   I : WORD_FREQUENCY_MAP_OPS.INDEX;
begin
   WORD_FILE.OPEN (IN_FILE, WORD_FILE_NAME);
   while not WORD_FILE.END_OF_FILE loop
      FIND_OR_INSERT
         (WORD_FREQUENCY_MAP, WORD_FILE.GET, I, WORD_EXISTS);
      if WORD_EXISTS then
         SET_INFO (WORD_FREQUENCY_MAP, I, 1);
      else
         SET_INFO (WORD_FREQUENCY_MAP, I,
                   GET_INFO (WORD_FREQUENCY_MAP, I) + 1);
      end if;
   end loop;
   WORD_FILE.CLOSE;
end GET_WORDS;
```

```
   procedure FIND_HIGH_SCORES is
      procedure INSERT_WORD_SCORE
                      (W         : WORD;
                       FREQUENCY : POSITIVE;
                       I         : WORD_FREQUENCY_MAP_OPS.INDEX) is
         WS : WORD_SCORE;
         use WORD_SCORE_ORDER_OPS.ORDER_OPERATIONS;
      begin
         WS := (INDEX => I, SCORE => WORD_SCORE (W, FREQUENCY));
         if WS.SCORE > 0 and then
            (IS_EMPTY (HIGH_SCORES) or else
               MIN (HIGH_SCORES) < WS) then
            if COUNT (HIGH_SCORES) = NR_OF_CODES then
               REMOVE_MIN (HIGH_SCORES);
            end if;
            INSERT (HIGH_SCORES, WS);
         end if;
      end INSERT_WORD_SCORE;

      procedure INSERT_WORD_SCORES is
         new WORD_FREQUENCY_MAP_OPS.ITERATE
               (ACTION_WITH_INDEX => INSERT_WORD_SCORE);
   begin
      INSERT_WORD_SCORES (WORD_FREQUENCY_MAP);
   end FIND_HIGH_SCORES;

   procedure PUT_CODED_WORDS (CODED_WORD_FILE_NAME : STRING) is
      procedure PUT_CODED_WORD (WS : WORD_SCORE) is
      begin
         PUT_CODED_WORD (GET_KEY (WORD_FREQUENCY_MAP, WS.INDEX));
      end PUT_CODED_WORD;
      procedure PUT is
         new WORD_SCORE_ORDER_OPS.ITERATE (PUT_CODED_WORD);
   begin
      CODED_WORD_FILE.OPEN (OUT_FILE, CODED_WORD_FILE_NAME);
      PUT (HIGH_SCORES);
      CODED_WORD_FILE.CLOSE;
   end PUT_CODED_WORDS;

end WORD_FREQUENCY_COLLECTION;
```

### 8.5.3  The Word-Code Map

For the compression of a file, that is split into a sequence of words, we must determine
for each word, whether it shall be coded or not. If it is coded, we put the code-item to
the compressed file, otherwise the word itself. In order to efficiently find the code, if
any, that is associated to a word, the word-code relationship is represented by a map
from words to codes. This structure is first installed by reading the "coded-word"
file. The rest is straightforward.

The key type of our map is WORD, which might be an unconstrained type, so that we
need the variant with indirect_keys. The number of map entries is bounded by the
number of codes. Since we have a good estimate for the number of map entries, a
hash table representation of the map seems to be the best solution.

```
with WORD_CODE_MAPS;
package body WORD_CODE_MAP is

    package WORD_CODE_MAP_OPS is
        new WORD_CODE_MAPS (KEY_TYPE => WORD, INFO_TYPE=> CODE);
    use WORD_CODE_MAP_OPS;

    WORD_CODE_MAP : WORD_CODE_MAP_OPS.STRUCT (NR_OF_CODES);

    procedure INITIALIZE (CODED_WORD_FILE_NAME : STRING) is
        C : CODE := CODE'FIRST;
    begin
        CODED_WORD_FILE.OPEN (IN_FILE, CODED_WORD_FILE_NAME);
        while not CODED_WORD_FILE.END_OF_FILE loop
            INSERT (WORD_CODE_MAP, CODED_WORD_FILE.GET, C);
            if C < CODE'LAST then
                C := CODE'SUCC (C);
            end if;
        end loop;
        CODED_WORD_FILE.CLOSE;
    end INITIALIZE;
```

```
function MAKE_ITEM (W : WORD) return ITEM is
   IX : WORD_CODE_MAP_OPS.INDEX := FIND (WORD_CODE_MAP, W);
begin
   if IX /= NIL then
      MAKE_ITEM (GET_INFO (WORD_CODE_MAP, IX));
   else
      MAKE_ITEM (W);
   end if;
end MAKE_ITEM;
end WORD_CODE_MAP;
```

## 8.5.4  Decompression

Decompression is just the inverse to compression. We need the map from codes to words. The CODE type is discrete and sufficiently small, so we can use the map variant that is implemented by an array. The info type is WORD, so we need an indirect_info variant. The number of entries is bounded as it is for compression.

```
with CODE_WORD_MAPS;
package body CODE_WORD_MAP is

   package CODE_WORD_MAP_OPS is
      new CODE_WORD_MAPS (KEY_TYPE => WORD, INFO_TYPE=> CODE);
   use CODE_WORD_MAP_OPS;

   CODE_WORD_MAP : CODE_WORD_MAP_OPS.STRUCT (NR_OF_CODES);

   procedure INITIALIZE (CODED_WORD_FILE_NAME : STRING) is
      C : CODE := CODE'FIRST;
   begin
      CODED_WORD_FILE.OPEN (IN_FILE, CODED_WORD_FILE_NAME);
      while not CODED_WORD_FILE.END_OF_FILE loop
         INSERT (CODE_WORD_MAP, C, CODED_WORD_FILE.GET);
         if C < CODE'LAST then
            C := CODE'SUCC (C);
         end if;
      end loop;
      CODED_WORD_FILE.CLOSE;
   end INITIALIZE;
```

```
function MAKE_WORD (I : ITEM) return WORD is
   IX : CODE_WORD_MAP_OPS.INDEX;
begin
   if IS_WORD (I) then
      return WORD_OF (I);
   else
      return GET_INFO (CODE_WORD_MAP,
                        FIND (CODE_WORD_MAP, CODE_OF (I)));
   end if;
end MAKE_WORD;

end CODE_WORD_MAP;
```

# Bibliography

[1] A.V. Aho, J.E. Hopcroft, J.D. Ullman; *Data Structures and Algorithms;* Addison-Wesley, 1983

[2] B.W. Kerninghan, P. Pike; *The Unix Programming Environment;* Prentice Hall, 1984

[3] T. Biggerstaff; *Foreword to Special Issue on Software Reusability;* IEEE Transactions on Software Engineering, SE-10, No. 5, 1984

[4] G. Booch; *Software Components with Ada – Structures, Tools, and Subsystems;* Benjamin Cummings, 1987

[5] U. Braun, H.A. Schmid; *Wiederverwendbare abstrakte Datentypen und deren Auswahl durch ein Expertensystem;* Informatik Forschung und Entwicklung, (1988) 3, pp. 164-181, Springer-Verlag 1988

[6] E. Horowitz, S. Sahni; *Fundamentals of Data Structures in Pascal;* Pitman, 1984

[7] J.T. Schwartz, R.B.K. Dewar, E. Dubinsky, E. Schonberg; *Programming with Sets – An introduction to SETL;* Springer-Verlag, 1986

[8] K. Kleine; *Catalogue of Data Types;* Technical Report, TR 05.371, IBM Laboratory Böblingen, April 1986

[9] D.E. Knuth; *The Art of Computer Programming, Vol. 1;* Fundamental Algorithms, 2nd edition, Addison-Wesley, 1973

[10] D.E. Knuth; *The Art of Computer Programming, Vol. 3;* Sorting and Searching, Addison-Wesley, 1973

[11] C. Lins; *The Modula-2 Software Component Library;* Springer-Verlag, 1989

[12] M. Lenz, H.A. Schmid, P.F. Wolf; *Software Reuse through Building Blocks –
Concept and Experience –;* IEEE Software, pp. 34-42, July 1987

[13] K. Mehlhorn; *Data Structures and Algorithms 1: Sorting and Searching;*
Springer-Verlag, 1984

[14] D.R. Musser, A.A. Stepanov; *The Ada Generic Library – Linear List Processing
Packages;* Springer-Verlag, 1989

[15] G.L. Steele; *Common Lisp: The Language;* Burlington, Mass., Digital Press,
1984

[16] T.A. Standish; *Data Structure Techniques;* Addison-Wesley, 1980

# Appendix A

# Ada Specifications

## A.1   Building Block Utilities

```ada
package BUILDING_BLOCK_UTILITIES is

   ADT_USE_ERROR : exception;

   type ORDER_RELATION is (LESS, EQUAL, GREATER);

   generic
      type ELEM_TYPE is limited private;
      with function "<" (LEFT, RIGHT : in ELEM_TYPE)
                     return BOOLEAN is <>;
   function COMPARISON (LEFT, RIGHT : in ELEM_TYPE)
                     return ORDER_RELATION;

   generic
      type T is private;
   procedure DIRECT_COPY (TO : in out T; FROM : in T);

   generic
      type T is private;
   procedure DIRECT_TRANSFER (TO, FROM : in out T);
```

```ada
generic
   type T is private;
procedure EMPTY_DEALLOCATE (E : in out T);

generic
   type ELEM_TYPE is private;
package ELEM_OPS is
   function  EQUAL (LEFT, RIGHT : in ELEM_TYPE) return BOOLEAN;
   procedure COPY (TO : in out ELEM_TYPE; FROM : in ELEM_TYPE);
   procedure TRANSFER (TO, FROM : in out ELEM_TYPE);
   procedure DEALLOCATE (E : in out ELEM_TYPE);
end ELEM_OPS;

generic
   type ELEM_TYPE is limited private;
   with function  EQUAL (LEFT, RIGHT : in ELEM_TYPE)
                        return BOOLEAN is <>;
   with procedure COPY (TO   : in out ELEM_TYPE;
                        FROM : in ELEM_TYPE) is <>;
   with procedure TRANSFER (TO, FROM : in out ELEM_TYPE) is <>;
   with procedure DEALLOCATE (E : in out ELEM_TYPE) is <>;
package ACCESS_OPS is
   type ELEM_ACCESS is access ELEM_TYPE;
   function  EQUAL (LEFT, RIGHT : in ELEM_ACCESS) return BOOLEAN;
   procedure COPY (TO : in out ELEM_ACCESS; FROM : in ELEM_TYPE);
   procedure COPY (TO : in out ELEM_TYPE; FROM : in ELEM_ACCESS);
   procedure COPY (TO : in out ELEM_ACCESS; FROM : in ELEM_ACCESS);
   procedure TRANSFER (TO   : in out ELEM_ACCESS;
                       FROM : in out ELEM_TYPE);
   procedure TRANSFER (TO   : in out ELEM_TYPE;
                       FROM : in out ELEM_ACCESS);
   procedure TRANSFER (TO, FROM : in out ELEM_ACCESS);
   procedure INITIALIZE (A : in out ELEM_ACCESS);
   procedure DEALLOCATE (A : in out ELEM_ACCESS);
end ACCESS_OPS;
```

```
   generic
      type ELEM_TYPE is private;
      INITIAL_ELEM : ELEM_TYPE;
   package VARIABLE_ACCESS_OPS is
      type ELEM_ACCESS is access ELEM_TYPE;
      function  EQUAL (LEFT, RIGHT : in ELEM_ACCESS) return BOOLEAN;
      procedure COPY (TO : in out ELEM_ACCESS; FROM : in ELEM_TYPE);
      procedure COPY (TO : in out ELEM_TYPE; FROM : in ELEM_ACCESS);
      procedure COPY (TO : in out ELEM_ACCESS; FROM : in ELEM_ACCESS);
      procedure TRANSFER (TO   : in out ELEM_ACCESS;
                          FROM : in out ELEM_TYPE);
      procedure TRANSFER (TO   : in out ELEM_TYPE;
                          FROM : in out ELEM_ACCESS);
      procedure TRANSFER (TO, FROM : in out ELEM_ACCESS);
      procedure INITIALIZE (A : in out ELEM_ACCESS);
      procedure DEALLOCATE (A : in out ELEM_ACCESS);
   end VARIABLE_ACCESS_OPS;


   generic
      type ELEM_TYPE (D : INTEGER) is limited private;
      with function  EQUAL (LEFT, RIGHT : in ELEM_TYPE)
                           return BOOLEAN is <>;
      with procedure COPY (TO   : in out ELEM_TYPE;
                           FROM : in ELEM_TYPE) is <>;
      with procedure TRANSFER (TO, FROM : in out ELEM_TYPE) is <>;
      INITIAL_ELEM : INTEGER;
      with procedure DEALLOCATE (E : in out ELEM_TYPE) is <>;
   package ELEM_DISCR_OPS is
      type ELEM_ACCESS is access ELEM_TYPE;
      function  EQUAL (LEFT, RIGHT : in ELEM_ACCESS) return BOOLEAN;
      procedure COPY (TO : in out ELEM_ACCESS; FROM : in ELEM_TYPE);
      procedure COPY (TO : in out ELEM_TYPE; FROM : in ELEM_ACCESS);
      procedure COPY (TO : in out ELEM_ACCESS; FROM : in ELEM_ACCESS);
      procedure TRANSFER (TO   : in out ELEM_ACCESS;
                          FROM : in out ELEM_TYPE);
      procedure TRANSFER (TO   : in out ELEM_TYPE;
                          FROM : in out ELEM_ACCESS);
      procedure TRANSFER (TO, FROM : in out ELEM_ACCESS);
      procedure INITIALIZE (A : in out ELEM_ACCESS);
      procedure DEALLOCATE (A : in out ELEM_ACCESS);
   end ELEM_DISCR_OPS;
end BUILDING_BLOCK_UTILITIES;
```

# A.2   Generic Parameters

The generic parameters for the following specifications depend on the chosen variant
for the element type. This section specifies these generic parameters for the different
variants.

*Simple Elements*

```
type ELEM_TYPE is private; -- must not be an unconstrained
                           -- array or record type
```

*Indirect Elements*

```
type ELEM_TYPE is private; -- may be any private type
```

*General Elements*

```
type ELEM_TYPE is limited private;

with function EQUAL (LEFT, RIGHT : in ELEM_TYPE)
                   return BOOLEAN is <>;
with procedure COPY (TO   : in out ELEM_TYPE;
                    FROM : in ELEM_TYPE) is <>;
with procedure TRANSFER (TO, FROM : in out ELEM_TYPE) is <>;
with procedure DEALLOCATE (E : in out ELEM_TYPE) is <>;
```

*Variable(-Size) Elements*

```
type ELEM_TYPE (D : INTEGER) is limited private;

with function EQUAL (LEFT, RIGHT : in ELEM_TYPE)
                   return BOOLEAN is <>;
with procedure COPY (TO   : in out ELEM_TYPE;
                    FROM : in ELEM_TYPE) is <>;
with procedure TRANSFER (TO, FROM : in out ELEM_TYPE) is <>;
with procedure DEALLOCATE (E : in out ELEM_TYPE) is <>;
INITIAL_ELEM : INTEGER := 0;
```

## Accessed Elements

```
type ELEM_TYPE is limited private;

with function EQUAL (LEFT, RIGHT : in ELEM_TYPE)
                     return BOOLEAN is <>;
type ELEM_ACCESS is access ELEM_TYPE;
with procedure COPY (TO   : in out ELEM_ACCESS;
                     FROM : in ELEM_TYPE) is <>;
with procedure COPY (TO   : in out ELEM_TYPE;
                     FROM : in ELEM_ACCESS) is <>;
with procedure TRANSFER (TO : in out ELEM_ACCESS;
                         FROM : in out ELEM_TYPE) is <>;
with procedure TRANSFER (TO : in out ELEM_TYPE;
                         FROM : in out ELEM_ACCESS) is <>;
with procedure INITIALIZE (A : in out ELEM_ACCESS) is <>;
with procedure DEALLOCATE (A : in out ELEM_ACCESS) is <>;
```

## Compact Elements

```
type ELEM_TYPE is limited private;

with function EQUAL (LEFT, RIGHT : in ELEM_TYPE)
                     return BOOLEAN is <>;
with procedure COPY (TO   : in out ELEM_TYPE;
                     FROM : in ELEM_TYPE) is <>;
with procedure TRANSFER (TO, FROM : in out ELEM_TYPE) is <>;
```

# A.3   Linked Collections

## Variant Combinations

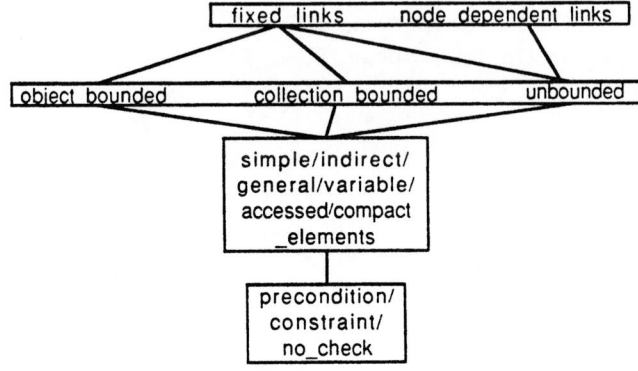

```
generic
   ... see A.2
 [ COLLECTION_SIZE : NATURAL; ]
 [ LINKS : POSITIVE; ]
package <LINKED_COLLECTIONS> is

   type STRUCT [ (SIZE : NATURAL) ] is limited private;
   subtype <LINKED_COLLECTION> is STRUCT;

   type INDEX is private;

   procedure ALLOCATE (S      : in out STRUCT;
                      [ LINKS : in NATURAL; ]
                        I      : out INDEX);

   procedure DEALLOCATE (S : in out STRUCT; I : in INDEX);

   function NIL return INDEX;

   function NR_OF_LINKS (S : in STRUCT; I : in INDEX) return NATURAL;

   function GET_LINK (S : in STRUCT;
                      I : in INDEX;
                      N : in POSITIVE) return INDEX;
```

```
    procedure SET_LINK (S : in out STRUCT;
                        I : in INDEX;
                        N : in POSITIVE;
                        L : in INDEX);

    function GET_ELEM (S : in STRUCT; I : in INDEX) return ELEM_TYPE;

    procedure SET_ELEM (S : in out STRUCT;
                        I : in INDEX;
                        E : in ELEM_TYPE);

    procedure TRANSFER_ELEM (TO     : in out ELEM_TYPE;
                             FROM   : in out STRUCT;
                             FROM_I : in INDEX);

    procedure TRANSFER_ELEM (TO   : in out STRUCT;
                             FROM : in out ELEM_TYPE;
                             TO_I : in INDEX);

    generic
        with procedure MODIFICATION (E : in out ELEM_TYPE);
    procedure MODIFY_ELEM (S : in out STRUCT; I : in INDEX);

private

    ...

end <LINKED_COLLECTIONS>;
```

# A.4   Tabular Collections

**Variant Combinations**

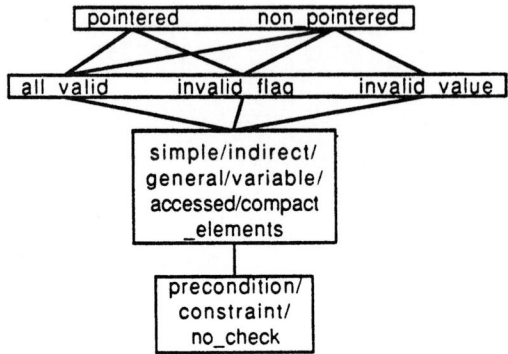

```
generic
    ... see A.2
 [ with function IS_VALID (E : in ELEM_TYPE) return BOOLEAN is <>;
   with procedure INVALIDATE (E : in out ELEM_TYPE) is <>; ]
package <TABULAR_COLLECTIONS> is

    type STRUCT (SIZE : NATURAL) is limited private;
    subtype <TABULAR_COLLECTION> is STRUCT;

    -- Indices
    -- =======

    subtype INDEX is NATURAL;

    NIL : constant INDEX := 0;

    function IS_VALID (S : in STRUCT; I : in INDEX) return BOOLEAN;

    procedure VALIDATE (S : in out STRUCT; I : in INDEX);

    procedure INVALIDATE (S : in out STRUCT; I : in INDEX);

    procedure SWAP (S : in out STRUCT; I1, I2 : in INDEX);
```

```
    procedure TRANSFER_ELEM (TO     : in out ELEM_TYPE;
                             FROM   : in out STRUCT;
                             FROM_I : in INDEX);

    procedure TRANSFER_ELEM (TO   : in out STRUCT;
                             FROM : in out ELEM_TYPE;
                             TO_I : in INDEX);

    procedure TRANSFER_ELEM (TO     : in out STRUCT;
                             FROM   : in out STRUCT;
                             FROM_I : in INDEX;
                             TO_I   : in INDEX);

    procedure TRANSFER_ELEM (S      : in out STRUCT;
                             FROM_I : in INDEX;
                             TO_I   : in INDEX);

    function GET_ELEM (S : in STRUCT; I : in INDEX) return ELEM_TYPE;

    procedure SET_ELEM (S : in out STRUCT;
                        I : in INDEX;
                        E : in ELEM_TYPE);

    generic
       with procedure MODIFICATION (E : in out ELEM_TYPE);
    procedure MODIFY_ELEM (S : in out STRUCT; I : in INDEX);

private

    ...

end <TABULAR_COLLECTIONS>;
```

# A.5   Hash Tables

**Variant Combinations**

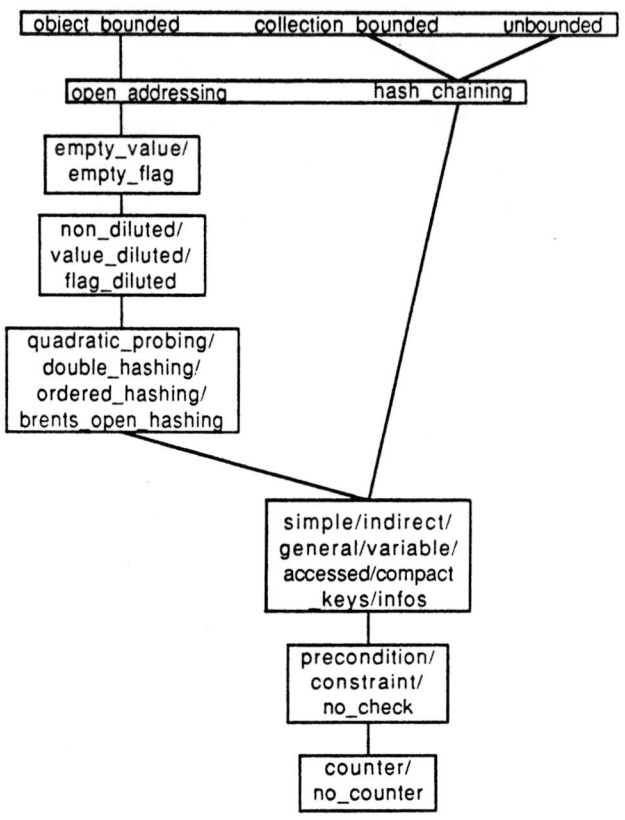

```
generic
    ... see A.2
  [ COLLECTION_SIZE : NATURAL; ]
    HASH_TABLE_SIZE : NATURAL;
    with function HASH (K : in KEY_TYPE) return NATURAL is <>;
package <HASH_TABLES> is

    type STRUCT [ (SIZE : NATURAL) ] is limited private;
    subtype <HASH_TABLE> is STRUCT;
```

```
-- Indices
-- =======

type INDEX is private;

function NIL return INDEX;

function GET_KEY  (S : in STRUCT; I : in INDEX) return KEY_TYPE;

function GET_INFO (S : in STRUCT; I : in INDEX) return INFO_TYPE;

procedure SET_INFO (S    : in out STRUCT;
                    I    : in INDEX;
                    INFO : in INFO_TYPE);

procedure TRANSFER_INFO (TO     : in out INFO_TYPE;
                         FROM   : in out STRUCT;
                         FROM_I : in INDEX);

procedure TRANSFER_INFO (TO   : in out STRUCT;
                         FROM : in out INFO_TYPE;
                         TO_I : in INDEX);

generic
   with procedure MODIFICATION (A : in out INFO_TYPE);
procedure MODIFY_INFO (S : in out STRUCT; I : in INDEX);

-- Insert and remove positions
-- ===========================

subtype REMOVE_POSITION is INDEX;

-- Constructor operations
-- ======================

procedure CLEAR (S : in out STRUCT);

procedure FIND_OR_INSERT (S     : in out STRUCT;
                          K     : in KEY_TYPE;
                          I     : out INDEX;
                          FOUND : out BOOLEAN);
```

```
generic
   with procedure ABSORB (K      : in out KEY_TYPE;
                          INFO : in out INFO_TYPE);
procedure GENERIC_REMOVE (S         : in out STRUCT;
                          FROM_POS : in REMOVE_POSITION);

procedure MOVE (TO         : in out STRUCT;
                FROM_KEY  : in out KEY_TYPE;
                FROM_INFO : in out INFO_TYPE);

-- Selector operations
-- ===================

function COUNT (S : in STRUCT) return NATURAL;

function IS_EMPTY (S : in STRUCT) return BOOLEAN;

function FIND (S : in STRUCT; K : in KEY_TYPE) return INDEX;

-- Iteration
-- =========

package DEFAULTS is
   function TRUE  (S : in STRUCT; I : in INDEX) return BOOLEAN;
   function FALSE (S : in STRUCT; I : in INDEX) return BOOLEAN;
   function TRUE  (K    : in KEY_TYPE;
                   INFO : in INFO_TYPE) return BOOLEAN;
   function FALSE (K    : in KEY_TYPE;
                   INFO : in INFO_TYPE) return BOOLEAN;

   procedure NONE  (K : in KEY_TYPE; INFO : in INFO_TYPE);
   procedure NONE1 (K : in KEY_TYPE; INFO : in out INFO_TYPE);
   procedure NONE  (K    : in KEY_TYPE;
                    INFO : in INFO_TYPE; I : in INDEX);
   procedure NONE1 (K    : in KEY_TYPE;
                    INFO : in out INFO_TYPE; I : in INDEX);
end DEFAULTS;
use DEFAULTS;
```

```
generic
   with procedure ACTION
                     (K    : in KEY_TYPE;
                      INFO : in out INFO_TYPE) is NONE1;
   with function  SELECTION
                     (K    : in KEY_TYPE;
                      INFO : in INFO_TYPE) return BOOLEAN is TRUE;
   with function  UNTIL
                     (S : in STRUCT;
                      I : in INDEX) return BOOLEAN is FALSE;
   with procedure ACTION_WITH_INDEX
                     (K    : in KEY_TYPE;
                      INFO : in out INFO_TYPE;
                      I    : in INDEX) is NONE1;
   with function  SELECTION_WITH_INDEX
                     (S : in STRUCT;
                      I : in INDEX) return BOOLEAN is TRUE;
procedure APPLY (S    : in out STRUCT);

generic
   with procedure ACTION
                     (K    : in KEY_TYPE;
                      INFO : in INFO_TYPE) is NONE;
   with function  SELECTION
                     (K    : in KEY_TYPE;
                      INFO : in INFO_TYPE) return BOOLEAN is TRUE;
   with function  UNTIL
                     (S : in STRUCT;
                      I : in INDEX) return BOOLEAN is FALSE;
   with procedure ACTION_WITH_INDEX
                     (K    : in KEY_TYPE;
                      INFO : in INFO_TYPE;
                      I    : in INDEX) is NONE;
   with function  SELECTION_WITH_INDEX
                     (S : in STRUCT;
                      I : in INDEX) return BOOLEAN is TRUE;
procedure ITERATE (S    : in STRUCT);
```

```ada
   generic
      with procedure ACTION (S : in out STRUCT; I : in INDEX);
      with function SELECTION
                        (S : in STRUCT;
                         I : in INDEX) return BOOLEAN is TRUE;
      with function UNTIL
                        (S : in STRUCT;
                         I : in INDEX) return BOOLEAN is FALSE;
   procedure ITERATE_MOVE (S : in STRUCT);

private

   ...

end <HASH_TABLES>;
```

# A.6 Lists

**Variant Combinations**

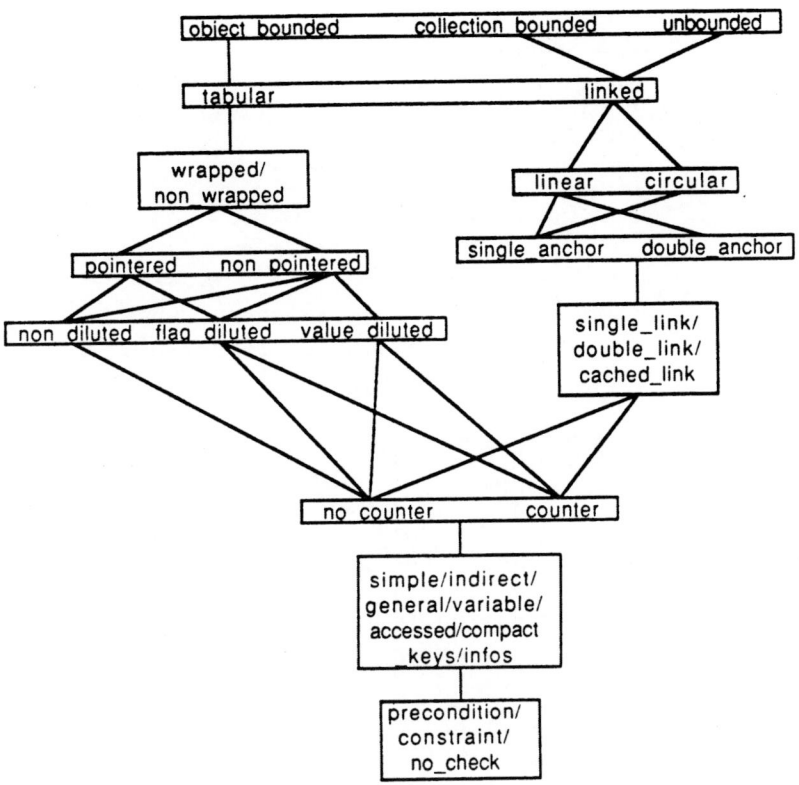

```
generic
    ... see A.2
  [ COLLECTION_SIZE : NATURAL; ]
  [ with function IS_VALID (E : in ELEM_TYPE) return BOOLEAN is <>;
    with procedure INVALIDATE (E : in out ELEM_TYPE) is <>; ]
package <LISTS> is

    type STRUCT [ (SIZE : NATURAL) ] is limited private;
    subtype <LIST> is STRUCT;
```

```
-- Indices
-- =======

type INDEX is private;

function NIL return INDEX;

function GET_ELEM (S : in STRUCT; I : in INDEX) return ELEM_TYPE;

procedure SET_ELEM (S : in out STRUCT;
                    I : in INDEX;
                    E : in ELEM_TYPE);

procedure TRANSFER_ELEM (TO     : in out ELEM_TYPE;
                         FROM   : in out STRUCT;
                         FROM_I : in INDEX);

procedure TRANSFER_ELEM (TO   : in out STRUCT;
                         FROM : in out ELEM_TYPE;
                         TO_I : in INDEX);

generic
   with procedure MODIFICATION (E : in out ELEM_TYPE);
procedure MODIFY_ELEM (S : in out STRUCT; I : in INDEX);

-- Insert and remove positions
-- ===========================

type INSERT_POSITION is private;

function BEFORE (I : in INDEX) return INSERT_POSITION;
function AFTER  (I : in INDEX) return INSERT_POSITION;
function FIRST     return INSERT_POSITION;
function LAST      return INSERT_POSITION;
function DONT_CARE return INSERT_POSITION;

type REMOVE_POSITION is private;

function AT_INDEX (I : in INDEX) return REMOVE_POSITION;
function AFTER    (I : in INDEX) return REMOVE_POSITION;
function FIRST       return REMOVE_POSITION;
function LAST        return REMOVE_POSITION;
```

```
-- Structure parts
-- ================

type PART is private;

function WHOLE_STRUCT return PART;
function SUBLIST (FROM     : in INDEX;
                  TO       : in INDEX := NIL;
                  CIRCULAR : in BOOLEAN := FALSE) return PART;


-- Constructor operations
-- ======================

procedure CLEAR (S : in out STRUCT);

procedure INSERT (S      : in out STRUCT;
                  E      : in ELEM_TYPE;
                  TO_POS : in INSERT_POSITION := LAST);
procedure INSERT (S      : in out STRUCT;
                  E      : in ELEM_TYPE;
                  TO_POS : in INSERT_POSITION := LAST;
                  I      : out INDEX);
procedure INSERT (S      : in out STRUCT;
                  TO_POS : in INSERT_POSITION := LAST;
                  I      : out INDEX);

procedure INSERT (TO     : in out STRUCT;
                  FROM   : in STRUCT;
                  SUB    : in PART := WHOLE_STRUCT;
                  TO_POS : in INSERT_POSITION := LAST);

procedure FIND_OR_INSERT (S      : in out STRUCT;
                          E      : in ELEM_TYPE;
                          TO_POS : in INSERT_POSITION := LAST;
                          I      : out INDEX;
                          FOUND  : out BOOLEAN);

procedure REMOVE (S        : in out STRUCT;
                  FROM_POS : in REMOVE_POSITION);

procedure REMOVE (S : in out STRUCT; SUB : in PART);
```

```
procedure REMOVE (S : in out STRUCT; E : in ELEM_TYPE);

procedure REMOVE_ALL (S : in out STRUCT; E : in ELEM_TYPE);

generic
   with procedure ABSORB (E : in out ELEM_TYPE);
procedure GENERIC_REMOVE (S        : in out STRUCT;
                          FROM_POS : in REMOVE_POSITION);

procedure MOVE (S        : in out STRUCT;
                FROM_POS : in REMOVE_POSITION;
                TO_POS   : in INSERT_POSITION);

procedure MOVE (S       : in out STRUCT;
                SUB     : in PART;
                TO_POS  : in INSERT_POSITION);

procedure MOVE (TO       : in out STRUCT;
                FROM     : in out STRUCT;
                FROM_POS : in REMOVE_POSITION;
                TO_POS   : in INSERT_POSITION := LAST);

procedure MOVE (TO       : in out STRUCT;
                FROM     : in out STRUCT;
                SUB      : in PART := WHOLE_STRUCT;
                TO_POS   : in INSERT_POSITION := LAST);

procedure MOVE (TO       : in out STRUCT;
                FROM     : in out ELEM_TYPE;
                TO_POS   : in INSERT_POSITION := LAST);

procedure MOVE (TO       : in out ELEM_TYPE;
                FROM     : in out STRUCT;
                FROM_POS : in REMOVE_POSITION);

procedure COPY (TO   : in out STRUCT;
                FROM : in STRUCT;
                SUB  : in PART);
procedure COPY (TO : in out STRUCT; FROM : in STRUCT);

procedure TRANSFER (TO, FROM : in out STRUCT; SUB : in PART);
```

```
procedure TRANSFER (TO, FROM : in out STRUCT);

procedure SWAP (S          : in out STRUCT;
                POS1, POS2 : in REMOVE_POSITION);

procedure SLICE (S : in out STRUCT; SUB : in PART);

procedure SHIFT (S : in out STRUCT; BY : in INTEGER);

procedure INVERT (S : in out STRUCT);

procedure DEALLOCATE (S : in out STRUCT);

-- Selector operations
-- ===================

function COUNT (S   : in STRUCT;
               SUB : in PART := WHOLE_STRUCT) return NATURAL;

function IS_EMPTY (S : in STRUCT) return BOOLEAN;

function FIND (S   : in STRUCT;
              E   : in ELEM_TYPE;
              SUB : in PART := WHOLE_STRUCT) return INDEX;

function SKIP (S   : in STRUCT;
              E   : in ELEM_TYPE;
              SUB : in PART := WHOLE_STRUCT) return INDEX;

function COUNT_ELEM (S   : in STRUCT;
                    E   : in ELEM_TYPE;
                    SUB : in PART := WHOLE_STRUCT) return NATURAL;

function IS_ELEM (S   : in STRUCT;
                 E   : in ELEM_TYPE;
                 SUB : in PART := WHOLE_STRUCT) return BOOLEAN;

function "=" (LEFT, RIGHT : in STRUCT) return BOOLEAN;
function EQUAL (LEFT,
               RIGHT : in STRUCT) return BOOLEAN renames "=";

function FIRST (S : in STRUCT) return INDEX;
```

```
function FIRST (S : in STRUCT) return ELEM_TYPE;

function LAST (S : in STRUCT) return INDEX;

function LAST (S : in STRUCT) return ELEM_TYPE;

function NEXT (S        : in STRUCT;
               I        : in INDEX;
               CIRCULAR : in BOOLEAN := FALSE) return INDEX;

function PREVIOUS (S        : in STRUCT;
                   I        : in INDEX;
                   CIRCULAR : in BOOLEAN := FALSE) return INDEX;

-- Access by position count
-- ========================

function INDEX_VAL (S : in STRUCT; P : in POSITIVE) return INDEX;
function INDEX_POS (S : in STRUCT; I : in INDEX) return POSITIVE;

function GET_ELEM (S : in STRUCT;
                   P : in POSITIVE) return ELEM_TYPE;

procedure SET_ELEM (S : in out STRUCT;
                    P : in POSITIVE;
                    E : in ELEM_TYPE);

procedure TRANSFER_ELEM (TO     : in out ELEM_TYPE;
                         FROM   : in out STRUCT;
                         FROM_P : in POSITIVE);

procedure TRANSFER_ELEM (TO   : in out STRUCT;
                         FROM : in out ELEM_TYPE;
                         TO_P : in POSITIVE);

generic
   with procedure MODIFICATION (E : in out ELEM_TYPE);
procedure MODIFY_ELEM_BY_POS (S : in out STRUCT;
                              P : in POSITIVE);
```

```
-- Iteration
-- =========

type ITERATION_ORDER is (FROM_FIRST, FROM_LAST, DONT_CARE);

package DEFAULTS is
   function TRUE  (E : in ELEM_TYPE) return BOOLEAN;
   function FALSE (E : in ELEM_TYPE) return BOOLEAN;
   function TRUE  (S : in STRUCT; I : in INDEX) return BOOLEAN;
   function FALSE (S : in STRUCT; I : in INDEX) return BOOLEAN;

   procedure NONE (E : in ELEM_TYPE);
   procedure NONE (E : in ELEM_TYPE; I : in INDEX);
   procedure NONE1 (E : in out ELEM_TYPE);
   procedure NONE1 (E : in out ELEM_TYPE; I : in INDEX);

   function TRUE  (LEFT  : in ELEM_TYPE;
                   RIGHT : in ELEM_TYPE) return BOOLEAN;
   function FALSE (LEFT  : in ELEM_TYPE;
                   RIGHT : in ELEM_TYPE) return BOOLEAN;
   function TRUE  (LEFT    : in STRUCT;
                   LEFT_I  : in INDEX;
                   RIGHT   : in STRUCT;
                   RIGHT_I : in INDEX) return BOOLEAN;
   function FALSE (LEFT    : in STRUCT;
                   LEFT_I  : in INDEX;
                   RIGHT   : in STRUCT;
                   RIGHT_I : in INDEX) return BOOLEAN;

   procedure NONE (LEFT  : in ELEM_TYPE;
                   RIGHT : in ELEM_TYPE);
   procedure NONE (LEFT    : in ELEM_TYPE;
                   LEFT_I  : in INDEX;
                   RIGHT   : in ELEM_TYPE;
                   RIGHT_I : in INDEX);
   procedure NONE1 (LEFT  : in out ELEM_TYPE;
                    RIGHT : in out ELEM_TYPE);
   procedure NONE1 (LEFT    : in out ELEM_TYPE;
                    LEFT_I  : in INDEX;
                    RIGHT   : in out ELEM_TYPE;
                    RIGHT_I : in INDEX);
```

```
      procedure NONE2 (LEFT  : in out ELEM_TYPE;
                       RIGHT : in ELEM_TYPE);
      procedure NONE2 (LEFT    : in out ELEM_TYPE;
                       LEFT_I  : in INDEX;
                       RIGHT   : in ELEM_TYPE;
                       RIGHT_I : in INDEX);
end DEFAULTS;
use DEFAULTS;


generic
   with procedure ACTION (E : in out ELEM_TYPE) is NONE1;
   with function  SELECTION
                     (E : in ELEM_TYPE) return BOOLEAN is TRUE;
   with function  UNTIL
                     (S : in STRUCT;
                      I : in INDEX) return BOOLEAN is FALSE;
   with procedure ACTION_WITH_INDEX
                     (E : in ELEM_TYPE;
                      I : in INDEX) is NONE;
   with function  SELECTION_WITH_INDEX
                     (S : in STRUCT;
                      I : in INDEX) return BOOLEAN is TRUE;
procedure APPLY (S   : in out STRUCT;
                 SUB : in PART := WHOLE_STRUCT;
                 ORD : in ITERATION_ORDER := FROM_FIRST);


generic
   with procedure ACTION (E : in ELEM_TYPE) is NONE;
   with function  SELECTION
                     (E : in ELEM_TYPE) return BOOLEAN is TRUE;
   with function  UNTIL
                     (S : in STRUCT;
                      I : in INDEX) return BOOLEAN is FALSE;
   with procedure ACTION_WITH_INDEX
                     (E : in ELEM_TYPE;
                      I : in INDEX) is NONE;
   with function  SELECTION_WITH_INDEX
                     (S : in STRUCT;
                      I : in INDEX) return BOOLEAN is TRUE;
procedure ITERATE (S   : in STRUCT;
                   SUB : in PART := WHOLE_STRUCT;
                   ORD : in ITERATION_ORDER := FROM_FIRST);
```

```
generic
   with procedure ACTION (S : in out STRUCT; I : in INDEX);
   with function  SELECTION
                     (S : in STRUCT;
                      I : in INDEX) return BOOLEAN is TRUE;
   with function  UNTIL
                     (S : in STRUCT;
                      I : in INDEX) return BOOLEAN is FALSE;
procedure ITERATE_MOVE (S   : in STRUCT;
                        SUB : in PART := WHOLE_STRUCT;
                        ORD : in ITERATION_ORDER := FROM_FIRST);


-- Reduction
-- =========

generic
   with function  OPERATION
                     (LEFT, RIGHT : in ELEM_TYPE) return ELEM_TYPE;
   with function  SELECTION
                     (E : in ELEM_TYPE) return BOOLEAN is TRUE;
   with function  UNTIL
                     (S : in STRUCT;
                      I : in INDEX) return BOOLEAN is FALSE;
function REDUCE (S   : in STRUCT;
                 SUB : in PART := WHOLE_STRUCT;
                 ORD : in ITERATION_ORDER := DONT_CARE)
             return ELEM_TYPE;
```

```
generic
   with function  OPERATION
                     (LEFT, RIGHT : in ELEM_TYPE) return ELEM_TYPE;
   with function  UNIT return ELEM_TYPE;
   with function  SELECTION
                     (E : in ELEM_TYPE) return BOOLEAN is TRUE;
   with function  UNTIL
                     (S : in STRUCT;
                      I : in INDEX) return BOOLEAN is FALSE;
function UREDUCE (S   : in STRUCT;
                  SUB : in PART := WHOLE_STRUCT;
                  ORD : in ITERATION_ORDER := DONT_CARE)
                return ELEM_TYPE;


generic
   type RESULT_TYPE is limited private;
   with function  OPERATION
                     (LEFT  : in RESULT_TYPE;
                      RIGHT : in ELEM_TYPE) return RESULT_TYPE;
   with function  UNIT return RESULT_TYPE;
   with function  SELECTION
                     (E : in ELEM_TYPE) return BOOLEAN is TRUE;
   with function  UNTIL
                     (S : in STRUCT;
                      I : in INDEX) return BOOLEAN is FALSE;
function AREDUCE (S   : in STRUCT;
                  SUB : in PART := WHOLE_STRUCT;
                  ORD : in ITERATION_ORDER := DONT_CARE)
                return RESULT_TYPE;
```

```
-- Find, skip and count
-- =====================

generic
   with function PROPERTY (E : in ELEM_TYPE) return BOOLEAN;
function FIND_PROPERTY
            (S   : in STRUCT;
             SUB : in PART := WHOLE_STRUCT;
             ORD : in ITERATION_ORDER := DONT_CARE) return INDEX;

generic
   with function PROPERTY (E : in ELEM_TYPE) return BOOLEAN;
function SKIP_PROPERTY
            (S   : in STRUCT;
             SUB : in PART := WHOLE_STRUCT;
             ORD : in ITERATION_ORDER := DONT_CARE) return INDEX;

generic
   with function PROPERTY (E : in ELEM_TYPE) return BOOLEAN;
function COUNT_PROPERTY
            (S   : in STRUCT;
             SUB : in PART := WHOLE_STRUCT;
             ORD : in ITERATION_ORDER := DONT_CARE) return NATURAL;

-- Existential and universal quantification
-- ========================================

generic
   with function PROPERTY (E : in ELEM_TYPE) return BOOLEAN;
function EXISTS (S   : in STRUCT;
                 SUB : in PART := WHOLE_STRUCT;
                 ORD : in ITERATION_ORDER := DONT_CARE)
                return BOOLEAN;

generic
   with function PROPERTY (E : in ELEM_TYPE) return BOOLEAN;
function FORALL (S   : in STRUCT;
                 SUB : in PART := WHOLE_STRUCT;
                 ORD : in ITERATION_ORDER := DONT_CARE)
                return BOOLEAN;
```

```
-- Double iterations
-- =================

generic
   with procedure ACTION
                     (LEFT    : in out ELEM_TYPE;
                      RIGHT   : in out ELEM_TYPE) is NONE1;
   with function  SELECTION
                     (LEFT, RIGHT : in ELEM_TYPE)
                      return BOOLEAN is TRUE;
   with function  UNTIL
                     (LEFT    : in STRUCT;
                      LEFT_I  : in INDEX;
                      RIGHT   : in STRUCT;
                      RIGHT_I : in INDEX)
                      return BOOLEAN is FALSE;
   with procedure ACTION_WITH_INDEX
                     (LEFT    : in out ELEM_TYPE;
                      LEFT_I  : in INDEX;
                      RIGHT   : in out ELEM_TYPE;
                      RIGHT_I : in INDEX) is NONE1;
   with function  SELECTION_WITH_INDEX
                     (LEFT    : in STRUCT;
                      LEFT_I  : in INDEX;
                      RIGHT   : in STRUCT;
                      RIGHT_I : in INDEX)
                      return BOOLEAN is TRUE;
   procedure APPLY_CORRESPONDING
                 (LEFT      : in out STRUCT;
                  RIGHT     : in out STRUCT;
                  LEFT_SUB  : in PART := WHOLE_STRUCT;
                  RIGHT_SUB : in PART := WHOLE_STRUCT;
                  LENGTH    : out ORDER_RELATION);
```

```
generic
  with procedure ACTION
                     (LEFT     : in ELEM_TYPE;
                      RIGHT    : in ELEM_TYPE) is NONE;
  with function  SELECTION
                     (LEFT, RIGHT : in ELEM_TYPE)
                     return BOOLEAN is TRUE;
  with function  UNTIL
                     (LEFT    : in STRUCT;
                      LEFT_I  : in INDEX;
                      RIGHT   : in STRUCT;
                      RIGHT_I : in INDEX)
                     return BOOLEAN is FALSE;
  with procedure ACTION_WITH_INDEX
                     (LEFT    : in ELEM_TYPE;
                      LEFT_I  : in INDEX;
                      RIGHT   : in ELEM_TYPE;
                      RIGHT_I : in INDEX) is NONE;
  with function  SELECTION_WITH_INDEX
                     (LEFT    : in STRUCT;
                      LEFT_I  : in INDEX;
                      RIGHT   : in STRUCT;
                      RIGHT_I : in INDEX)
                     return BOOLEAN is TRUE;
procedure ITERATE_CORRESPONDING
                 (LEFT      : in STRUCT;
                  RIGHT     : in STRUCT;
                  LEFT_SUB  : in PART := WHOLE_STRUCT;
                  RIGHT_SUB : in PART := WHOLE_STRUCT;
                  LENGTH    : out ORDER_RELATION);
```

```
generic
   with procedure ACTION
                      (LEFT    : in out ELEM_TYPE;
                       RIGHT   : in ELEM_TYPE) is NONE2;
   with function  SELECTION
                      (LEFT, RIGHT : in ELEM_TYPE)
                      return BOOLEAN is TRUE;
   with function  UNTIL
                      (LEFT    : in STRUCT;
                       LEFT_I  : in INDEX;
                       RIGHT   : in STRUCT;
                       RIGHT_I : in INDEX)
                      return BOOLEAN is FALSE;
   with procedure ACTION_WITH_INDEX
                      (LEFT    : in out ELEM_TYPE;
                       LEFT_I  : in INDEX;
                       RIGHT   : in ELEM_TYPE;
                       RIGHT_I : in INDEX) is NONE2;
   with function  SELECTION_WITH_INDEX
                      (LEFT    : in STRUCT;
                       LEFT_I  : in INDEX;
                       RIGHT   : in STRUCT;
                       RIGHT_I : in INDEX)
                      return BOOLEAN is TRUE;
procedure MODIFY_CORRESPONDING
              (LEFT      : in out STRUCT;
               RIGHT     : in STRUCT;
               LEFT_SUB  : in PART := WHOLE_STRUCT;
               RIGHT_SUB : in PART := WHOLE_STRUCT;
               LENGTH    : out ORDER_RELATION);


-- Runs
-- ====


procedure RUN (S          : in STRUCT;
               E          : in ELEM_TYPE;
               MIN_LENGTH : in NATURAL;
               SUB        : in PART := WHOLE_STRUCT;
               RUN_START  : out INDEX);
```

```
    procedure LONGEST_RUN (S          : in STRUCT;
                           E          : in ELEM_TYPE;
                           SUB        : in PART := WHOLE_STRUCT;
                           RUN_START  : out INDEX;
                           RUN_LENGTH : out NATURAL);

    procedure MAX_RUN (S          : in STRUCT;
                       SUB        : in PART := WHOLE_STRUCT;
                       RUN_START  : out INDEX;
                       RUN_LENGTH : out NATURAL);

-- Order dependent operations
-- ==========================

generic
    with function COMPARE (LEFT, RIGHT : in ELEM_TYPE)
                          return ORDER_RELATION is <>;
package ORDER_OPERATIONS is

    -- Lexicographic comparison
    -- ========================

    function COMPARE (LEFT, RIGHT : in STRUCT)
                      return ORDER_RELATION;

    function "<"  (LEFT, RIGHT : in STRUCT) return BOOLEAN;
    function "<=" (LEFT, RIGHT : in STRUCT) return BOOLEAN;
    function ">"  (LEFT, RIGHT : in STRUCT) return BOOLEAN;
    function ">=" (LEFT, RIGHT : in STRUCT) return BOOLEAN;

    -- Maximum and minimum
    -- ===================

    function MAX (S   : in STRUCT;
                  SUB : in PART := WHOLE_STRUCT) return INDEX;
    function MAX (S   : in STRUCT;
                  SUB : in PART := WHOLE_STRUCT) return ELEM_TYPE;

    function MIN (S   : in STRUCT;
                  SUB : in PART := WHOLE_STRUCT) return INDEX;
    function MIN (S   : in STRUCT;
                  SUB : in PART := WHOLE_STRUCT) return ELEM_TYPE;
```

```
      procedure REMOVE_MAX (S   : in out STRUCT;
                            SUB : in PART := WHOLE_STRUCT);
      procedure REMOVE_MIN (S   : in out STRUCT;
                            SUB : in PART := WHOLE_STRUCT);

   end ORDER_OPERATIONS;

   -- Hash Operation
   -- ==============

   generic
      with function HASH (E : in ELEM_TYPE) return INTEGER is <>;
   function HASH_FUNCTION (S : in STRUCT) return INTEGER;

private

   ...

end <LISTS>;
```

# A.7  Stacks

## Variant Combinations

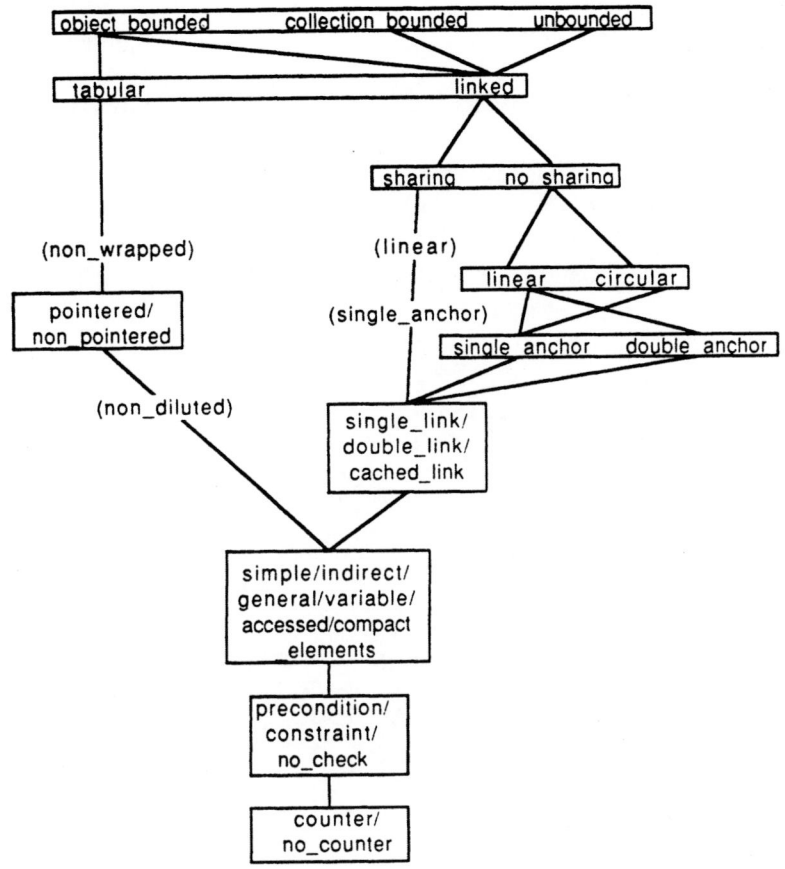

```
generic
   ... see A.2
 [ COLLECTION_SIZE : NATURAL; ]
 [ with function IS_VALID (E : in ELEM_TYPE) return BOOLEAN is <>;
   with procedure INVALIDATE (E : in out ELEM_TYPE) is <>; ]
package <STACKS> is

   type STRUCT [ (SIZE : NATURAL) ] is limited private;
   subtype <STACK> is STRUCT;
```

```
-- Indices
-- =======

type INDEX is private;

function NIL return INDEX;

function GET_ELEM (S : in STRUCT; I : in INDEX) return ELEM_TYPE;

-- Insert and remove positions
-- ===========================

type INSERT_POSITION is private;

function FIRST     return INSERT_POSITION;

type REMOVE_POSITION is private;

function FIRST     return REMOVE_POSITION;

-- Structure parts
-- ===============

type PART is private;

function WHOLE_STRUCT return PART;

-- Stack specific operations
-- =========================

procedure PUSH (S : in out STRUCT; E : in ELEM_TYPE);

procedure POP (S : in out STRUCT);

function TOP (S : in STRUCT) return ELEM_TYPE;
```

```
-- Constructor operations
-- =====================

procedure CLEAR (S : in out STRUCT);
procedure INSERT (S      : in out STRUCT;
                  E      : in ELEM_TYPE;
                  TO_POS : in INSERT_POSITION := LAST);
procedure INSERT (S      : in out STRUCT;
                  E      : in ELEM_TYPE;
                  TO_POS : in INSERT_POSITION := LAST;
                  I      : out INDEX);
procedure INSERT (S      : in out STRUCT;
                  TO_POS : in INSERT_POSITION := LAST;
                  I      : out INDEX);

procedure FIND_OR_INSERT (S      : in out STRUCT;
                          E      : in ELEM_TYPE;
                          TO_POS : in INSERT_POSITION := LAST;
                          I      : out INDEX;
                          FOUND  : out BOOLEAN);

procedure REMOVE (S        : in out STRUCT;
                  FROM_POS : in REMOVE_POSITION);

generic
   with procedure ABSORB (E : in out ELEM_TYPE);
procedure GENERIC_REMOVE (S        : in out STRUCT;
                          FROM_POS : in REMOVE_POSITION);

procedure MOVE (TO       : in out STRUCT;
                FROM     : in out STRUCT;
                FROM_POS : in REMOVE_POSITION;
                TO_POS   : in INSERT_POSITION := LAST);

procedure MOVE (TO     : in out STRUCT;
                FROM   : in out ELEM_TYPE;
                TO_POS : in INSERT_POSITION := LAST);

procedure MOVE (TO       : in out ELEM_TYPE;
                FROM     : in out STRUCT;
                FROM_POS : in REMOVE_POSITION);
```

```
procedure COPY (TO   : in out STRUCT;
                FROM : in STRUCT;
                SUB  : in PART);
procedure COPY (TO : in out STRUCT; FROM : in STRUCT);

procedure TRANSFER (TO, FROM : in out STRUCT; SUB : in PART);
procedure TRANSFER (TO, FROM : in out STRUCT);

procedure DEALLOCATE (S : in out STRUCT);

-- Selector operations
-- ===================

function COUNT (S   : in STRUCT;
               SUB : in PART := WHOLE_STRUCT) return NATURAL;

function IS_EMPTY (S : in STRUCT) return BOOLEAN;

function FIND (S   : in STRUCT;
              E   : in ELEM_TYPE;
              SUB : in PART := WHOLE_STRUCT) return INDEX;

function SKIP (S   : in STRUCT;
              E   : in ELEM_TYPE;
              SUB : in PART := WHOLE_STRUCT) return INDEX;

function COUNT_ELEM (S   : in STRUCT;
                    E   : in ELEM_TYPE;
                    SUB : in PART := WHOLE_STRUCT) return NATURAL;

function IS_ELEM (S   : in STRUCT;
                 E   : in ELEM_TYPE;
                 SUB : in PART := WHOLE_STRUCT) return BOOLEAN;

function "=" (LEFT, RIGHT : in STRUCT) return BOOLEAN;
function EQUAL (LEFT,
               RIGHT : in STRUCT) return BOOLEAN renames "=";
```

```
function FIRST (S : in STRUCT) return INDEX;

function FIRST (S : in STRUCT) return ELEM_TYPE;

function LAST (S : in STRUCT) return INDEX;

function LAST (S : in STRUCT) return ELEM_TYPE;

function NEXT (S        : in STRUCT;
               I        : in INDEX;
               CIRCULAR : in BOOLEAN := FALSE) return INDEX;

function PREVIOUS (S        : in STRUCT;
                   I        : in INDEX;
                   CIRCULAR : in BOOLEAN := FALSE) return INDEX;

-- Access by position count
-- ========================

function INDEX_VAL (S : in STRUCT; P : in POSITIVE) return INDEX;
function INDEX_POS (S : in STRUCT; I : in INDEX) return POSITIVE;

function GET_ELEM (S : in STRUCT;
                   P : in POSITIVE) return ELEM_TYPE;

-- Iteration
-- =========

type ITERATION_ORDER is (FROM_FIRST, FROM_LAST, DONT_CARE);

package DEFAULTS is
    function TRUE  (E : in ELEM_TYPE) return BOOLEAN;
    function FALSE (E : in ELEM_TYPE) return BOOLEAN;
    function TRUE  (S : in STRUCT; I : in INDEX) return BOOLEAN;
    function FALSE (S : in STRUCT; I : in INDEX) return BOOLEAN;

    procedure NONE (E : in ELEM_TYPE);
    procedure NONE (E : in ELEM_TYPE; I : in INDEX);
    procedure NONE1 (E : in out ELEM_TYPE);
    procedure NONE1 (E : in out ELEM_TYPE; I : in INDEX);
```

```
    function TRUE   (LEFT   : in ELEM_TYPE;
                     RIGHT : in ELEM_TYPE) return BOOLEAN;
    function FALSE  (LEFT   : in ELEM_TYPE;
                     RIGHT : in ELEM_TYPE) return BOOLEAN;
    function TRUE   (LEFT    : in STRUCT;
                     LEFT_I  : in INDEX;
                     RIGHT   : in STRUCT;
                     RIGHT_I : in INDEX) return BOOLEAN;
    function FALSE  (LEFT    : in STRUCT;
                     LEFT_I  : in INDEX;
                     RIGHT   : in STRUCT;
                     RIGHT_I : in INDEX) return BOOLEAN;

    procedure NONE (LEFT   : in ELEM_TYPE;
                    RIGHT : in ELEM_TYPE);
    procedure NONE (LEFT    : in ELEM_TYPE;
                    LEFT_I  : in INDEX;
                    RIGHT   : in ELEM_TYPE;
                    RIGHT_I : in INDEX);
    procedure NONE1 (LEFT   : in out ELEM_TYPE;
                     RIGHT : in out ELEM_TYPE);
    procedure NONE1 (LEFT    : in out ELEM_TYPE;
                     LEFT_I  : in INDEX;
                     RIGHT   : in out ELEM_TYPE;
                     RIGHT_I : in INDEX);
    procedure NONE2 (LEFT   : in out ELEM_TYPE;
                     RIGHT : in ELEM_TYPE);
    procedure NONE2 (LEFT    : in out ELEM_TYPE;
                     LEFT_I  : in INDEX;
                     RIGHT   : in ELEM_TYPE;
                     RIGHT_I : in INDEX);
end DEFAULTS;
use DEFAULTS;
```

```
generic
   with procedure ACTION (E : in ELEM_TYPE) is NONE;
   with function  SELECTION
                     (E : in ELEM_TYPE) return BOOLEAN is TRUE;
   with function  UNTIL
                     (S : in STRUCT;
                      I : in INDEX) return BOOLEAN is FALSE;
   with procedure ACTION_WITH_INDEX
                     (E : in ELEM_TYPE;
                      I : in INDEX) is NONE;
   with function  SELECTION_WITH_INDEX
                     (S : in STRUCT;
                      I : in INDEX) return BOOLEAN is TRUE;
procedure ITERATE (S   : in STRUCT;
                   SUB : in PART := WHOLE_STRUCT;
                   ORD : in ITERATION_ORDER := FROM_FIRST);

-- Reduction
-- =========

generic
   with function  OPERATION
                     (LEFT, RIGHT : in ELEM_TYPE) return ELEM_TYPE;
   with function  SELECTION
                     (E : in ELEM_TYPE) return BOOLEAN is TRUE;
   with function  UNTIL
                     (S : in STRUCT;
                      I : in INDEX) return BOOLEAN is FALSE;
function REDUCE (S   : in STRUCT;
                 SUB : in PART := WHOLE_STRUCT;
                 ORD : in ITERATION_ORDER := DONT_CARE)
             return ELEM_TYPE;
```

```
generic
   with function  OPERATION
                       (LEFT, RIGHT : in ELEM_TYPE) return ELEM_TYPE;
   with function  UNIT return ELEM_TYPE;
   with function  SELECTION
                       (E : in ELEM_TYPE) return BOOLEAN is TRUE;
   with function  UNTIL
                       (S : in STRUCT;
                        I : in INDEX) return BOOLEAN is FALSE;
function UREDUCE (S   : in STRUCT;
                  SUB : in PART := WHOLE_STRUCT;
                  ORD : in ITERATION_ORDER := DONT_CARE)
                 return ELEM_TYPE;


generic
   type RESULT_TYPE is limited private;
   with function  OPERATION
                       (LEFT  : in RESULT_TYPE;
                        RIGHT : in ELEM_TYPE) return RESULT_TYPE;
   with function  UNIT return RESULT_TYPE;
   with function  SELECTION
                       (E : in ELEM_TYPE) return BOOLEAN is TRUE;
   with function  UNTIL
                       (S : in STRUCT;
                        I : in INDEX) return BOOLEAN is FALSE;
function AREDUCE (S   : in STRUCT;
                  SUB : in PART := WHOLE_STRUCT;
                  ORD : in ITERATION_ORDER := DONT_CARE)
                 return RESULT_TYPE;
```

```
-- Find, skip and count
-- ===================

generic
   with function PROPERTY (E : in ELEM_TYPE) return BOOLEAN;
function FIND_PROPERTY
            (S   : in STRUCT;
             SUB : in PART := WHOLE_STRUCT;
             ORD : in ITERATION_ORDER := DONT_CARE) return INDEX;

generic
   with function PROPERTY (E : in ELEM_TYPE) return BOOLEAN;
function SKIP_PROPERTY
            (S   : in STRUCT;
             SUB : in PART := WHOLE_STRUCT;
             ORD : in ITERATION_ORDER := DONT_CARE) return INDEX;

generic
   with function PROPERTY (E : in ELEM_TYPE) return BOOLEAN;
function COUNT_PROPERTY
            (S   : in STRUCT;
             SUB : in PART := WHOLE_STRUCT;
             ORD : in ITERATION_ORDER := DONT_CARE) return NATURAL;

-- Existential and universal quantification
-- ========================================

generic
   with function PROPERTY (E : in ELEM_TYPE) return BOOLEAN;
function EXISTS (S   : in STRUCT;
                 SUB : in PART := WHOLE_STRUCT;
                 ORD : in ITERATION_ORDER := DONT_CARE)
                return BOOLEAN;

generic
   with function PROPERTY (E : in ELEM_TYPE) return BOOLEAN;
function FORALL (S   : in STRUCT;
                 SUB : in PART := WHOLE_STRUCT;
                 ORD : in ITERATION_ORDER := DONT_CARE)
                return BOOLEAN;
```

```
-- Double iterations
-- =================

generic
   with procedure ACTION
                     (LEFT    : in ELEM_TYPE;
                      RIGHT   : in ELEM_TYPE) is NONE;
   with function  SELECTION
                     (LEFT, RIGHT : in ELEM_TYPE)
                     return BOOLEAN is TRUE;
   with function  UNTIL
                     (LEFT    : in STRUCT;
                      LEFT_I  : in INDEX;
                      RIGHT   : in STRUCT;
                      RIGHT_I : in INDEX)
                     return BOOLEAN is FALSE;
   with procedure ACTION_WITH_INDEX
                     (LEFT    : in ELEM_TYPE;
                      LEFT_I  : in INDEX;
                      RIGHT   : in ELEM_TYPE;
                      RIGHT_I : in INDEX) is NONE;
   with function  SELECTION_WITH_INDEX
                     (LEFT    : in STRUCT;
                      LEFT_I  : in INDEX;
                      RIGHT   : in STRUCT;
                      RIGHT_I : in INDEX)
                     return BOOLEAN is TRUE;
procedure ITERATE_CORRESPONDING
             (LEFT      : in STRUCT;
              RIGHT     : in STRUCT;
              LEFT_SUB  : in PART := WHOLE_STRUCT;
              RIGHT_SUB : in PART := WHOLE_STRUCT;
              LENGTH    : out ORDER_RELATION);


-- Runs
-- ====

procedure RUN (S          : in STRUCT;
               E          : in ELEM_TYPE;
               MIN_LENGTH : in NATURAL;
               SUB        : in PART := WHOLE_STRUCT;
               RUN_START  : out INDEX);
```

```
    procedure LONGEST_RUN (S          : in STRUCT;
                           E          : in ELEM_TYPE;
                           SUB        : in PART := WHOLE_STRUCT;
                           RUN_START  : out INDEX;
                           RUN_LENGTH : out NATURAL);

    procedure MAX_RUN (S          : in STRUCT;
                       SUB        : in PART := WHOLE_STRUCT;
                       RUN_START  : out INDEX;
                       RUN_LENGTH : out NATURAL);

    -- Order dependent operations
    -- ==========================

    generic
       with function COMPARE (LEFT, RIGHT : in ELEM_TYPE)
                             return ORDER_RELATION is <>;
    package ORDER_OPERATIONS is

       -- Lexicographic comparison
       -- ========================

       function COMPARE (LEFT, RIGHT : in STRUCT)
                        return ORDER_RELATION;

       function "<"  (LEFT, RIGHT : in STRUCT) return BOOLEAN;
       function "<=" (LEFT, RIGHT : in STRUCT) return BOOLEAN;
       function ">"  (LEFT, RIGHT : in STRUCT) return BOOLEAN;
       function ">=" (LEFT, RIGHT : in STRUCT) return BOOLEAN;

       -- Maximum and minimum
       -- ===================

       function MAX (S   : in STRUCT;
                     SUB : in PART := WHOLE_STRUCT) return INDEX;
       function MAX (S   : in STRUCT;
                     SUB : in PART := WHOLE_STRUCT) return ELEM_TYPE;

       function MIN (S   : in STRUCT;
                     SUB : in PART := WHOLE_STRUCT) return INDEX;
       function MIN (S   : in STRUCT;
                     SUB : in PART := WHOLE_STRUCT) return ELEM_TYPE;
```

```
      procedure REMOVE_MAX (S   : in out STRUCT;
                            SUB : in PART := WHOLE_STRUCT);
      procedure REMOVE_MIN (S   : in out STRUCT;
                            SUB : in PART := WHOLE_STRUCT);

   end ORDER_OPERATIONS;

   -- Hash Operation
   -- ==============

   generic
      with function HASH (E : in ELEM_TYPE) return INTEGER is <>;
   function HASH_FUNCTION (S : in STRUCT) return INTEGER;

private

   ...

end <STACKS>;
```

# A.8 Queues and Deques

**Variant Combinations**

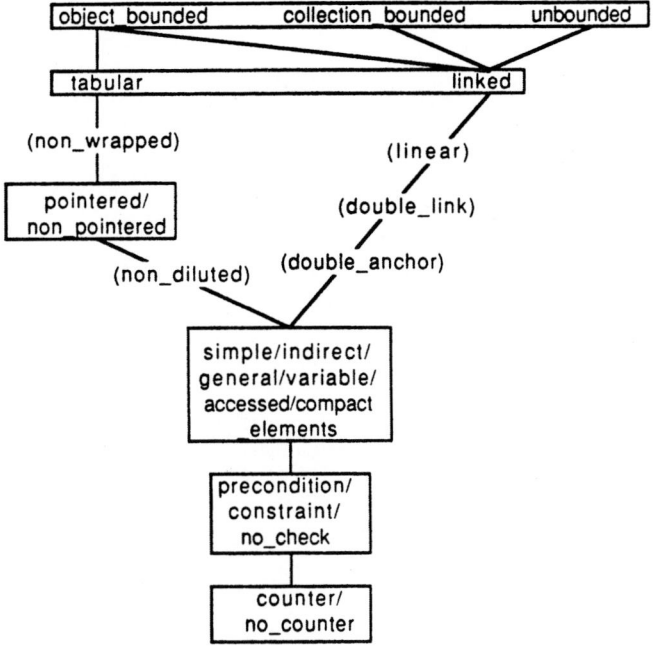

```
generic
    ... see A.2
[ COLLECTION_SIZE : NATURAL; ]
[ with function IS_VALID (E : in ELEM_TYPE) return BOOLEAN is <>;
  with procedure INVALIDATE (E : in out ELEM_TYPE) is <>; ]
package <QUEUES/DEQUES> is

    type STRUCT [ (SIZE : NATURAL) ] is limited private;
    subtype <QUEUE/DEQUE> is STRUCT;

    -- Indices
    -- =======

    type INDEX is private;

    function NIL return INDEX;
```

```
    function GET_ELEM (S : in STRUCT; I : in INDEX) return ELEM_TYPE;

    -- Insert and remove positions
    -- ===========================

    type INSERT_POSITION is private;
    function FIRST      return INSERT_POSITION;
[ function LAST        return INSERT_POSITION; ]

    type REMOVE_POSITION is private;
[ function FIRST       return REMOVE_POSITION; ]
    function LAST        return REMOVE_POSITION;

    -- Structure parts
    -- ===============

    type PART is private;

    function WHOLE_STRUCT return PART;

    -- Constructor operations
    -- ======================

    procedure CLEAR (S : in out STRUCT);

    procedure INSERT (S      : in out STRUCT;
                      E      : in ELEM_TYPE;
                      TO_POS : in INSERT_POSITION := LAST);
    procedure INSERT (S      : in out STRUCT;
                      E      : in ELEM_TYPE;
                      TO_POS : in INSERT_POSITION := LAST;
                      I      : out INDEX);
    procedure INSERT (S      : in out STRUCT;
                      TO_POS : in INSERT_POSITION := LAST;
                      I      : out INDEX);

    procedure FIND_OR_INSERT (S      : in out STRUCT;
                              E      : in ELEM_TYPE;
                              TO_POS : in INSERT_POSITION := LAST;
                              I      : out INDEX;
                              FOUND  : out BOOLEAN);
```

```
   procedure REMOVE (S        : in out STRUCT;
                     FROM_POS : in REMOVE_POSITION);


   generic
      with procedure ABSORB (E : in out ELEM_TYPE);
   procedure GENERIC_REMOVE (S        : in out STRUCT;
                             FROM_POS : in REMOVE_POSITION);

[ procedure MOVE (S        : in out STRUCT;
                  FROM_POS : in REMOVE_POSITION;
                  TO_POS   : in INSERT_POSITION); ]

   procedure MOVE (TO       : in out STRUCT;
                   FROM     : in out STRUCT;
                   FROM_POS : in REMOVE_POSITION;
                   TO_POS   : in INSERT_POSITION := LAST);

   procedure MOVE (TO     : in out STRUCT;
                   FROM   : in out ELEM_TYPE;
                   TO_POS : in INSERT_POSITION := LAST);

   procedure MOVE (TO       : in out ELEM_TYPE;
                   FROM     : in out STRUCT;
                   FROM_POS : in REMOVE_POSITION);

   procedure COPY (TO   : in out STRUCT;
                   FROM : in STRUCT;
                   SUB  : in PART);
   procedure COPY (TO : in out STRUCT; FROM : in STRUCT);

   procedure TRANSFER (TO, FROM : in out STRUCT; SUB : in PART);
   procedure TRANSFER (TO, FROM : in out STRUCT);

   procedure DEALLOCATE (S : in out STRUCT);

   -- Selector operations
   -- ===================

   function COUNT (S   : in STRUCT;
                   SUB : in PART := WHOLE_STRUCT) return NATURAL;
   function IS_EMPTY (S : in STRUCT) return BOOLEAN;
```

```
function FIND (S   : in STRUCT;
               E   : in ELEM_TYPE;
               SUB : in PART := WHOLE_STRUCT) return INDEX;
function SKIP (S   : in STRUCT;
               E   : in ELEM_TYPE;
               SUB : in PART := WHOLE_STRUCT) return INDEX;

function COUNT_ELEM (S   : in STRUCT;
                     E   : in ELEM_TYPE;
                     SUB : in PART := WHOLE_STRUCT) return NATURAL;
function IS_ELEM (S   : in STRUCT;
                  E   : in ELEM_TYPE;
                  SUB : in PART := WHOLE_STRUCT) return BOOLEAN;

function "=" (LEFT, RIGHT : in STRUCT) return BOOLEAN;
function EQUAL (LEFT,
                RIGHT : in STRUCT) return BOOLEAN renames "=";

function FIRST (S : in STRUCT) return INDEX;
function FIRST (S : in STRUCT) return ELEM_TYPE;

function LAST (S : in STRUCT) return INDEX;
function LAST (S : in STRUCT) return ELEM_TYPE;

function NEXT (S        : in STRUCT;
               I        : in INDEX;
               CIRCULAR : in BOOLEAN := FALSE) return INDEX;
function PREVIOUS (S        : in STRUCT;
                   I        : in INDEX;
                   CIRCULAR : in BOOLEAN := FALSE) return INDEX;

-- Access by position count
-- ========================

function INDEX_VAL (S : in STRUCT; P : in POSITIVE) return INDEX;
function INDEX_POS (S : in STRUCT; I : in INDEX) return POSITIVE;

function GET_ELEM (S : in STRUCT;
                   P : in POSITIVE) return ELEM_TYPE;
```

```
-- Iteration
-- =========

type ITERATION_ORDER is (FROM_FIRST, FROM_LAST, DONT_CARE);

package DEFAULTS is
   function TRUE  (E : in ELEM_TYPE) return BOOLEAN;
   function FALSE (E : in ELEM_TYPE) return BOOLEAN;
   function TRUE  (S : in STRUCT; I : in INDEX) return BOOLEAN;
   function FALSE (S : in STRUCT; I : in INDEX) return BOOLEAN;

   procedure NONE (E : in ELEM_TYPE);
   procedure NONE (E : in ELEM_TYPE; I : in INDEX);
   procedure NONE1 (E : in out ELEM_TYPE);
   procedure NONE1 (E : in out ELEM_TYPE; I : in INDEX);

   function TRUE  (LEFT  : in ELEM_TYPE;
                   RIGHT : in ELEM_TYPE) return BOOLEAN;
   function FALSE (LEFT  : in ELEM_TYPE;
                   RIGHT : in ELEM_TYPE) return BOOLEAN;
   function TRUE  (LEFT   : in STRUCT;
                   LEFT_I  : in INDEX;
                   RIGHT   : in STRUCT;
                   RIGHT_I : in INDEX) return BOOLEAN;
   function FALSE (LEFT   : in STRUCT;
                   LEFT_I  : in INDEX;
                   RIGHT   : in STRUCT;
                   RIGHT_I : in INDEX) return BOOLEAN;

   procedure NONE (LEFT  : in ELEM_TYPE;
                   RIGHT : in ELEM_TYPE);
   procedure NONE (LEFT   : in ELEM_TYPE;
                   LEFT_I  : in INDEX;
                   RIGHT   : in ELEM_TYPE;
                   RIGHT_I : in INDEX);
   procedure NONE1 (LEFT  : in out ELEM_TYPE;
                    RIGHT : in out ELEM_TYPE);
   procedure NONE1 (LEFT   : in out ELEM_TYPE;
                    LEFT_I  : in INDEX;
                    RIGHT   : in out ELEM_TYPE;
                    RIGHT_I : in INDEX);
```

```
      procedure NONE2 (LEFT   : in out ELEM_TYPE;
                       RIGHT  : in ELEM_TYPE);
      procedure NONE2 (LEFT     : in out ELEM_TYPE;
                       LEFT_I  : in INDEX;
                       RIGHT    : in ELEM_TYPE;
                       RIGHT_I : in INDEX);
   end DEFAULTS;
   use DEFAULTS;

   generic
      with procedure ACTION (E : in ELEM_TYPE) is NONE;
      with function  SELECTION
                     (E : in ELEM_TYPE) return BOOLEAN is TRUE;
      with function  UNTIL
                     (S : in STRUCT;
                      I : in INDEX) return BOOLEAN is FALSE;
      with procedure ACTION_WITH_INDEX
                     (E : in ELEM_TYPE;
                      I : in INDEX) is NONE;
      with function  SELECTION_WITH_INDEX
                     (S : in STRUCT;
                      I : in INDEX) return BOOLEAN is TRUE;
   procedure ITERATE (S   : in STRUCT;
                      SUB : in PART := WHOLE_STRUCT;
                      ORD : in ITERATION_ORDER := FROM_FIRST);

   -- Reduction
   -- =========

   generic
      with function  OPERATION
                     (LEFT, RIGHT : in ELEM_TYPE) return ELEM_TYPE;
      with function  SELECTION
                     (E : in ELEM_TYPE) return BOOLEAN is TRUE;
      with function  UNTIL
                     (S : in STRUCT;
                      I : in INDEX) return BOOLEAN is FALSE;
   function REDUCE (S   : in STRUCT;
                    SUB : in PART := WHOLE_STRUCT;
                    ORD : in ITERATION_ORDER := DONT_CARE)
                 return ELEM_TYPE;
```

```
generic
   with function  OPERATION
                     (LEFT, RIGHT : in ELEM_TYPE) return ELEM_TYPE;
   with function  UNIT return ELEM_TYPE;
   with function  SELECTION
                     (E : in ELEM_TYPE) return BOOLEAN is TRUE;
   with function  UNTIL
                     (S : in STRUCT;
                      I : in INDEX) return BOOLEAN is FALSE;
function UREDUCE (S   : in STRUCT;
                  SUB : in PART := WHOLE_STRUCT;
                  ORD : in ITERATION_ORDER := DONT_CARE)
                 return ELEM_TYPE;


generic
   with function  OPERATION
                     (LEFT  : in RESULT_TYPE;
                      RIGHT : in ELEM_TYPE) return RESULT_TYPE;
   with function  UNIT return RESULT_TYPE;
   with function  SELECTION
                     (E : in ELEM_TYPE) return BOOLEAN is TRUE;
   with function  UNTIL
                     (S : in STRUCT;
                      I : in INDEX) return BOOLEAN is FALSE;
function AREDUCE (S   : in STRUCT;
                  SUB : in PART := WHOLE_STRUCT;
                  ORD : in ITERATION_ORDER := DONT_CARE)
                 return RESULT_TYPE;
```

```
-- Find, skip and count
-- ====================

generic
   with function PROPERTY (E : in ELEM_TYPE) return BOOLEAN;
function FIND_PROPERTY
             (S   : in STRUCT;
              SUB : in PART := WHOLE_STRUCT;
              ORD : in ITERATION_ORDER := DONT_CARE) return INDEX;

generic
   with function PROPERTY (E : in ELEM_TYPE) return BOOLEAN;
function SKIP_PROPERTY
             (S   : in STRUCT;
              SUB : in PART := WHOLE_STRUCT;
              ORD : in ITERATION_ORDER := DONT_CARE) return INDEX;

generic
   with function PROPERTY (E : in ELEM_TYPE) return BOOLEAN;
function COUNT_PROPERTY
             (S   : in STRUCT;
              SUB : in PART := WHOLE_STRUCT;
              ORD : in ITERATION_ORDER := DONT_CARE) return NATURAL;

generic
   with function PROPERTY (E : in ELEM_TYPE) return BOOLEAN;
function EXISTS (S   : in STRUCT;
                 SUB : in PART := WHOLE_STRUCT;
                 ORD : in ITERATION_ORDER := DONT_CARE)
               return BOOLEAN;

generic
   with function PROPERTY (E : in ELEM_TYPE) return BOOLEAN;
function FORALL (S   : in STRUCT;
                 SUB : in PART := WHOLE_STRUCT;
                 ORD : in ITERATION_ORDER := DONT_CARE)
               return BOOLEAN;
```

```
-- Double iterations
-- ==================


generic
   with procedure ACTION
                     (LEFT     : in ELEM_TYPE;
                      RIGHT    : in ELEM_TYPE) is NONE;
   with function  SELECTION
                     (LEFT, RIGHT : in ELEM_TYPE)
                     return BOOLEAN is TRUE;
   with function  UNTIL
                     (LEFT     : in STRUCT;
                      LEFT_I   : in INDEX;
                      RIGHT    : in STRUCT;
                      RIGHT_I  : in INDEX)
                     return BOOLEAN is FALSE;
   with procedure ACTION_WITH_INDEX
                     (LEFT     : in ELEM_TYPE;
                      LEFT_I   : in INDEX;
                      RIGHT    : in ELEM_TYPE;
                      RIGHT_I  : in INDEX) is NONE;
   with function  SELECTION_WITH_INDEX
                     (LEFT     : in STRUCT;
                      LEFT_I   : in INDEX;
                      RIGHT    : in STRUCT;
                      RIGHT_I  : in INDEX)
                     return BOOLEAN is TRUE;
procedure ITERATE_CORRESPONDING
             (LEFT      : in STRUCT;
              RIGHT     : in STRUCT;
              LEFT_SUB  : in PART := WHOLE_STRUCT;
              RIGHT_SUB : in PART := WHOLE_STRUCT;
              LENGTH    : out ORDER_RELATION);


-- Runs
-- ====


procedure RUN (S          : in STRUCT;
               E          : in ELEM_TYPE;
               MIN_LENGTH : in NATURAL;
               SUB        : in PART := WHOLE_STRUCT;
               RUN_START  : out INDEX);
```

```ada
   procedure LONGEST_RUN (S          : in STRUCT;
                          E          : in ELEM_TYPE;
                          SUB        : in PART := WHOLE_STRUCT;
                          RUN_START  : out INDEX;
                          RUN_LENGTH : out NATURAL);

   procedure MAX_RUN (S          : in STRUCT;
                      SUB        : in PART := WHOLE_STRUCT;
                      RUN_START  : out INDEX;
                      RUN_LENGTH : out NATURAL);

-- Order dependent operations
-- ==========================

generic
   with function COMPARE (LEFT, RIGHT : in ELEM_TYPE)
                          return ORDER_RELATION is <>;
package ORDER_OPERATIONS is

   -- Lexicographic comparison
   -- =======================

   function COMPARE (LEFT, RIGHT : in STRUCT)
                     return ORDER_RELATION;

   function "<"  (LEFT, RIGHT : in STRUCT) return BOOLEAN;
   function "<=" (LEFT, RIGHT : in STRUCT) return BOOLEAN;
   function ">"  (LEFT, RIGHT : in STRUCT) return BOOLEAN;
   function ">=" (LEFT, RIGHT : in STRUCT) return BOOLEAN;

   -- Maximum and minimum
   -- ===================

   function MAX (S   : in STRUCT;
                 SUB : in PART := WHOLE_STRUCT) return INDEX;
   function MAX (S   : in STRUCT;
                 SUB : in PART := WHOLE_STRUCT) return ELEM_TYPE;
```

```
        function MIN (S   : in STRUCT;
                      SUB : in PART := WHOLE_STRUCT) return INDEX;
        function MIN (S   : in STRUCT;
                      SUB : in PART := WHOLE_STRUCT) return ELEM_TYPE;

        procedure REMOVE_MAX (S   : in out STRUCT;
                              SUB : in PART := WHOLE_STRUCT);
        procedure REMOVE_MIN (S   : in out STRUCT;
                              SUB : in PART := WHOLE_STRUCT);

    end ORDER_OPERATIONS;

    -- Hash Operation
    -- ==============

    generic
        with function HASH (E : in ELEM_TYPE) return INTEGER is <>;
    function HASH_FUNCTION (S : in STRUCT) return INTEGER;

private

    ...

end <QUEUES/DEQUES>;
```

# A.9   Trees

**Variant Combinations**

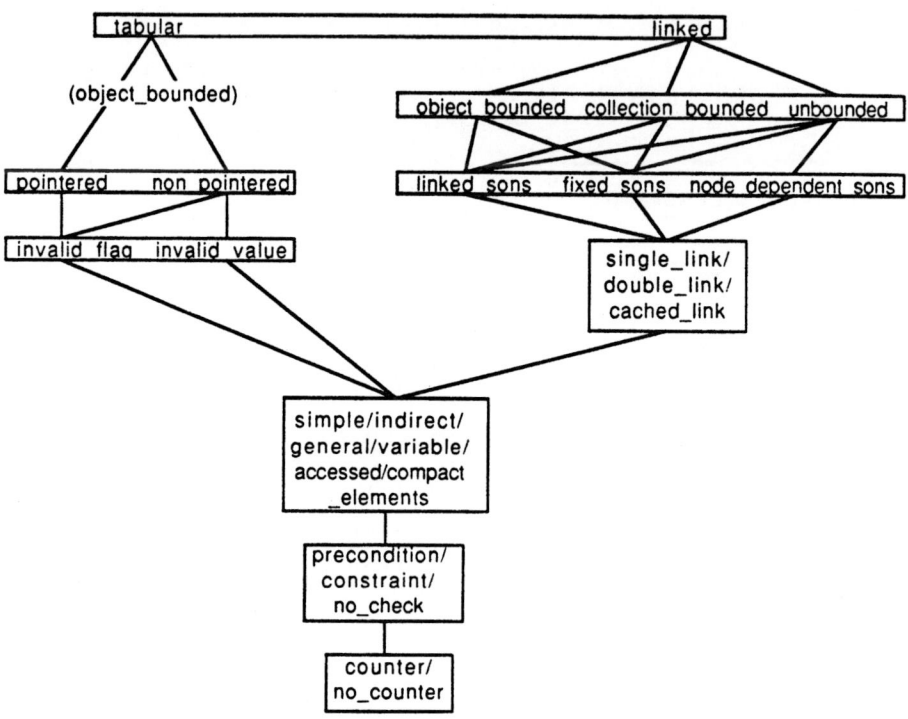

```
generic
    ... see A.2
  [ COLLECTION_SIZE : NATURAL; ]
  [ SONS : POSITIVE := 2; ]
  [ with function IS_VALID (E : in ELEM_TYPE) return BOOLEAN is <>;
    with procedure INVALIDATE (E : in out ELEM_TYPE) is <>; ]
package <TREES> is

    type STRUCT [ (SIZE : NATURAL) ] is limited private;
    subtype <TREE> is STRUCT;

    -- Indices
    -- =======

    type INDEX is private;
```

```
function NIL return INDEX;

function GET_ELEM (S : in STRUCT; I : in INDEX) return ELEM_TYPE;

procedure SET_ELEM (S : in out STRUCT;
                    I : in INDEX;
                    E : in ELEM_TYPE);

procedure TRANSFER_ELEM (TO     : in out ELEM_TYPE;
                         FROM   : in out STRUCT;
                         FROM_I : in INDEX);

procedure TRANSFER_ELEM (TO   : in out STRUCT;
                         FROM : in out ELEM_TYPE;
                         TO_I : in INDEX);

generic
   with procedure MODIFICATION (E : in out ELEM_TYPE);
procedure MODIFY_ELEM (S : in out STRUCT; I : in INDEX);

-- Insert and remove positions
-- ===========================

type INSERT_POSITION is private;

function FATHER_OF (SON      : in INDEX;
                    NR_OF_SON : POSITIVE := 1)
                   return INSERT_POSITION;

function SON_OF (FATHER        : in INDEX;
                 NR_OF_SON     : POSITIVE;
                 NR_OF_GRANDSON : NATURAL := 0)
                return INSERT_POSITION;

function ROOT (NR_OF_SON : NATURAL := 0) return INSERT_POSITION;

type REMOVE_POSITION is private;

function AT_INDEX (I        : in INDEX;
                   NR_OF_SON : in NATURAL := 0)
                  return REMOVE_POSITION;
```

```
function SON_OF (FATHER         : in INDEX;
                NR_OF_SON       : POSITIVE;
                NR_OF_GRANDSON : NATURAL := 0)
                return REMOVE_POSITION;

function ROOT (NR_OF_SON : NATURAL := 0) return REMOVE_POSITION;

-- Structure parts
-- ===============

type PART is private;

function WHOLE_STRUCT return PART;
function SUBTREE (ROOT : in INDEX) return PART;

-- Constructor operations
-- ======================

procedure CLEAR (S : in out STRUCT);

procedure INSERT (S      : in out STRUCT;
                  E      : in ELEM_TYPE;
                [ SONS   : in NATURAL; ]
                  TO_POS : in INSERT_POSITION);

procedure INSERT (S      : in out STRUCT;
                  E      : in ELEM_TYPE;
                [ SONS   : in NATURAL; ]
                  TO_POS : in INSERT_POSITION;
                  I      : out INDEX);

procedure INSERT (S      : in out STRUCT;
                [ SONS   : in NATURAL; ]
                  TO_POS : in INSERT_POSITION;
                  I      : out INDEX);

procedure INSERT (TO     : in out STRUCT;
                  FROM   : in STRUCT;
                  SUB    : in PART := WHOLE_STRUCT;
                  TO_POS : in INSERT_POSITION);
```

```
    procedure FIND_OR_INSERT (S       : in out STRUCT;
                              E       : in ELEM_TYPE;
                          [ SONS    : in NATURAL; ]
                            TO_POS : in INSERT_POSITION;
                            I       : out INDEX;
                            FOUND   : out BOOLEAN);


    procedure REMOVE (S        : in out STRUCT;
                      FROM_POS : in REMOVE_POSITION);


    procedure REMOVE (S : in out STRUCT; SUB : in PART);


    procedure REMOVE (S : in out STRUCT; E : in ELEM_TYPE);


    procedure REMOVE_ALL (S : in out STRUCT; E : in ELEM_TYPE);


    generic
       with procedure ABSORB (E : in out ELEM_TYPE);
    procedure GENERIC_REMOVE (S        : in out STRUCT;
                              FROM_POS : in REMOVE_POSITION);


    procedure MOVE (S        : in out STRUCT;
                    FROM_POS : in REMOVE_POSITION;
                    TO_POS   : in INSERT_POSITION);


    procedure MOVE (S      : in out STRUCT;
                    SUB    : in PART;
                    TO_POS : in INSERT_POSITION);


    procedure MOVE (TO       : in out STRUCT;
                    FROM     : in out STRUCT;
                    FROM_POS : in REMOVE_POSITION;
                    TO_POS   : in INSERT_POSITION);


    procedure MOVE (TO     : in out STRUCT;
                    FROM   : in out STRUCT;
                    SUB    : in PART := WHOLE_STRUCT;
                    TO_POS : in INSERT_POSITION);
```

```
   procedure MOVE (TO      : in out STRUCT;
                   FROM    : in out ELEM_TYPE;
                 [ SONS    : in NATURAL; ]
                   TO_POS  : in INSERT_POSITION);

   procedure MOVE (TO       : in out ELEM_TYPE;
                   FROM     : in out STRUCT;
                   FROM_POS : in REMOVE_POSITION);

[ procedure ROTATE (S : in out STRUCT; POS : in REMOVE_POSITION); ]

   procedure COPY (TO   : in out STRUCT;
                   FROM : in STRUCT;
                   SUB  : in PART);
   procedure COPY (TO : in out STRUCT; FROM : in STRUCT);

   procedure TRANSFER (TO, FROM : in out STRUCT; SUB : in PART);
   procedure TRANSFER (TO, FROM : in out STRUCT);

   procedure SWAP (S          : in out STRUCT;
                   POS1, POS2 : in REMOVE_POSITION);

   procedure SLICE (S : in out STRUCT; SUB : in PART);

   procedure DEALLOCATE (S : in out STRUCT);

   -- Selector operations
   -- ===================

   function COUNT (S   : in STRUCT;
                   SUB : in PART := WHOLE_STRUCT) return NATURAL;

   function IS_EMPTY (S : in STRUCT) return BOOLEAN;

   function FIND (S   : in STRUCT;
                  E   : in ELEM_TYPE;
                  SUB : in PART := WHOLE_STRUCT) return INDEX;

   function COUNT_ELEM (S   : in STRUCT;
                        E   : in ELEM_TYPE;
                        SUB : in PART := WHOLE_STRUCT) return NATURAL;
```

```
function IS_ELEM (S   : in STRUCT;
                  E   : in ELEM_TYPE;
                  SUB : in PART := WHOLE_STRUCT) return BOOLEAN;

function "=" (LEFT, RIGHT : in STRUCT) return BOOLEAN;
function EQUAL (LEFT,
               RIGHT : in STRUCT) return BOOLEAN renames "=";

function ROOT (S : in STRUCT) return INDEX;

function ROOT (S : in STRUCT) return ELEM_TYPE;

function NR_OF_SONS (S  : in STRUCT; I : in INDEX) return NATURAL;

function SON (S  : in STRUCT;
             I  : in INDEX;
             NR : in POSITIVE) return INDEX;

function FATHER (S : in STRUCT; I : in INDEX) return INDEX;

function NR_OF_SON (S      : in STRUCT;
                   FATHER : in INDEX;
                   SON    : in INDEX) return NATURAL;

procedure FIND_FATHER (S        : in STRUCT;
                       SON      : in INDEX;
                       FATHER   : out INDEX;
                       NR_OF_SON : out NATURAL);

procedure FIRST_VALID_SON (S        : in STRUCT;
                           FATHER   : in INDEX;
                           SON      : out INDEX;
                           NR_OF_SON : out NATURAL);

procedure NEXT_VALID_SON (S        : in STRUCT;
                          FATHER   : in INDEX;
                          SON      : out INDEX;
                          NR_OF_SON : in out NATURAL);
```

```
-- Iteration
-- =========

type ITERATION_ORDER is (PRE_ORDER,
                         IN_ORDER,
                         POST_ORDER,
                         DONT_CARE);

package DEFAULTS is
   function TRUE  (E : in ELEM_TYPE) return BOOLEAN;
   function FALSE (E : in ELEM_TYPE) return BOOLEAN;
   function TRUE  (S : in STRUCT; I : in INDEX) return BOOLEAN;
   function FALSE (S : in STRUCT; I : in INDEX) return BOOLEAN;

   procedure NONE (E : in ELEM_TYPE);
   procedure NONE (E : in ELEM_TYPE; I : in INDEX);
   procedure NONE1 (E : in out ELEM_TYPE);
   procedure NONE1 (E : in out ELEM_TYPE; I : in INDEX);
end DEFAULTS;
use DEFAULTS;

generic
   with procedure ACTION (E : in out ELEM_TYPE) is NONE1;
   with function  SELECTION
                  (E : in ELEM_TYPE) return BOOLEAN is TRUE;
   with function  UNTIL
                  (S : in STRUCT;
                   I : in INDEX) return BOOLEAN is FALSE;
   with procedure ACTION_WITH_INDEX
                  (E : in out ELEM_TYPE;
                   I : in INDEX) is NONE1;
   with function  SELECTION_WITH_INDEX
                  (S : in STRUCT;
                   I : in INDEX) return BOOLEAN is TRUE;
procedure APPLY (S   : in out STRUCT;
                 SUB : in PART := WHOLE_STRUCT;
                 ORD : in ITERATION_ORDER := PRE_ORDER);
```

```
generic
   with procedure ACTION (E : in ELEM_TYPE) is NONE;
   with function  SELECTION
                      (E : in ELEM_TYPE) return BOOLEAN is TRUE;
   with function  UNTIL
                      (S : in STRUCT;
                       I : in INDEX) return BOOLEAN is FALSE;
   with procedure ACTION_WITH_INDEX
                      (E : in ELEM_TYPE;
                       I : in INDEX) is NONE;
   with function  SELECTION_WITH_INDEX
                      (S : in STRUCT;
                       I : in INDEX) return BOOLEAN is TRUE;
procedure ITERATE (S   : in STRUCT;
                   SUB : in PART := WHOLE_STRUCT;
                   ORD : in ITERATION_ORDER := PRE_ORDER);


generic
   with procedure ACTION (S : in out STRUCT; I : in INDEX);
   with function  SELECTION
                      (S : in STRUCT;
                       I : in INDEX) return BOOLEAN is TRUE;
   with function  UNTIL
                      (S : in STRUCT;
                       I : in INDEX) return BOOLEAN is FALSE;
procedure ITERATE_MOVE (S   : in STRUCT;
                        SUB : in PART := WHOLE_STRUCT;
                        ORD : in ITERATION_ORDER := PRE_ORDER);


generic
   with procedure ACTION (S        : in out STRUCT;
                          FATHER,
                          SON      : in INDEX;
                          NR_OF_SON : in POSITIVE);
   with function  SELECTION (E : in ELEM_TYPE)
                          return BOOLEAN is TRUE;
   with function  UNTIL
                      (S : in STRUCT;
                       I : in INDEX) return BOOLEAN is FALSE;
procedure APPLY_TO_SONS (S : in out STRUCT; I : in INDEX);
```

```
generic
   with procedure ACTION (S           : in STRUCT;
                          FATHER,
                          SON         : in INDEX;
                          NR_OF_SON : in POSITIVE);
   with function  SELECTION (E : in ELEM_TYPE)
                          return BOOLEAN is TRUE;
   with function  UNTIL
                 (S : in STRUCT;
                  I : in INDEX) return BOOLEAN is FALSE;
procedure ITERATE_OVER_SONS (S : in STRUCT; I : in INDEX);

-- Reduction
-- =========

generic
   with function  OPERATION
                     (LEFT, RIGHT : in ELEM_TYPE) return ELEM_TYPE;
   with function  SELECTION
                     (E : in ELEM_TYPE) return BOOLEAN is TRUE;
   with function  UNTIL
                 (S : in STRUCT;
                  I : in INDEX) return BOOLEAN is FALSE;
function REDUCE (S   : in STRUCT;
                 SUB : in PART := WHOLE_STRUCT;
                 ORD : in ITERATION_ORDER := DONT_CARE)
               return ELEM_TYPE;

generic
   with function  OPERATION
                     (LEFT, RIGHT : in ELEM_TYPE) return ELEM_TYPE;
   with function  UNIT return ELEM_TYPE;
   with function  SELECTION
                     (E : in ELEM_TYPE) return BOOLEAN is TRUE;
   with function  UNTIL
                 (S : in STRUCT;
                  I : in INDEX) return BOOLEAN is FALSE;
function UREDUCE (S   : in STRUCT;
                  SUB : in PART := WHOLE_STRUCT;
                  ORD : in ITERATION_ORDER := DONT_CARE)
                return ELEM_TYPE;
```

```
generic
   type RESULT_TYPE is limited private;
   with function  OPERATION
                     (LEFT  : in RESULT_TYPE;
                      RIGHT : in ELEM_TYPE) return RESULT_TYPE;
   with function  UNIT return RESULT_TYPE;
   with function  SELECTION
                     (E : in ELEM_TYPE) return BOOLEAN is TRUE;
   with function  UNTIL
                     (S : in STRUCT;
                      I : in INDEX) return BOOLEAN is FALSE;
function AREDUCE (S   : in STRUCT;
                  SUB : in PART := WHOLE_STRUCT;
                  ORD : in ITERATION_ORDER := DONT_CARE)
                return RESULT_TYPE;

-- Find and count
-- ==============

generic
   with function PROPERTY (E : in ELEM_TYPE) return BOOLEAN;
function FIND_PROPERTY
           (S   : in STRUCT;
            SUB : in PART := WHOLE_STRUCT;
            ORD : in ITERATION_ORDER := DONT_CARE) return INDEX;

generic
   with function PROPERTY (E : in ELEM_TYPE) return BOOLEAN;
function COUNT_PROPERTY
           (S   : in STRUCT;
            SUB : in PART := WHOLE_STRUCT;
            ORD : in ITERATION_ORDER := DONT_CARE) return NATURAL;

-- Existential and universal quantification
-- ========================================

generic
   with function PROPERTY (E : in ELEM_TYPE) return BOOLEAN;
function EXISTS (S   : in STRUCT;
                 SUB : in PART := WHOLE_STRUCT;
                 ORD : in ITERATION_ORDER := DONT_CARE)
               return BOOLEAN;
```

```ada
generic
   with function PROPERTY (E : in ELEM_TYPE) return BOOLEAN;
function FORALL (S   : in STRUCT;
                 SUB : in PART := WHOLE_STRUCT;
                 ORD : in ITERATION_ORDER := DONT_CARE)
              return BOOLEAN;

-- Order dependent operations
-- ==========================

generic
   with function COMPARE (LEFT, RIGHT : in ELEM_TYPE)
                          return ORDER_OPERATION is <>;
package ORDER_OPERATIONS is

   -- Lexicographic comparison
   -- ========================

   function COMPARE (LEFT, RIGHT : in STRUCT)
                     return ORDER_RELATION;

   function "<"  (LEFT, RIGHT : in STRUCT) return BOOLEAN;
   function "<=" (LEFT, RIGHT : in STRUCT) return BOOLEAN;
   function ">"  (LEFT, RIGHT : in STRUCT) return BOOLEAN;
   function ">=" (LEFT, RIGHT : in STRUCT) return BOOLEAN;

   -- Maximum and minimum
   -- ===================

   function MAX (S   : in STRUCT;
                 SUB : in PART := WHOLE_STRUCT) return INDEX;
   function MAX (S   : in STRUCT;
                 SUB : in PART := WHOLE_STRUCT) return ELEM_TYPE;

   function MIN (S   : in STRUCT;
                 SUB : in PART := WHOLE_STRUCT) return INDEX;
   function MIN (S   : in STRUCT;
                 SUB : in PART := WHOLE_STRUCT) return ELEM_TYPE;
```

```
        procedure REMOVE_MAX (S   : in out STRUCT;
                              SUB : in PART := WHOLE_STRUCT);
        procedure REMOVE_MIN (S   : in out STRUCT;
                              SUB : in PART := WHOLE_STRUCT);

    end ORDER_OPERATIONS;

    -- Hash Operation
    -- ==============

    generic
       with function HASH (E : in ELEM_TYPE) return INTEGER is <>;
    function HASH_FUNCTION (S : in STRUCT) return INTEGER;

private

       ...

end <TREES>;
```

# A.10   Orders

## Variant Combinations

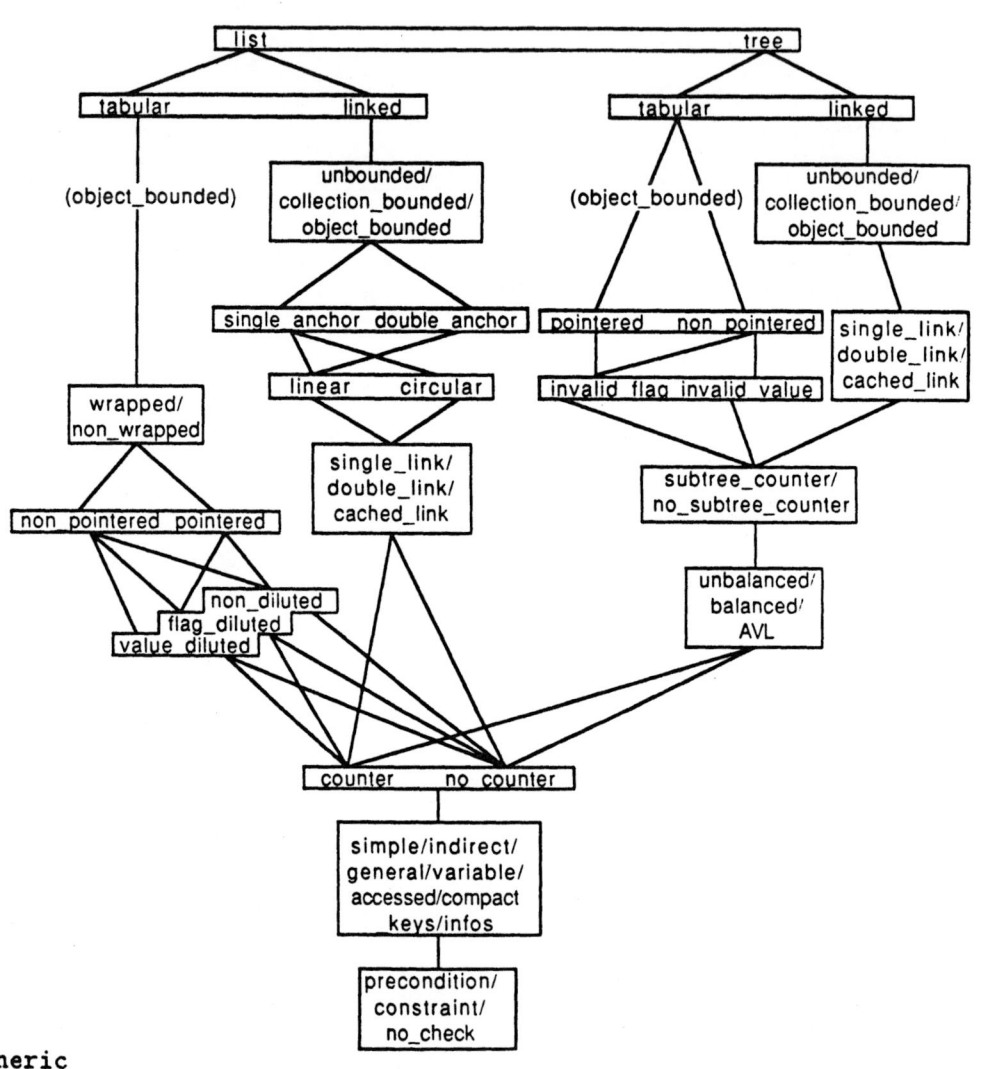

```
generic
    ... see A.2
  [ COLLECTION_SIZE : NATURAL; ]
    with function "<" (LEFT,
                        RIGHT : in ELEM_TYPE) return BOOLEAN is <>;
package <ORDERS> is
```

```
type STRUCT [ (SIZE : NATURAL) ] is limited private;
subtype <ORDER> is STRUCT;


-- Indices
-- =======

type INDEX is private;

function NIL return INDEX;

function GET_ELEM (S : in STRUCT; I : in INDEX) return ELEM_TYPE;


-- Remove positions
-- ================

type REMOVE_POSITION is private;

function AT_INDEX (I : in INDEX) return REMOVE_POSITION;
function FIRST return REMOVE_POSITION;
function LAST  return REMOVE_POSITION;


-- Structure parts
-- ===============

type PART is private;

function WHOLE_STRUCT return PART;
function SUBLIST (FROM : in INDEX;
                  TO   : in INDEX := NIL) return PART;


-- Constructor operations
-- ======================

procedure CLEAR (S : in out STRUCT);

procedure INSERT (S : in out STRUCT; E : in ELEM_TYPE);

procedure INSERT (S : in out STRUCT;
                  E : in ELEM_TYPE;
                  I : out INDEX);
```

```
procedure INSERT (TO      : in out STRUCT;
                  FROM    : in STRUCT;
                  SUB     : in PART := WHOLE_STRUCT);

procedure FIND_OR_INSERT (S     : in out STRUCT;
                          E     : in ELEM_TYPE;
                          I     : out INDEX;
                          FOUND : out BOOLEAN);

procedure REMOVE (S        : in out STRUCT;
                  FROM_POS : in REMOVE_POSITION);

procedure REMOVE (S : in out STRUCT; SUB : in PART);

procedure REMOVE (S : in out STRUCT; E : in ELEM_TYPE);

procedure REMOVE_ALL (S : in out STRUCT; E : in ELEM_TYPE);

generic
   with procedure ABSORB (E : in out ELEM_TYPE);
procedure GENERIC_REMOVE (S        : in out STRUCT;
                          FROM_POS : in REMOVE_POSITION);

procedure MOVE (TO       : in out STRUCT;
                FROM     : in out STRUCT;
                FROM_POS : in REMOVE_POSITION);

procedure MOVE (TO   : in out STRUCT;
                FROM : in out STRUCT;
                SUB  : in PART := WHOLE_STRUCT);

procedure MOVE (TO       : in out STRUCT;
                FROM     : in out ELEM_TYPE);

procedure MOVE (TO       : in out ELEM_TYPE;
                FROM     : in out STRUCT;
                FROM_POS : in REMOVE_POSITION);

procedure COPY (TO   : in out STRUCT;
                FROM : in STRUCT;
                SUB  : in PART);
```

```
procedure COPY (TO : in out STRUCT; FROM : in STRUCT);

procedure TRANSFER (TO, FROM : in out STRUCT; SUB : in PART);

procedure TRANSFER (TO, FROM : in out STRUCT);

procedure SLICE (S : in out STRUCT; SUB : in PART);

procedure DEALLOCATE (S : in out STRUCT);

-- Selector operations
-- ===================

function COUNT (S   : in STRUCT;
               SUB : in PART := WHOLE_STRUCT) return NATURAL;

function IS_EMPTY (S : in STRUCT) return BOOLEAN;

function FIND (S   : in STRUCT;
              E   : in ELEM_TYPE;
              SUB : in PART := WHOLE_STRUCT) return INDEX;

function SKIP (S   : in STRUCT;
              E   : in ELEM_TYPE;
              SUB : in PART := WHOLE_STRUCT) return INDEX;

function COUNT_ELEM (S   : in STRUCT;
                     E   : in ELEM_TYPE;
                     SUB : in PART := WHOLE_STRUCT) return NATURAL;

function IS_ELEM (S   : in STRUCT;
                 E   : in ELEM_TYPE;
                 SUB : in PART := WHOLE_STRUCT) return BOOLEAN;

function "=" (LEFT, RIGHT : in STRUCT) return BOOLEAN;
function EQUAL (LEFT,
               RIGHT : in STRUCT) return BOOLEAN renames "=";

function FIRST (S : in STRUCT) return INDEX;

function FIRST (S : in STRUCT) return ELEM_TYPE;
```

```
function LAST (S : in STRUCT) return INDEX;

function LAST (S : in STRUCT) return ELEM_TYPE;

function NEXT (S        : in STRUCT;
              I         : in INDEX;
              CIRCULAR : in BOOLEAN := FALSE) return INDEX;

function PREVIOUS (S        : in STRUCT;
                   I         : in INDEX;
                   CIRCULAR : in BOOLEAN := FALSE) return INDEX;

-- Access by position count
-- ========================

function INDEX_VAL (S : in STRUCT; P : in POSITIVE) return INDEX;

function INDEX_POS (S : in STRUCT; I : in INDEX) return POSITIVE;

function GET_ELEM (S : in STRUCT;
                   P : in POSITIVE) return ELEM_TYPE;

-- Iteration
-- =========

type ITERATION_ORDER is (FROM_FIRST, FROM_LAST, DONT_CARE);

package DEFAULTS is
    function TRUE  (E : in ELEM_TYPE) return BOOLEAN;
    function FALSE (E : in ELEM_TYPE) return BOOLEAN;
    function TRUE  (S : in STRUCT; I : in INDEX) return BOOLEAN;
    function FALSE (S : in STRUCT; I : in INDEX) return BOOLEAN;
```

```
      procedure NONE (E : in ELEM_TYPE);
      procedure NONE (E : in ELEM_TYPE; I : in INDEX);
      procedure NONE1 (E : in out ELEM_TYPE);
      procedure NONE1 (E : in out ELEM_TYPE; I : in INDEX);
   end DEFAULTS;
   use DEFAULTS;

   generic
      with procedure ACTION (E : in ELEM_TYPE) is NONE;
      with function  SELECTION
                        (E : in ELEM_TYPE) return BOOLEAN is TRUE;
      with function  UNTIL
                        (S : in STRUCT;
                         I : in INDEX) return BOOLEAN is FALSE;
      with procedure ACTION_WITH_INDEX
                        (E : in out ELEM_TYPE;
                         I : in INDEX) is NONE1;
      with function  SELECTION_WITH_INDEX
                        (S : in STRUCT;
                         I : in INDEX) return BOOLEAN is TRUE;
   procedure ITERATE (S   : in STRUCT;
                      SUB : in PART := WHOLE_STRUCT;
                      ORD : in ITERATION_ORDER := FROM_FIRST);

   generic
      with procedure ACTION (S : in out STRUCT; I : in INDEX);
      with function  SELECTION
                        (S : in STRUCT;
                         I : in INDEX) return BOOLEAN is TRUE;
      with function  UNTIL
                        (S : in STRUCT;
                         I : in INDEX) return BOOLEAN is FALSE;
   procedure ITERATE_MOVE (S   : in STRUCT;
                           SUB : in PART := WHOLE_STRUCT;
                           ORD : in ITERATION_ORDER := FROM_FIRST);
```

```
-- Reduction
-- =========

generic
   with function  OPERATION
                     (LEFT, RIGHT : in ELEM_TYPE) return ELEM_TYPE;
   with function  SELECTION
                     (E : in ELEM_TYPE) return BOOLEAN is TRUE;
   with function  UNTIL
                     (S : in STRUCT;
                      I : in INDEX) return BOOLEAN is FALSE;
function REDUCE (S   : in STRUCT;
                 SUB : in PART := WHOLE_STRUCT;
                 ORD : in ITERATION_ORDER := DONT_CARE)
              return ELEM_TYPE;

generic
   with function  OPERATION
                     (LEFT, RIGHT : in ELEM_TYPE) return ELEM_TYPE;
   with function  UNIT return ELEM_TYPE;
   with function  SELECTION
                     (E : in ELEM_TYPE) return BOOLEAN is TRUE;
   with function  UNTIL
                     (S : in STRUCT;
                      I : in INDEX) return BOOLEAN is FALSE;
function UREDUCE (S   : in STRUCT;
                  SUB : in PART := WHOLE_STRUCT;
                  ORD : in ITERATION_ORDER := DONT_CARE)
              return ELEM_TYPE;
```

```
generic
   type RESULT_TYPE is limited private;
   with function  OPERATION
                      (LEFT  : in RESULT_TYPE;
                       RIGHT : in ELEM_TYPE) return RESULT_TYPE;
   with function  UNIT return RESULT_TYPE;
   with function  SELECTION
                      (E : in ELEM_TYPE) return BOOLEAN is TRUE;
   with function  UNTIL
                     (S : in STRUCT;
                      I : in INDEX) return BOOLEAN is FALSE;
function AREDUCE (S   : in STRUCT;
                  SUB : in PART := WHOLE_STRUCT;
                  ORD : in ITERATION_ORDER := DONT_CARE)
                 return RESULT_TYPE;

-- Find, skip and count
-- =====================

generic
   with function PROPERTY (E : in ELEM_TYPE) return BOOLEAN;
function FIND_PROPERTY
            (S   : in STRUCT;
             SUB : in PART := WHOLE_STRUCT;
             ORD : in ITERATION_ORDER := DONT_CARE) return INDEX;

generic
   with function PROPERTY (E : in ELEM_TYPE) return BOOLEAN;
function SKIP_PROPERTY
            (S   : in STRUCT;
             SUB : in PART := WHOLE_STRUCT;
             ORD : in ITERATION_ORDER := DONT_CARE) return INDEX;

generic
   with function PROPERTY (E : in ELEM_TYPE) return BOOLEAN;
function COUNT_PROPERTY
            (S   : in STRUCT;
             SUB : in PART := WHOLE_STRUCT;
             ORD : in ITERATION_ORDER := DONT_CARE) return NATURAL;
```

```
-- Existential and universal quantification
-- =========================================

generic
   with function PROPERTY (E : in ELEM_TYPE) return BOOLEAN;
function EXISTS (S   : in STRUCT;
                 SUB : in PART := WHOLE_STRUCT;
                 ORD : in ITERATION_ORDER := DONT_CARE)
                return BOOLEAN;

generic
   with function PROPERTY (E : in ELEM_TYPE) return BOOLEAN;
function FORALL (S   : in STRUCT;
                 SUB : in PART := WHOLE_STRUCT;
                 ORD : in ITERATION_ORDER := DONT_CARE)
                return BOOLEAN;

-- Order dependent operations
-- ==========================

package ORDER_OPERATIONS is

   -- Lexicographic comparison
   -- ========================

   function COMPARE (LEFT, RIGHT : in STRUCT)
                    return ORDER_RELATION;

   function "<"  (LEFT, RIGHT : in STRUCT) return BOOLEAN;
   function "<=" (LEFT, RIGHT : in STRUCT) return BOOLEAN;
   function ">"  (LEFT, RIGHT : in STRUCT) return BOOLEAN;
   function ">=" (LEFT, RIGHT : in STRUCT) return BOOLEAN;

   -- Maximum and minimum
   -- ===================

   function MAX (S   : in STRUCT;
                 SUB : in PART := WHOLE_STRUCT) return INDEX;
   function MAX (S   : in STRUCT;
                 SUB : in PART := WHOLE_STRUCT) return ELEM_TYPE;
```

```
        function MIN (S   : in STRUCT;
                      SUB : in PART := WHOLE_STRUCT) return INDEX;
        function MIN (S   : in STRUCT;
                      SUB : in PART := WHOLE_STRUCT) return ELEM_TYPE;

        procedure REMOVE_MAX (S   : in out STRUCT;
                              SUB : in PART := WHOLE_STRUCT);
        procedure REMOVE_MIN (S   : in out STRUCT;
                              SUB : in PART := WHOLE_STRUCT);

    end ORDER_OPERATIONS;

    -- Hash Operation
    -- ==============

    generic
        with function HASH (E : in ELEM_TYPE) return INTEGER is <>;
    function HASH_FUNCTION (S : in STRUCT) return INTEGER;

private

    ...

end <ORDERS>;
```

# A.11  Key-Info Orders

**Variant Combinations**

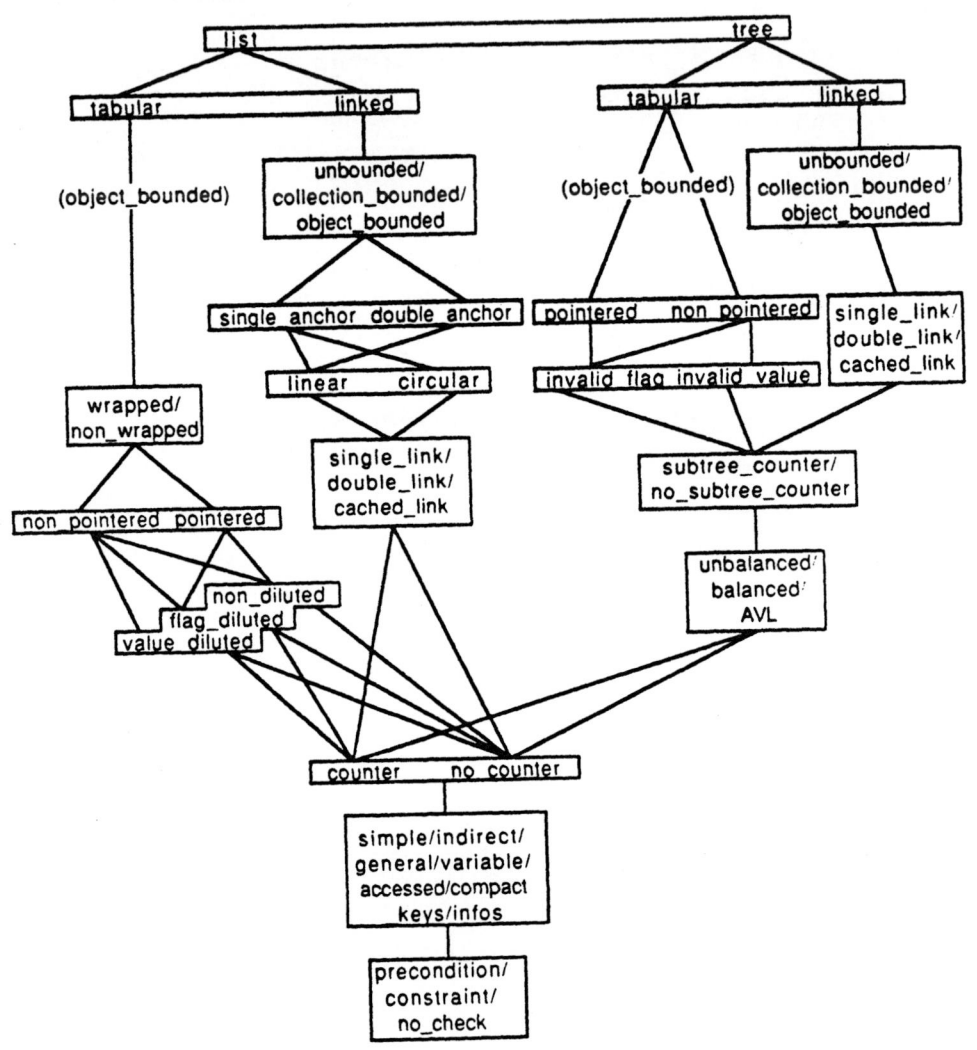

```
generic
    ... see A.2
[ COLLECTION_SIZE : NATURAL; ]
    with function "<" (LEFT, RIGHT : in KEY_TYPE) return BOOLEAN is <>;
package <KEY_INFO_ORDERS> is
```

```
type STRUCT [ (SIZE : NATURAL) ] is limited private;
subtype <KEY_INFO_ORDER> is STRUCT;

-- Indices
-- =======

type INDEX is private;

function NIL return INDEX;

function GET_KEY (S : in STRUCT; I : in INDEX) return KEY_TYPE;

function GET_INFO (S : in STRUCT; I : in INDEX) return INFO_TYPE;

procedure SET_INFO (S    : in out STRUCT;
                    I    : in INDEX;
                    INFO : in INFO_TYPE);

procedure TRANSFER_INFO (TO     : in out INFO_TYPE;
                         FROM   : in out STRUCT;
                         FROM_I : in INDEX);

procedure TRANSFER_INFO (TO   : in out STRUCT;
                         FROM : in out INFO_TYPE;
                         TO_I : in INDEX);

generic
   with procedure MODIFICATION (INFO : in out INFO_TYPE);
procedure MODIFY_INFO (S : in out STRUCT; I : in INDEX);

-- Remove positions
-- ================

type REMOVE_POSITION is private;

function AT_INDEX (I : in INDEX) return REMOVE_POSITION;
function FIRST return REMOVE_POSITION;
function LAST  return REMOVE_POSITION;
```

```
-- Structure parts
-- ===============

type PART is private;

function WHOLE_STRUCT return PART;
function SUBLIST (FROM : in INDEX;
                  TO   : in INDEX := NIL) return PART;

-- Constructor operations
-- ======================

procedure CLEAR (S : in out STRUCT);

procedure INSERT (S    : in out STRUCT;
                  K    : in KEY_TYPE;
                  INFO : in INFO_TYPE);
procedure INSERT (S    : in out STRUCT;
                  K    : in KEY_TYPE;
                  INFO : in INFO_TYPE;
                  I    : out INDEX);
procedure INSERT (S : in out STRUCT;
                  K : in KEY_TYPE;
                  I : out INDEX);

procedure INSERT (TO    : in out STRUCT;
                  FROM  : in STRUCT;
                  SUB   : in PART := WHOLE_STRUCT);

procedure FIND_OR_INSERT (S    : in out STRUCT;
                          K    : in KEY_TYPE;
                          INFO : in INFO_TYPE;
                          I    : out INDEX;
                          FOUND : out BOOLEAN);

procedure REMOVE (S        : in out STRUCT;
                  FROM_POS : in REMOVE_POSITION);

procedure REMOVE (S : in out STRUCT; SUB : in PART);

procedure REMOVE (S : in out STRUCT; K : in KEY_TYPE);
```

```
procedure REMOVE_ALL (S : in out STRUCT; K : in KEY_TYPE);

generic
   with procedure ABSORB (K    : in out KEY_TYPE;
                          INFO : in out INFO_TYPE);
procedure GENERIC_REMOVE (S        : in out STRUCT;
                          FROM_POS : in REMOVE_POSITION);

procedure MOVE (TO       : in out STRUCT;
                FROM     : in out STRUCT;
                FROM_POS : in REMOVE_POSITION);

procedure MOVE (TO     : in out STRUCT;
                FROM   : in out STRUCT;
                SUB    : in PART := WHOLE_STRUCT);

procedure MOVE (TO   : in out STRUCT;
                FROM : in out KEY_TYPE);

procedure MOVE (TO_KEY   : in out KEY_TYPE;
                TO_INFO  : in out INFO_TYPE;
                FROM     : in out STRUCT;
                FROM_POS : in REMOVE_POSITION);

procedure COPY (TO   : in out STRUCT;
                FROM : in STRUCT;
                SUB  : in PART);

procedure COPY (TO : in out STRUCT; FROM : in STRUCT);

procedure TRANSFER (TO, FROM : in out STRUCT; SUB : in PART);

procedure TRANSFER (TO, FROM : in out STRUCT);

procedure SLICE (S : in out STRUCT; SUB : in PART);

procedure DEALLOCATE (S : in out STRUCT);
```

```
-- Selector operations
-- ===================

function COUNT (S   : in STRUCT;
               SUB : in PART := WHOLE_STRUCT) return NATURAL;

function IS_EMPTY (S : in STRUCT) return BOOLEAN;

function FIND (S   : in STRUCT;
              K   : in KEY_TYPE;
              SUB : in PART := WHOLE_STRUCT) return INDEX;

function SKIP (S   : in STRUCT;
              K   : in KEY_TYPE;
              SUB : in PART := WHOLE_STRUCT) return INDEX;

function COUNT_KEY (S   : in STRUCT;
                   K   : in KEY_TYPE;
                   SUB : in PART := WHOLE_STRUCT) return NATURAL;

function IS_KEY (S   : in STRUCT;
                K   : in KEY_TYPE;
                SUB : in PART := WHOLE_STRUCT) return BOOLEAN;

function FIND_INFO (S    : in STRUCT;
                   INFO : in INFO_TYPE;
                   SUB  : in PART := WHOLE_STRUCT) return INDEX;

function SKIP_INFO (S    : in STRUCT;
                   INFO : in INFO_TYPE;
                   SUB  : in PART := WHOLE_STRUCT) return INDEX;

function COUNT_INFO (S    : in STRUCT;
                    INFO : in INFO_TYPE;
                    SUB  : in PART := WHOLE_STRUCT)
                    return NATURAL;

function IS_INFO (S    : in STRUCT;
                 INFO : in INFO_TYPE;
                 SUB  : in PART := WHOLE_STRUCT) return BOOLEAN;

function "=" (LEFT, RIGHT : in STRUCT) return BOOLEAN;
```

```
function EQUAL (LEFT,
               RIGHT : in STRUCT) return BOOLEAN renames "=";

function FIRST (S : in STRUCT) return INDEX;

function FIRST (S : in STRUCT) return KEY_TYPE;

function LAST (S : in STRUCT) return INDEX;

function LAST (S : in STRUCT) return KEY_TYPE;

function NEXT (S        : in STRUCT;
               I        : in INDEX;
               CIRCULAR : in BOOLEAN := FALSE) return INDEX;

function PREVIOUS (S        : in STRUCT;
                   I        : in INDEX;
                   CIRCULAR : in BOOLEAN := FALSE) return INDEX;

-- Access by position count
-- =======================

function INDEX_VAL (S : in STRUCT; P : in POSITIVE) return INDEX;

function INDEX_POS (S : in STRUCT; I : in INDEX) return POSITIVE;

function GET_KEY (S : in STRUCT; P : in POSITIVE) return KEY_TYPE;

function GET_INFO (S : in STRUCT;
                   P : in POSITIVE) return INFO_TYPE;

procedure SET_INFO (S    : in out STRUCT;
                    P    : in POSITIVE;
                    INFO : in INFO_TYPE);

procedure TRANSFER_INFO (TO    : in out INFO_TYPE;
                         FROM  : in out STRUCT;
                         FROM_P : in POSITIVE);

procedure TRANSFER_INFO (TO   : in out STRUCT;
                         FROM : in out INFO_TYPE;
                         TO_P : in POSITIVE);
```

```ada
generic
   with procedure MODIFICATION (INFO : in out INFO_TYPE);
procedure MODIFY_INFO_BY_POS (S : in out STRUCT; P : in POSITIVE);

-- Iteration
-- =========

type ITERATION_ORDER is (FROM_FIRST, FROM_LAST, DONT_CARE);

package DEFAULTS is
   function TRUE  (K : in KEY_TYPE) return BOOLEAN;
   function FALSE (K : in KEY_TYPE) return BOOLEAN;
   function TRUE  (INFO : in INFO_TYPE) return BOOLEAN;
   function FALSE (INFO : in INFO_TYPE) return BOOLEAN;
   function TRUE  (K    : in KEY_TYPE;
                   INFO : in INFO_TYPE) return BOOLEAN;
   function FALSE (K    : in KEY_TYPE;
                   INFO : in INFO_TYPE) return BOOLEAN;
   function TRUE  (S : in STRUCT; I : in INDEX) return BOOLEAN;
   function FALSE (S : in STRUCT; I : in INDEX) return BOOLEAN;

   procedure NONE (K : in KEY_TYPE; INFO : in INFO_TYPE);
   procedure NONE (K    : in KEY_TYPE;
                   INFO : in INFO_TYPE;
                   I    : in INDEX);
   procedure NONE1 (K : in KEY_TYPE; INFO : in out INFO_TYPE);
   procedure NONE1 (K    : in KEY_TYPE;
                    INFO : in out INFO_TYPE;
                    I    : in INDEX);
end DEFAULTS;
use DEFAULTS;
```

```
generic
   with procedure ACTION
                     (K    : in KEY_TYPE;
                      INFO : in out INFO_TYPE) is NONE1;
   with function  SELECTION
                     (K    : in KEY_TYPE;
                      INFO : in INFO_TYPE) return BOOLEAN is TRUE;
   with function  UNTIL
                     (S : in STRUCT;
                      I : in INDEX) return BOOLEAN is FALSE;
   with procedure ACTION_WITH_INDEX
                     (K    : in KEY_TYPE;
                      INFO : in out INFO_TYPE;
                      I    : in INDEX) is NONE1;
   with function  SELECTION_WITH_INDEX
                     (S : in STRUCT;
                      I : in INDEX) return BOOLEAN is TRUE;
   procedure APPLY (S   : in out STRUCT;
                    SUB : in PART := WHOLE_STRUCT;
                    ORD : in ITERATION_ORDER := FROM_FIRST);


generic
   with procedure ACTION
                     (K    : in KEY_TYPE;
                      INFO : in INFO_TYPE) is NONE;
   with function  SELECTION
                     (K    : in KEY_TYPE;
                      INFO : in INFO_TYPE) return BOOLEAN is TRUE;
   with function  UNTIL
                     (S : in STRUCT;
                      I : in INDEX) return BOOLEAN is FALSE;
   with procedure ACTION_WITH_INDEX
                     (K    : in KEY_TYPE;
                      INFO : in INFO_TYPE;
                      I    : in INDEX) is NONE;
   with function  SELECTION_WITH_INDEX
                     (S : in STRUCT;
                      I : in INDEX) return BOOLEAN is TRUE;
   procedure ITERATE (S   : in STRUCT;
                      SUB : in PART := WHOLE_STRUCT;
                      ORD : in ITERATION_ORDER := FROM_FIRST);
```

```
generic
   with procedure ACTION (S : in out STRUCT; I : in INDEX);
   with function SELECTION
                   (S : in STRUCT;
                    I : in INDEX) return BOOLEAN is TRUE;
   with function UNTIL
                   (S : in STRUCT;
                    I : in INDEX) return BOOLEAN is FALSE;
procedure ITERATE_MOVE (S   : in STRUCT;
                        SUB : in PART := WHOLE_STRUCT;
                        ORD : in ITERATION_ORDER := FROM_FIRST);


-- Reduction
-- =========

generic
   with function  OPERATION
                   (LEFT, RIGHT : in KEY_TYPE) return KEY_TYPE;
   with function  SELECTION
                   (K : in KEY_TYPE) return BOOLEAN is TRUE;
   with function  UNTIL
                   (S : in STRUCT;
                    I : in INDEX) return BOOLEAN is FALSE;
function REDUCE (S   : in STRUCT;
                 SUB : in PART := WHOLE_STRUCT;
                 ORD : in ITERATION_ORDER := DONT_CARE)
               return KEY_TYPE;


generic
   with function  OPERATION
                   (LEFT, RIGHT : in KEY_TYPE) return KEY_TYPE;
   with function  UNIT return KEY_TYPE;
   with function  SELECTION
                   (K : in KEY_TYPE) return BOOLEAN is TRUE;
   with function  UNTIL
                   (S : in STRUCT;
                    I : in INDEX) return BOOLEAN is FALSE;
function UREDUCE (S   : in STRUCT;
                  SUB : in PART := WHOLE_STRUCT;
                  ORD : in ITERATION_ORDER := DONT_CARE)
               return KEY_TYPE;
```

```
generic
   type RESULT_TYPE is limited private;
   with function  OPERATION
                      (LEFT  : in RESULT_TYPE;
                       RIGHT : in KEY_TYPE) return RESULT_TYPE;
   with function  UNIT return RESULT_TYPE;
   with function  SELECTION
                      (K : in KEY_TYPE) return BOOLEAN is TRUE;
   with function  UNTIL
                      (S : in STRUCT;
                       I : in INDEX) return BOOLEAN is FALSE;
function AREDUCE (S   : in STRUCT;
                  SUB : in PART := WHOLE_STRUCT;
                  ORD : in ITERATION_ORDER := DONT_CARE)
                return RESULT_TYPE;


generic
   with function  OPERATION
                      (LEFT, RIGHT : in INFO_TYPE) return INFO_TYPE;
   with function  SELECTION
                      (INFO : in INFO_TYPE) return BOOLEAN is TRUE;
   with function  UNTIL
                      (S : in STRUCT;
                       I : in INDEX) return BOOLEAN is FALSE;
function REDUCE_INFO (S   : in STRUCT;
                      SUB : in PART := WHOLE_STRUCT;
                      ORD : in ITERATION_ORDER := DONT_CARE)
                    return INFO_TYPE;


generic
   with function  OPERATION
                      (LEFT, RIGHT : in INFO_TYPE) return INFO_TYPE;
   with function  UNIT return INFO_TYPE;
   with function  SELECTION
                      (INFO : in INFO_TYPE) return BOOLEAN is TRUE;
   with function  UNTIL
                      (S : in STRUCT;
                       I : in INDEX) return BOOLEAN is FALSE;
function UREDUCE_INFO (S   : in STRUCT;
                       SUB : in PART := WHOLE_STRUCT;
                       ORD : in ITERATION_ORDER := DONT_CARE)
                     return INFO_TYPE;
```

```
generic
   type RESULT_TYPE is limited private;
   with function  OPERATION
                     (LEFT  : in RESULT_TYPE;
                      RIGHT : in INFO_TYPE) return RESULT_TYPE;
   with function  UNIT return RESULT_TYPE;
   with function  SELECTION
                     (INFO : in INFO_TYPE) return BOOLEAN is TRUE;
   with function  UNTIL
                     (S : in STRUCT;
                      I : in INDEX) return BOOLEAN is FALSE;
function AREDUCE_INFO (S   : in STRUCT;
                       SUB : in PART := WHOLE_STRUCT;
                       ORD : in ITERATION_ORDER := DONT_CARE)
                       return RESULT_TYPE;

-- Find, skip and count
-- ====================

generic
   with function PROPERTY (K : in KEY_TYPE) return BOOLEAN;
function FIND_PROPERTY
            (S   : in STRUCT;
             SUB : in PART := WHOLE_STRUCT;
             ORD : in ITERATION_ORDER := DONT_CARE) return INDEX;

generic
   with function PROPERTY (K : in KEY_TYPE) return BOOLEAN;
function SKIP_PROPERTY
            (S   : in STRUCT;
             SUB : in PART := WHOLE_STRUCT;
             ORD : in ITERATION_ORDER := DONT_CARE) return INDEX;

generic
   with function PROPERTY (K : in KEY_TYPE) return BOOLEAN;
function COUNT_PROPERTY
            (S   : in STRUCT;
             SUB : in PART := WHOLE_STRUCT;
             ORD : in ITERATION_ORDER := DONT_CARE) return NATURAL;
```

```
generic
   with function PROPERTY (INFO : in INFO_TYPE) return BOOLEAN;
function FIND_INFO_PROPERTY
             (S   : in STRUCT;
              SUB : in PART := WHOLE_STRUCT;
              ORD : in ITERATION_ORDER := DONT_CARE) return INDEX;


generic
   with function PROPERTY (INFO : in INFO_TYPE) return BOOLEAN;
function SKIP_INFO_PROPERTY
             (S   : in STRUCT;
              SUB : in PART := WHOLE_STRUCT;
              ORD : in ITERATION_ORDER := DONT_CARE) return INDEX;


generic
   with function PROPERTY (INFO : in INFO_TYPE) return BOOLEAN;
function COUNT_INFO_PROPERTY
             (S   : in STRUCT;
              SUB : in PART := WHOLE_STRUCT;
              ORD : in ITERATION_ORDER := DONT_CARE) return NATURAL;


-- Existential and universal quantification
-- =======================================


generic
   with function PROPERTY (K : in KEY_TYPE) return BOOLEAN;
function EXISTS (S   : in STRUCT;
                 SUB : in PART := WHOLE_STRUCT;
                 ORD : in ITERATION_ORDER := DONT_CARE)
              return BOOLEAN;


generic
   with function PROPERTY (K : in KEY_TYPE) return BOOLEAN;
function FORALL (S   : in STRUCT;
                 SUB : in PART := WHOLE_STRUCT;
                 ORD : in ITERATION_ORDER := DONT_CARE)
              return BOOLEAN;
```

```
    generic
       with function PROPERTY (INFO : in INFO_TYPE) return BOOLEAN;
    function EXISTS_INFO (S   : in STRUCT;
                          SUB : in PART := WHOLE_STRUCT;
                          ORD : in ITERATION_ORDER := DONT_CARE)
                      return BOOLEAN;

    generic
       with function PROPERTY (INFO : in INFO_TYPE) return BOOLEAN;
    function FORALL_INFO (S   : in STRUCT;
                          SUB : in PART := WHOLE_STRUCT;
                          ORD : in ITERATION_ORDER := DONT_CARE)
                      return BOOLEAN;

    -- Order dependent operations
    -- =========================

    generic
       with function COMPARE (LEFT, RIGHT : in INFO_TYPE)
                          return ORDER_RELATION is <>;
    package ORDER_OPERATIONS is

       -- Lexicographic comparison
       -- ========================

       function COMPARE (LEFT, RIGHT : in STRUCT)
                      return ORDER_RELATION;

       function "<"  (LEFT, RIGHT : in STRUCT) return BOOLEAN;
       function "<=" (LEFT, RIGHT : in STRUCT) return BOOLEAN;
       function ">"  (LEFT, RIGHT : in STRUCT) return BOOLEAN;
       function ">=" (LEFT, RIGHT : in STRUCT) return BOOLEAN;

       -- Maximum and minimum
       -- ===================

       function MAX (S   : in STRUCT;
                     SUB : in PART := WHOLE_STRUCT) return INDEX;
       function MAX (S   : in STRUCT;
                     SUB : in PART := WHOLE_STRUCT) return KEY_TYPE;
```

```
      function MIN (S   : in STRUCT;
                    SUB : in PART := WHOLE_STRUCT) return INDEX;
      function MIN (S   : in STRUCT;
                    SUB : in PART := WHOLE_STRUCT) return KEY_TYPE;

      procedure REMOVE_MAX (S   : in out STRUCT;
                            SUB : in PART := WHOLE_STRUCT);
      procedure REMOVE_MIN (S   : in out STRUCT;
                            SUB : in PART := WHOLE_STRUCT);

  end ORDER_OPERATIONS;

  -- Hash Operation
  -- ==============

  generic
      with function HASH (K : in KEY_TYPE) return INTEGER is <>;
      with function HASH (INFO : in INFO_TYPE) return INTEGER is <>;
  function HASH_FUNCTION (S : in STRUCT) return INTEGER;

private

      ...


end <KEY_INFO_ORDERS>;
```

# A.12    Sets

## Variant Combinations

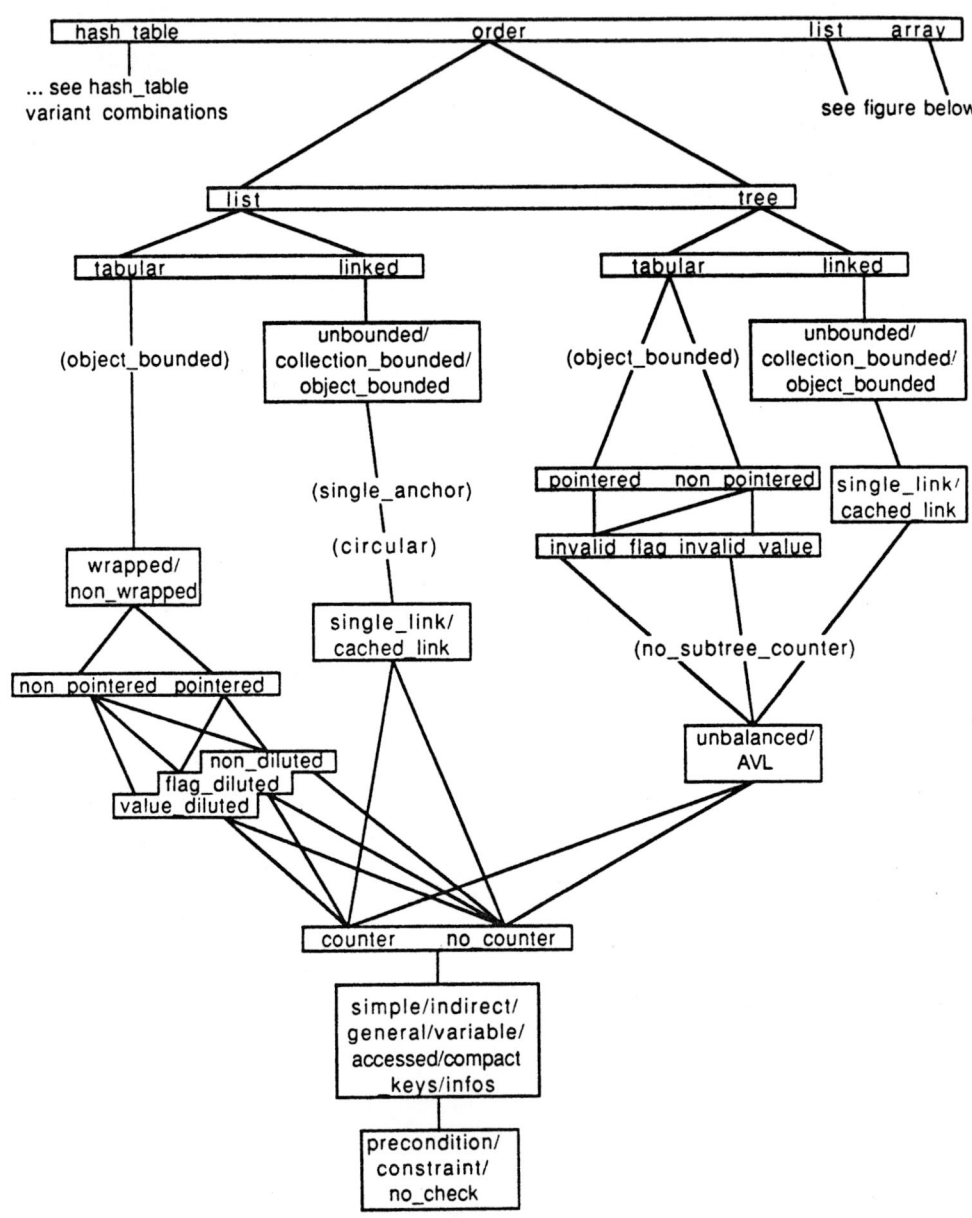

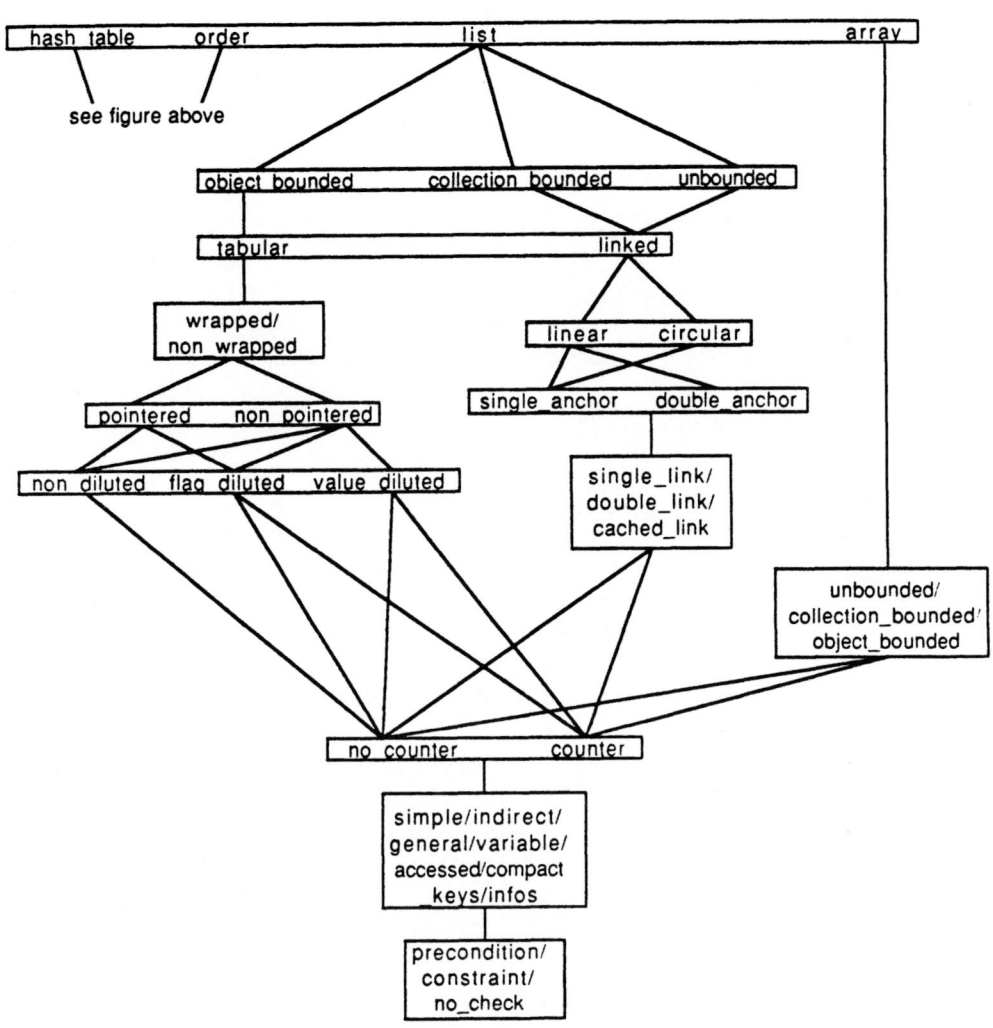

```
generic
    ... see A.2
  [ COLLECTION_SIZE : NATURAL; ]
  [ with function "<" (LEFT,
                       RIGHT : in ELEM_TYPE) return BOOLEAN is <>; ]
  [ HASH_TABLE_SIZE : NATURAL;
    with function HASH (E : in ELEM_TYPE) return NATURAL is <>; ]
package <SETS> is
```

```
type STRUCT [ (SIZE : NATURAL) ] is limited private;
subtype <SET> is STRUCT;


-- Indices
-- =======


type INDEX is private;

function NIL return INDEX;

function GET_ELEM  (S : in STRUCT; I : in INDEX) return ELEM_TYPE;

-- Insert and remove positions
-- ===========================

subtype REMOVE_POSITION is INDEX;

-- Set specific operations
-- =======================

procedure UNION (LEFT : in out STRUCT; RIGHT : in STRUCT);
procedure INTERSECTION (LEFT : in out STRUCT; RIGHT : in STRUCT);
procedure DIFFERENCE (LEFT : in out STRUCT; RIGHT : in STRUCT);

function SUBSET (LEFT, RIGHT : in STRUCT) return BOOLEAN;
function PROPER_SUBSET (LEFT, RIGHT : in STRUCT) return BOOLEAN;
function SUPERSET (LEFT, RIGHT : in STRUCT) return BOOLEAN;
function PROPER_SUPERSET (LEFT, RIGHT : in STRUCT) return BOOLEAN;

-- Constructor operations
-- ======================

procedure CLEAR (S : in out STRUCT);

procedure INSERT (S : in out STRUCT; E : in ELEM_TYPE);
procedure INSERT (S : in out STRUCT;
                  E : in ELEM_TYPE;
                  I : out INDEX);

procedure INSERT (TO : in out STRUCT; FROM : in STRUCT);
```

```
    procedure FIND_OR_INSERT (S     : in out STRUCT;
                              E     : in ELEM_TYPE;
                              I     : out INDEX;
                              FOUND : out BOOLEAN);


    procedure REMOVE (S        : in out STRUCT;
                      FROM_POS : in REMOVE_POSITION);


    procedure REMOVE (S : in out STRUCT; E : in ELEM_TYPE);


    procedure REMOVE_ALL (S : in out STRUCT; E : in ELEM_TYPE);


    generic
       with procedure ABSORB (E : in out ELEM_TYPE);
    procedure GENERIC_REMOVE (S        : in out STRUCT;
                              FROM_POS : in REMOVE_POSITION);


    procedure MOVE (TO       : in out STRUCT;
                    FROM     : in out STRUCT;
                    FROM_POS : in REMOVE_POSITION);


    procedure MOVE (TO   : in out STRUCT;
                    FROM : in out ELEM_TYPE);


    procedure MOVE (TO       : in out ELEM_TYPE;
                    FROM     : in out STRUCT;
                    FROM_POS : in REMOVE_POSITION);


    procedure MOVE (TO, FROM : in out STRUCT);

    procedure COPY (TO : in out STRUCT; FROM : in STRUCT);

    procedure TRANSFER (TO : in out STRUCT; FROM : in STRUCT);

    procedure DEALLOCATE (S : in out STRUCT);

    -- Selector operations
    -- ====================

    function COUNT (S : in STRUCT) return NATURAL;

    function IS_EMPTY (S : in STRUCT) return BOOLEAN;
```

```
function FIND (S : in STRUCT; E : in ELEM_TYPE) return INDEX;

function COUNT_ELEM (S : in STRUCT;
                     E : in ELEM_TYPE) return NATURAL;

function IS_ELEM (S : in STRUCT; E : in ELEM_TYPE) return BOOLEAN;

function "=" (LEFT, RIGHT : in STRUCT) return BOOLEAN;
function EQUAL (LEFT,
               RIGHT : in STRUCT) return BOOLEAN renames "=";

-- Iteration
-- =========

package DEFAULTS is
   function TRUE  (E : in ELEM_TYPE) return BOOLEAN;
   function FALSE (E : in ELEM_TYPE) return BOOLEAN;
   function TRUE  (S : in STRUCT; I : in INDEX) return BOOLEAN;
   function FALSE (S : in STRUCT; I : in INDEX) return BOOLEAN;

   procedure NONE (E : in ELEM_TYPE);
   procedure NONE (E : in ELEM_TYPE; I : in INDEX);
   procedure NONE1 (E : in out ELEM_TYPE);
   procedure NONE1 (E : in out ELEM_TYPE; I : in INDEX);
end DEFAULTS;
use DEFAULTS;

generic
   with procedure ACTION (E : in ELEM_TYPE) is NONE;
   with function  SELECTION
                  (E : in ELEM_TYPE) return BOOLEAN is TRUE;
   with function  UNTIL
                  (S : in STRUCT;
                   I : in INDEX) return BOOLEAN is FALSE;
   with procedure ACTION_WITH_INDEX
                  (E : in ELEM_TYPE;
                   I : in INDEX) is NONE;
   with function  SELECTION_WITH_INDEX
                  (S : in STRUCT;
                   I : in INDEX) return BOOLEAN is TRUE;
procedure ITERATE (S : in STRUCT);
```

```
generic
   with procedure ACTION (S : in out STRUCT; I : in INDEX);
   with function  SELECTION
                     (S : in STRUCT;
                      I : in INDEX) return BOOLEAN is TRUE;
   with function  UNTIL
                     (S : in STRUCT;
                      I : in INDEX) return BOOLEAN is FALSE;
procedure ITERATE_MOVE (S : in out STRUCT);

-- Reduction
-- =========

generic
   with function  OPERATION
                     (LEFT, RIGHT : in ELEM_TYPE) return ELEM_TYPE;
   with function  SELECTION
                     (E : in ELEM_TYPE) return BOOLEAN is TRUE;
   with function  UNTIL
                     (S : in STRUCT;
                      I : in INDEX) return BOOLEAN is FALSE;
function REDUCE (S : in STRUCT) return ELEM_TYPE;

generic
   with function  OPERATION
                     (LEFT, RIGHT : in ELEM_TYPE) return ELEM_TYPE;
   with function  UNIT return ELEM_TYPE;
   with function  SELECTION
                     (E : in ELEM_TYPE) return BOOLEAN is TRUE;
   with function  UNTIL
                     (S : in STRUCT;
                      I : in INDEX) return BOOLEAN is FALSE;
function UREDUCE (S : in STRUCT) return ELEM_TYPE;
```

```
generic
   type RESULT_TYPE is private;
   with function  OPERATION
                     (LEFT  : in RESULT_TYPE;
                      RIGHT : in ELEM_TYPE) return RESULT_TYPE;
   with function  UNIT return RESULT_TYPE;
   with function  SELECTION
                     (E : in ELEM_TYPE) return BOOLEAN is TRUE;
   with function  UNTIL
                     (S : in STRUCT;
                      I : in INDEX) return BOOLEAN is FALSE;
function AREDUCE (S : in STRUCT) return RESULT_TYPE;

-- Find and count
-- ==============

generic
   with function PROPERTY (E : in ELEM_TYPE) return BOOLEAN;
function FIND_PROPERTY (S : in STRUCT) return INDEX;

generic
   with function PROPERTY (E : in ELEM_TYPE) return BOOLEAN;
function COUNT_PROPERTY (S : in STRUCT) return NATURAL;

-- Existential and universal quantification
-- ========================================

generic
   with function PROPERTY (E : in ELEM_TYPE) return BOOLEAN;
function EXISTS (S : in STRUCT) return BOOLEAN;

generic
   with function PROPERTY (E : in ELEM_TYPE) return BOOLEAN;
function FORALL (S : in STRUCT) return BOOLEAN;

-- Order dependent operations
-- ==========================

generic
   with function COMPARE (LEFT, RIGHT : in ELEM_TYPE)
                     return ORDER_RELATION is <>;
package ORDER_OPERATIONS is
```

```
     -- Lexicographic comparison
     -- =========================

     function COMPARE (LEFT, RIGHT : in STRUCT)
                       return ORDER_RELATION;

     function "<"  (LEFT, RIGHT : in STRUCT) return BOOLEAN;
     function "<=" (LEFT, RIGHT : in STRUCT) return BOOLEAN;
     function ">"  (LEFT, RIGHT : in STRUCT) return BOOLEAN;
     function ">=" (LEFT, RIGHT : in STRUCT) return BOOLEAN;

     -- Maximum and minimum
     -- ===================

     function MAX (S : in STRUCT) return INDEX;
     function MAX (S : in STRUCT) return ELEM_TYPE;

     function MIN (S : in STRUCT) return INDEX;
     function MIN (S : in STRUCT) return ELEM_TYPE;

     procedure REMOVE_MAX (S : in out STRUCT);
     procedure REMOVE_MIN (S : in out STRUCT);
  end ORDER_OPERATIONS;

  -- Hash Operation
  -- ==============

  generic
     with function HASH (E : in ELEM_TYPE)
                      return INTEGER [ is <SETS>.HASH ] ;
  function HASH_FUNCTION (S : in STRUCT) return INTEGER;

private

  ...

end <SETS>;
```

# A.13   Maps

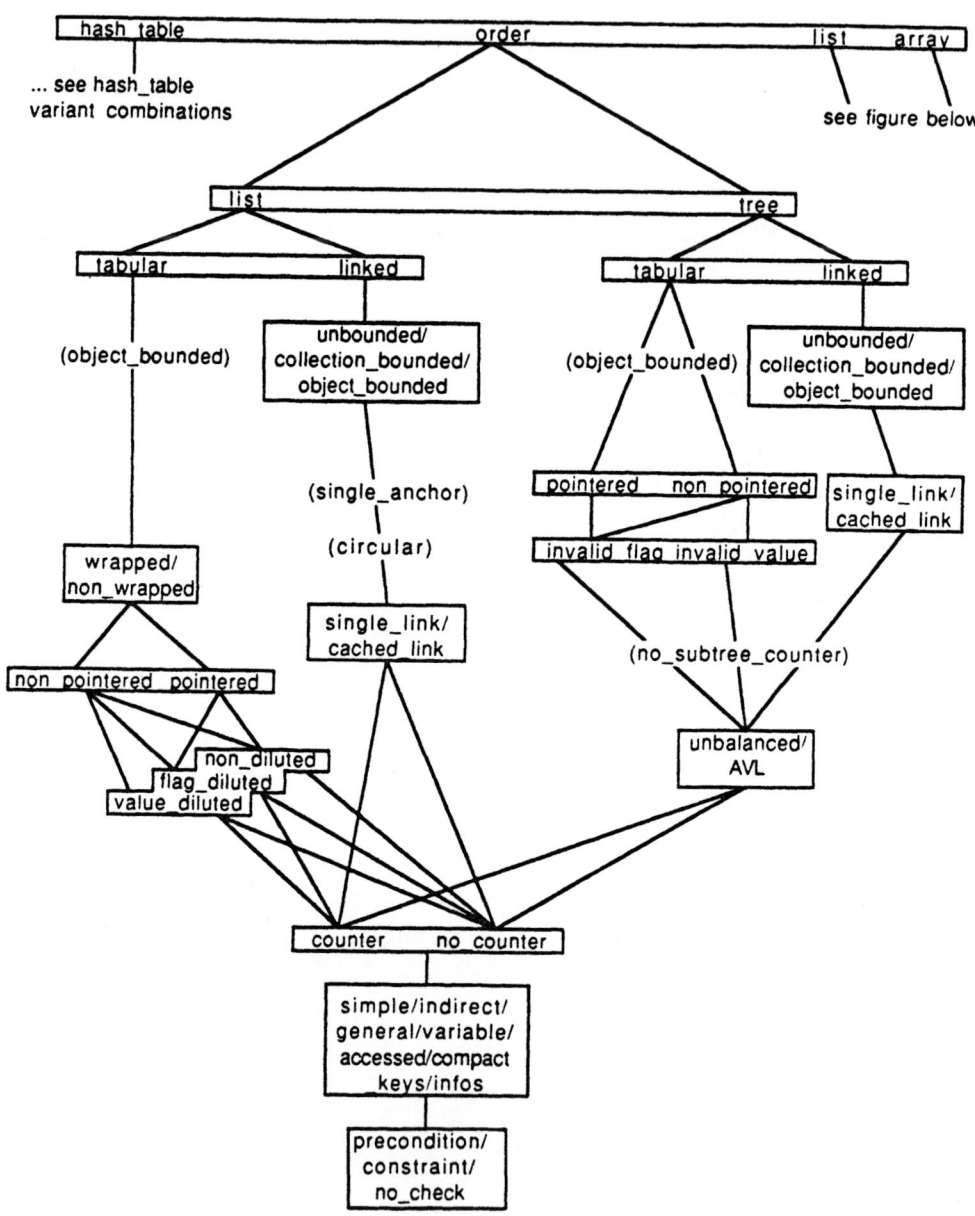

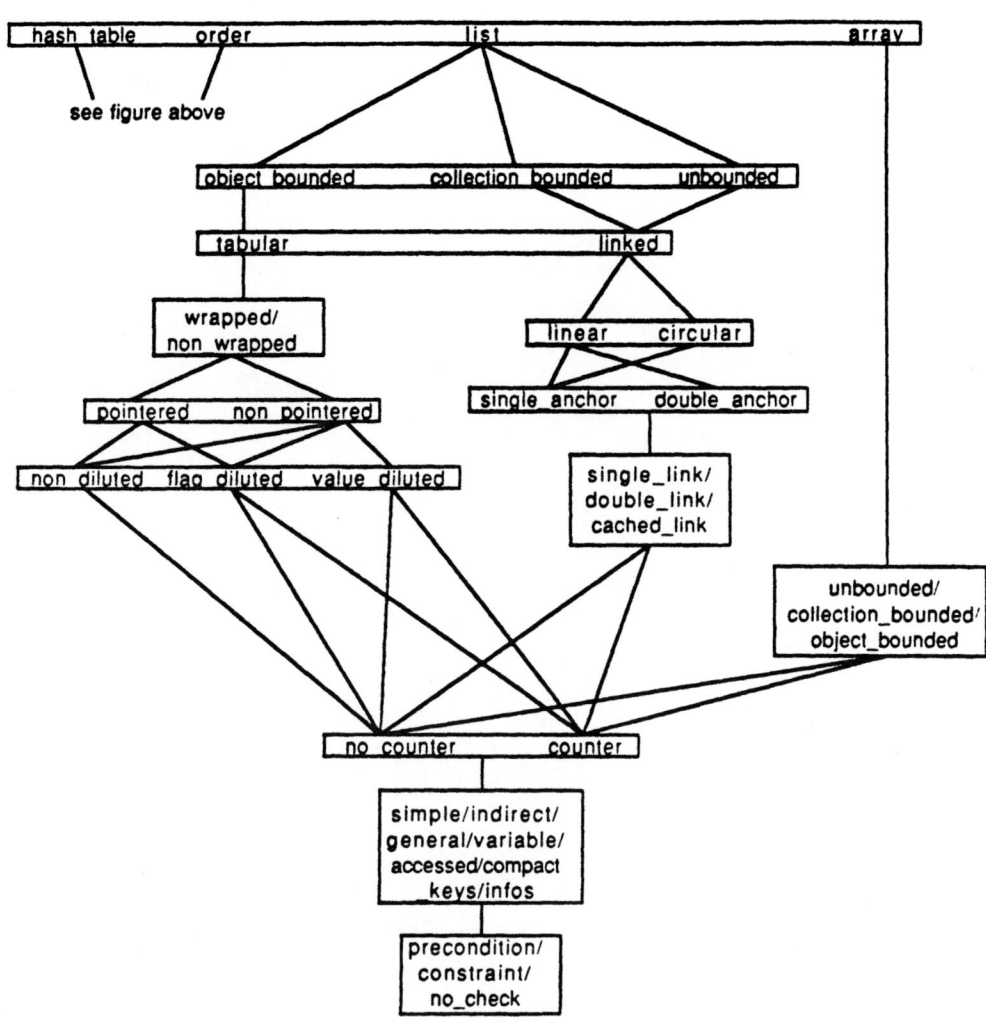

```
generic
    ... see A.2
  [ COLLECTION_SIZE : NATURAL; ]
  [ with function "<" (LEFT,
                       RIGHT : in KEY_TYPE) return BOOLEAN is <>; ]
  [ HASH_TABLE_SIZE : NATURAL;
    with function HASH (K : in KEY_TYPE) return NATURAL is <>; ]
package <MAPS> is
```

```
type STRUCT [ (SIZE : NATURAL) ] is limited private;
subtype <MAP> is STRUCT;

-- Indices
-- =======

type INDEX is private;

function NIL return INDEX;

function GET_KEY  (S : in STRUCT; I : in INDEX) return KEY_TYPE;

function GET_INFO (S : in STRUCT; I : in INDEX) return INFO_TYPE;

procedure SET_INFO (S    : in out STRUCT;
                    I    : in INDEX;
                    INFO : in INFO_TYPE);

procedure TRANSFER_INFO (TO     : in out INFO_TYPE;
                         FROM   : in out STRUCT;
                         FROM_I : in INDEX);

procedure TRANSFER_INFO (TO   : in out STRUCT;
                         FROM : in out INFO_TYPE;
                         TO_I : in INDEX);

generic
   with procedure MODIFICATION (INFO : in out INFO_TYPE);
procedure MODIFY_INFO (S : in out STRUCT; I : in INDEX);

-- Insert and remove positions
-- ===========================

subtype REMOVE_POSITION is INDEX;

-- Map specific operations
-- =======================

procedure UNION (LEFT : in out STRUCT; RIGHT : in STRUCT);
procedure INTERSECTION (LEFT : in out STRUCT; RIGHT : in STRUCT);
procedure DIFFERENCE (LEFT : in out STRUCT; RIGHT : in STRUCT);
```

```
function SUBSET (LEFT, RIGHT : in STRUCT) return BOOLEAN;
function PROPER_SUBSET (LEFT, RIGHT : in STRUCT) return BOOLEAN;
function SUPERSET (LEFT, RIGHT : in STRUCT) return BOOLEAN;
function PROPER_SUPERSET (LEFT, RIGHT : in STRUCT) return BOOLEAN;

-- Constructor operations
-- ======================

procedure CLEAR (S : in out STRUCT);

procedure INSERT (S    : in out STRUCT;
                  K    : in KEY_TYPE;
                  INFO : in INFO_TYPE);
procedure INSERT (S    : in out STRUCT;
                  K    : in KEY_TYPE;
                  INFO : in INFO_TYPE;
                  I    : out INDEX);
procedure INSERT (S : in out STRUCT;
                  K : in KEY_TYPE;
                  I : out INDEX);

procedure INSERT (TO : in out STRUCT; FROM : in STRUCT);

procedure FIND_OR_INSERT (S     : in out STRUCT;
                          K     : in KEY_TYPE;
                          I     : out INDEX;
                          FOUND : out BOOLEAN);

procedure REMOVE (S        : in out STRUCT;
                  FROM_POS : in REMOVE_POSITION);

procedure REMOVE (S : in out STRUCT; K : in KEY_TYPE);

procedure REMOVE_ALL (S : in out STRUCT; K : in KEY_TYPE);

generic
   with procedure ABSORB (K    : in out KEY_TYPE;
                          INFO : in out INFO_TYPE);
procedure GENERIC_REMOVE (S        : in out STRUCT;
                          FROM_POS : in REMOVE_POSITION);
```

```
procedure MOVE (TO       : in out STRUCT;
                FROM     : in out STRUCT;
                FROM_POS : in REMOVE_POSITION);

procedure MOVE (TO        : in out STRUCT;
                FROM_KEY  : in out KEY_TYPE;
                FROM_INFO : in out INFO_TYPE);

procedure MOVE (TO_KEY   : in out KEY_TYPE;
                TO_INFO  : in out INFO_TYPE;
                FROM     : in out STRUCT;
                FROM_POS : in REMOVE_POSITION);

procedure MOVE (TO, FROM : in out STRUCT);

procedure COPY (TO : in out STRUCT; FROM : in STRUCT);

procedure TRANSFER (TO, FROM : in out STRUCT);

procedure DEALLOCATE (S : in out STRUCT);

-- Selector operations
-- ===================

function COUNT (S : in STRUCT) return NATURAL;

function IS_EMPTY (S : in STRUCT) return BOOLEAN;

function FIND (S : in STRUCT; K : in KEY_TYPE) return INDEX;

function COUNT_KEY (S : in STRUCT; K : in KEY_TYPE) return NATURAL;

function IS_KEY (S : in STRUCT; K : in KEY_TYPE) return BOOLEAN;

function FIND_INFO (S    : in STRUCT;
                    INFO : in INFO_TYPE) return INDEX;

function COUNT_INFO (S    : in STRUCT;
                     INFO : in INFO_TYPE) return NATURAL;
```

```
   function IS_INFO (S    : in STRUCT;
                     INFO : in INFO_TYPE) return BOOLEAN;

   function "=" (LEFT, RIGHT : in STRUCT) return BOOLEAN;
   function EQUAL (LEFT,
                   RIGHT : in STRUCT) return BOOLEAN renames "=";

   -- Iteration
   -- =========

   package DEFAULTS is
      function TRUE  (K : in KEY_TYPE) return BOOLEAN;
      function FALSE (K : in KEY_TYPE) return BOOLEAN;
      function TRUE  (INFO : in INFO_TYPE) return BOOLEAN;
      function FALSE (INFO : in INFO_TYPE) return BOOLEAN;
      function TRUE  (K    : in KEY_TYPE;
                      INFO : in INFO_TYPE) return BOOLEAN;
      function FALSE (K    : in KEY_TYPE;
                      INFO : in INFO_TYPE) return BOOLEAN;
      function TRUE  (S : in STRUCT; I : in INDEX) return BOOLEAN;
      function FALSE (S : in STRUCT; I : in INDEX) return BOOLEAN;

      procedure NONE (K : in KEY_TYPE; INFO : in INFO_TYPE);
      procedure NONE (K    : in KEY_TYPE;
                      INFO : in INFO_TYPE; I : in INDEX);
      procedure NONE1 (K : in KEY_TYPE; INFO : in out INFO_TYPE);
      procedure NONE1 (K    : in KEY_TYPE;
                       INFO : in out INFO_TYPE; I : in INDEX);
   end DEFAULTS;
   use DEFAULTS;
```

```ada
generic
   with procedure ACTION
                     (K    : in KEY_TYPE;
                      INFO : in out INFO_TYPE) is NONE1;
   with function  SELECTION
                     (K    : in KEY_TYPE;
                      INFO : in INFO_TYPE) return BOOLEAN is TRUE;
   with function  UNTIL
                     (S : in STRUCT;
                      I : in INDEX) return BOOLEAN is FALSE;
   with procedure ACTION_WITH_INDEX
                     (K    : in KEY_TYPE;
                      INFO : in out INFO_TYPE;
                      I    : in INDEX) is NONE1;
   with function  SELECTION_WITH_INDEX
                     (S : in STRUCT;
                      I : in INDEX) return BOOLEAN is TRUE;
procedure APPLY (S : in out STRUCT);

generic
   with procedure ACTION
                     (K    : in KEY_TYPE;
                      INFO : in INFO_TYPE) is NONE;
   with function  SELECTION
                     (K    : in KEY_TYPE;
                      INFO : in INFO_TYPE) return BOOLEAN is TRUE;
   with function  UNTIL
                     (S : in STRUCT;
                      I : in INDEX) return BOOLEAN is FALSE;
   with procedure ACTION_WITH_INDEX
                     (K    : in KEY_TYPE;
                      INFO : in INFO_TYPE;
                      I    : in INDEX) is NONE;
   with function  SELECTION_WITH_INDEX
                     (S : in STRUCT;
                      I : in INDEX) return BOOLEAN is TRUE;
procedure ITERATE (S : in STRUCT);
```

```
generic
   with procedure ACTION (S : in out STRUCT; I : in INDEX);
   with function SELECTION
                    (S : in STRUCT;
                     I : in INDEX) return BOOLEAN is TRUE;
   with function UNTIL
                    (S : in STRUCT;
                     I : in INDEX) return BOOLEAN is FALSE;
procedure ITERATE_MOVE (S : in STRUCT);

-- Reduction
-- =========

generic
   with function  OPERATION
                    (LEFT, RIGHT : in KEY_TYPE) return KEY_TYPE;
   with function  SELECTION
                    (K : in KEY_TYPE) return BOOLEAN is TRUE;
   with function  UNTIL
                    (S : in STRUCT;
                     I : in INDEX) return BOOLEAN is FALSE;
function REDUCE (S : in STRUCT) return KEY_TYPE;

generic
   with function  OPERATION
                    (LEFT, RIGHT : in KEY_TYPE) return KEY_TYPE;
   with function  UNIT return KEY_TYPE;
   with function  SELECTION
                    (K : in KEY_TYPE) return BOOLEAN is TRUE;
   with function  UNTIL
                    (S : in STRUCT;
                     I : in INDEX) return BOOLEAN is FALSE;
function UREDUCE (S : in STRUCT) return KEY_TYPE;
```

```
generic
   type RESULT_TYPE is limited private;
   with function  OPERATION
                      (LEFT  : in RESULT_TYPE;
                       RIGHT : in KEY_TYPE) return RESULT_TYPE;
   with function  UNIT return RESULT_TYPE;
   with function  SELECTION
                      (K : in KEY_TYPE) return BOOLEAN is TRUE;
   with function  UNTIL
                      (S : in STRUCT;
                       I : in INDEX) return BOOLEAN is FALSE;
function AREDUCE (S : in STRUCT) return RESULT_TYPE;


generic
   with function  OPERATION
                      (LEFT, RIGHT : in INFO_TYPE) return INFO_TYPE;
   with function  SELECTION
                      (INFO : in INFO_TYPE) return BOOLEAN is TRUE;
   with function  UNTIL
                      (S : in STRUCT;
                       I : in INDEX) return BOOLEAN is FALSE;
function REDUCE_INFO (S : in STRUCT) return INFO_TYPE;


generic
   with function  OPERATION
                      (LEFT, RIGHT : in INFO_TYPE) return INFO_TYPE;
   with function  UNIT return INFO_TYPE;
   with function  SELECTION
                      (INFO : in INFO_TYPE) return BOOLEAN is TRUE;
   with function  UNTIL
                      (S : in STRUCT;
                       I : in INDEX) return BOOLEAN is FALSE;
function UREDUCE_INFO (S : in STRUCT) return INFO_TYPE;
```

```
generic
   type RESULT_TYPE is limited private;
   with function  OPERATION
                       (LEFT  : in RESULT_TYPE;
                        RIGHT : in INFO_TYPE) return RESULT_TYPE;
   with function  UNIT return RESULT_TYPE;
   with function  SELECTION
                       (INFO : in INFO_TYPE) return BOOLEAN is TRUE;
   with function  UNTIL
                       (S : in STRUCT;
                        I : in INDEX) return BOOLEAN is FALSE;
function AREDUCE_INFO (S : in STRUCT) return RESULT_TYPE;

-- Find and count
-- ====================

generic
   with function PROPERTY (K : in KEY_TYPE) return BOOLEAN;
function FIND_PROPERTY (S : in STRUCT) return INDEX;

generic
   with function PROPERTY (K : in KEY_TYPE) return BOOLEAN;
function COUNT_PROPERTY (S : in STRUCT) return NATURAL;

generic
   with function PROPERTY (INFO : in INFO_TYPE) return BOOLEAN;
function FIND_INFO_PROPERTY (S : in STRUCT) return INDEX;

generic
   with function PROPERTY (INFO : in INFO_TYPE) return BOOLEAN;
function COUNT_INFO_PROPERTY (S : in STRUCT) return NATURAL;

-- Existential and universal quantification
-- =========================================

generic
   with function PROPERTY (K : in KEY_TYPE) return BOOLEAN;
function EXISTS (S : in STRUCT) return BOOLEAN;

generic
   with function PROPERTY (K : in KEY_TYPE) return BOOLEAN;
function FORALL (S : in STRUCT) return BOOLEAN;
```

```
generic
   with function PROPERTY (INFO : in INFO_TYPE) return BOOLEAN;
function EXISTS_INFO (S : in STRUCT) return BOOLEAN;

generic
   with function PROPERTY (INFO : in INFO_TYPE) return BOOLEAN;
function FORALL_INFO (S : in STRUCT) return BOOLEAN;

-- Order dependent operations
-- ==========================

generic
   with function COMPARE (LEFT, RIGHT : in KEY_TYPE)
                        return ORDER_RELATION is <>;
   with function COMPARE (LEFT, RIGHT : in INFO_TYPE)
                        return ORDER_RELATION is <>;
package ORDER_OPERATIONS is

   -- Lexicographic comparison
   -- ========================

   function COMPARE (LEFT,
                     RIGHT : in STRUCT) return ORDER_RELATION;

   function "<"  (LEFT, RIGHT : in STRUCT) return BOOLEAN;
   function "<=" (LEFT, RIGHT : in STRUCT) return BOOLEAN;
   function ">"  (LEFT, RIGHT : in STRUCT) return BOOLEAN;
   function ">=" (LEFT, RIGHT : in STRUCT) return BOOLEAN;

   -- Maximum and minimum
   -- ===================

   function MAX (S : in STRUCT) return INDEX;
   function MAX (S : in STRUCT) return KEY_TYPE;

   function MIN (S : in STRUCT) return INDEX;
   function MIN (S : in STRUCT) return KEY_TYPE;

   procedure REMOVE_MAX (S : in out STRUCT);
   procedure REMOVE_MIN (S : in out STRUCT);
end ORDER_OPERATIONS;
```

```
-- Hash Operation
-- ==============

generic
   with function HASH (K : in KEY_TYPE)
                      return INTEGER [ is _name.HASH ] ;
   with function HASH (INFO : in INFO_TYPE) return INTEGER is <>;
function HASH_FUNCTION (S : in STRUCT) return INTEGER;

private

   ...

end <MAPS>;
```

# A.14   Bags

**Variant Combinations**

```
  ┌─order────────────┬─list────────────────┬─map────────┐
  │                  │                     │            │
  │                  │                     │            │

... same as for     ... same as for       ... see map variant
sets and maps       sets and maps         combinations
```

```
generic
   ... see A.2
 [ COLLECTION_SIZE : NATURAL; ]
 [ with function "<" (LEFT,
                      RIGHT : in ELEM_TYPE) return BOOLEAN is <>; ]
 [ HASH_TABLE_SIZE : NATURAL;
   with function HASH (E : in ELEM_TYPE) return NATURAL is <>; ]
 [ SONS : POSITIVE := 2; ]
package <BAGS> is

    type STRUCT [ (SIZE : NATURAL) ] is limited private;
    subtype <BAG> is STRUCT;

    -- Indices
    -- =======

    type INDEX is private;

    function NIL return INDEX;

    function GET_ELEM (S : in STRUCT; I : in INDEX) return ELEM_TYPE;

    -- Insert and remove positions
    -- ===========================

    subtype REMOVE_POSITION is INDEX;

    -- Bag specific operations
    -- =======================

    function SUBSET (LEFT, RIGHT : in STRUCT) return BOOLEAN;
    function PROPER_SUBSET (LEFT, RIGHT : in STRUCT) return BOOLEAN;
```

```
function SUPERSET (LEFT, RIGHT : in STRUCT) return BOOLEAN;
function PROPER_SUPERSET (LEFT, RIGHT : in STRUCT) return BOOLEAN;

-- Constructor operations
-- ======================

procedure CLEAR (S : in out STRUCT);

procedure INSERT (S : in out STRUCT; E : in ELEM_TYPE);

procedure INSERT (S      : in out STRUCT;
                  E      : in ELEM_TYPE;
                  I      : out INDEX);

procedure INSERT (TO : in out STRUCT; FROM : in STRUCT);

procedure FIND_OR_INSERT (S     : in out STRUCT;
                          E     : in ELEM_TYPE;
                          I     : out INDEX;
                          FOUND : out BOOLEAN);

procedure REMOVE (S        : in out STRUCT;
                  FROM_POS : in REMOVE_POSITION);

procedure REMOVE (S : in out STRUCT; E : in ELEM_TYPE);

procedure REMOVE_ALL (S : in out STRUCT; E : in ELEM_TYPE);

generic
   with procedure ABSORB (K    : in out KEY_TYPE;
                          INFO : in out INFO_TYPE);
procedure GENERIC_REMOVE (S        : in out STRUCT;
                          FROM_POS : in REMOVE_POSITION);

procedure MOVE (TO       : in out STRUCT;
                FROM     : in out STRUCT;
                FROM_POS : in REMOVE_POSITION);

procedure MOVE (TO   : in out STRUCT;
                FROM : in out ELEM_TYPE);
```

```
procedure MOVE (TO        : in out ELEM_TYPE;
                FROM      : in out STRUCT;
                FROM_POS  : in REMOVE_POSITION);

procedure MOVE (TO, FROM : in out STRUCT);

procedure COPY (TO : in out STRUCT; FROM : in STRUCT);

procedure TRANSFER (TO, FROM : in out STRUCT);

procedure DEALLOCATE (S : in out STRUCT);

-- Selector operations
-- ===================

function COUNT (S : in STRUCT) return NATURAL;

function IS_EMPTY (S : in STRUCT) return BOOLEAN;

function FIND (S : in STRUCT; E : in ELEM_TYPE) return INDEX;

function COUNT_ELEM (S : in STRUCT;
                     E : in ELEM_TYPE) return NATURAL;

function IS_ELEM (S : in STRUCT; E : in ELEM_TYPE) return BOOLEAN;

function "=" (LEFT, RIGHT : in STRUCT) return BOOLEAN;
function EQUAL (LEFT,
               RIGHT : in STRUCT) return BOOLEAN renames "=";

-- Iteration
-- =========

package DEFAULTS is
   function TRUE  (E : in ELEM_TYPE) return BOOLEAN;
   function FALSE (E : in ELEM_TYPE) return BOOLEAN;
   function TRUE  (S : in STRUCT; I : in INDEX) return BOOLEAN;
   function FALSE (S : in STRUCT; I : in INDEX) return BOOLEAN;

   procedure NONE (E : in ELEM_TYPE);
   procedure NONE (E : in ELEM_TYPE; I : in INDEX);
```

```
      procedure NONE1 (E : in out ELEM_TYPE);
      procedure NONE1 (E : in out ELEM_TYPE; I : in INDEX);
   end DEFAULTS;
   use DEFAULTS;

   generic
      with procedure ACTION (E : in ELEM_TYPE) is NONE;
      with function  SELECTION
                        (E : in ELEM_TYPE) return BOOLEAN is TRUE;
      with function  UNTIL
                        (S : in STRUCT;
                         I : in INDEX) return BOOLEAN is FALSE;
      with procedure ACTION_WITH_INDEX
                        (E : in ELEM_TYPE;
                         I : in INDEX) is NONE;
      with function  SELECTION_WITH_INDEX
                        (S : in STRUCT;
                         I : in INDEX) return BOOLEAN is TRUE;
   procedure ITERATE (S : in STRUCT);

   generic
      with procedure ACTION (S : in out STRUCT; I : in INDEX);
      with function  SELECTION
                        (S : in STRUCT;
                         I : in INDEX) return BOOLEAN is TRUE;
      with function  UNTIL
                        (S : in STRUCT;
                         I : in INDEX) return BOOLEAN is FALSE;
   procedure ITERATE_MOVE (S : in out STRUCT);

   -- Reduction
   -- =========

   generic
      with function  OPERATION
                        (LEFT, RIGHT : in ELEM_TYPE) return ELEM_TYPE;
      with function  SELECTION
                        (E : in ELEM_TYPE) return BOOLEAN is TRUE;
      with function  UNTIL
                        (S : in STRUCT;
                         I : in INDEX) return BOOLEAN is FALSE;
   function REDUCE (S : in STRUCT) return ELEM_TYPE;
```

```
generic
   with function  OPERATION
                      (LEFT, RIGHT : in ELEM_TYPE) return ELEM_TYPE;
   with function  UNIT return ELEM_TYPE;
   with function  SELECTION
                      (E : in ELEM_TYPE) return BOOLEAN is TRUE;
   with function  UNTIL
                      (S : in STRUCT;
                       I : in INDEX) return BOOLEAN is FALSE;
function UREDUCE (S : in STRUCT) return ELEM_TYPE;

generic
   type RESULT_TYPE is private;
   with function  OPERATION
                      (LEFT  : in RESULT_TYPE;
                       RIGHT : in ELEM_TYPE) return RESULT_TYPE;
   with function  UNIT return RESULT_TYPE;
   with function  SELECTION
                      (E : in ELEM_TYPE) return BOOLEAN is TRUE;
   with function  UNTIL
                      (S : in STRUCT;
                       I : in INDEX) return BOOLEAN is FALSE;
function AREDUCE (S : in STRUCT) return RESULT_TYPE;

-- Find and count
-- ==============

generic
   with function PROPERTY (E : in ELEM_TYPE) return BOOLEAN;
function FIND_PROPERTY (S : in STRUCT) return INDEX;

generic
   with function PROPERTY (E : in ELEM_TYPE) return BOOLEAN;
function COUNT_PROPERTY (S : in STRUCT) return NATURAL;

-- Existential and universal quantification
-- ========================================

generic
   with function PROPERTY (E : in ELEM_TYPE) return BOOLEAN;
function EXISTS (S : in STRUCT) return BOOLEAN;
```

```
generic
   with function PROPERTY (E : in ELEM_TYPE) return BOOLEAN;
function FORALL (S : in STRUCT) return BOOLEAN;

-- Order dependent operations
-- =========================

generic
   with function COMPARE (LEFT, RIGHT : in ELEM_TYPE)
                         return ORDER_RELATION is <>;
package ORDER_OPERATIONS is

   -- Lexicographic comparison
   -- ========================

   function COMPARE (LEFT, RIGHT : in STRUCT)
                     return ORDER_RELATION;

   function "<"  (LEFT, RIGHT : in STRUCT) return BOOLEAN;
   function "<=" (LEFT, RIGHT : in STRUCT) return BOOLEAN;
   function ">"  (LEFT, RIGHT : in STRUCT) return BOOLEAN;
   function ">=" (LEFT, RIGHT : in STRUCT) return BOOLEAN;

   -- Maximum and minimum
   -- ===================

   function MAX (S : in STRUCT) return INDEX;
   function MAX (S : in STRUCT) return ELEM_TYPE;

   function MIN (S : in STRUCT) return INDEX;
   function MIN (S : in STRUCT) return ELEM_TYPE;

   procedure REMOVE_MAX (S : in out STRUCT);
   procedure REMOVE_MIN (S : in out STRUCT);

end ORDER_OPERATIONS;
```

```
-- Hash Operation
-- ==============

generic
    with function HASH (E : in ELEM_TYPE)
                       return INTEGER [ is <BAGS>.HASH ] ;
    function HASH_FUNCTION (S : in STRUCT) return INTEGER;

private

    . . .

end <BAGS>;
```

Vol. 408: M. Leeser, G. Brown (Eds.),Hardware Specification, Verification and Synthesis: Mathematical Aspects. Proceedings, 1989. VI, 402 pages. 1990.

Vol. 409: A. Buchmann, O. Günther, T. R. Smith, Y.-F. Wang (Eds.), Design and Implementation of Large Spatial Databases. Proceedings, 1989. IX, 364 pages. 1990.

Vol. 410: F. Pichler, R. Moreno-Diaz (Eds.), Computer Aided Systems Theory – EUROCAST '89. Proceedings, 1989. VII, 427 pages. 1990.

Vol. 411: M. Nagl (Ed.), Graph-Theoretic Concepts in Computer Science. Proceedings, 1989. VII, 374 pages. 1990.

Vol. 412: L. B. Almeida, C. J. Wellekens (Eds.), Neural Networks. Proceedings, 1990. IX, 276 pages. 1990,

Vol. 413: R. Lenz, Group Theoretical Methods in Image Processing. VIII, 139 pages. 1990.

Vol. 414: A.Kreczmar, A. Salwicki, M. Warpechowski, LOGLAN '88 – Report on the Programming Language. X, 133 pages. 1990.

Vol. 415: C. Choffrut, T. Lengauer (Eds.), STACS 90. Proceedings, 1990. VI, 312 pages. 1990.

Vol. 416: F. Bancilhon, C. Thanos, D. Tsichritzis (Eds.), Advances in Database Technology – EDBT '90. Proceedings, 1990. IX, 452 pages. 1990.

Vol. 417: P. Martin-Löf, G. Mints (Eds.), COLOG-88. International Conference on Computer Logic. Proceedings, 1988. VI, 338 pages. 1990.

Vol. 418: K. H. Bläsius, U. Hedtstück, C.-R. Rollinger (Eds.), Sorts and Types in Artificial Intelligence. Proceedings, 1989. VIII, 307 pages. 1990. (Subseries LNAI).

Vol. 419: K. Weichselberger, S. Pöhlmann, A Methodology for Uncertainty in Knowledge-Based Systems. VIII, 136 pages. 1990 (Subseries LNAI).

Vol. 420: Z. Michalewicz (Ed.), Statistical and Scientific Database Management, V SSDBM. Proceedings, 1990. V, 256 pages. 1990.

Vol. 421: T. Onodera, S. Kawai, A Formal Model of Visualization in Computer Graphics Systems. X, 100 pages. 1990.

Vol. 422: B. Nebel, Reasoning and Revision in Hybrid Representation Systems. XII, 270 pages. 1990 (Subseries LNAI).

Vol. 423: L. E. Deimel (Ed.), Software Engineering Education. Proceedings, 1990. VI, 164 pages. 1990.

Vol. 424: G. Rozenberg (Ed.), Advances in Petri Nets 1989. VI, 524 pages. 1990.

Vol. 425: C. H. Bergman, R. D. Maddux, D. L. Pigozzi (Eds.), Algebraic Logic and Universal Algebra in Computer Science. Proceedings, 1988. XI, 292 pages. 1990.

Vol. 426: N. Houbak, SIL – a Simulation Language. VII, 192 pages. 1990.

Vol. 427: O. Faugeras (Ed.), Computer Vision – ECCV 90. Proceedings, 1990. XII, 619 pages. 1990.

Vol. 428: D. Bjørner, C. A. R. Hoare, H. Langmaack (Eds.), VDM '90. VDM and Z – Formal Methods in Software Development. Proceedings, 1990. XVII, 580 pages. 1990.

Vol. 429: A. Miola (Ed.), Design and Implementation of Symbolic Computation Systems. Proceedings, 1990. XII, 284 pages. 1990.

Vol. 430: J. W. de Bakker, W.-P. de Roever, G. Rozenberg (Eds.), Stepwise Refinement of Distributed Systems. Models, Formalisms, Correctness. Proceedings, 1989. X, 808 pages. 1990.

Vol. 431: A. Arnold (Ed.), CAAP '90. Proceedings, 1990. VI, 285 pages. 1990.

Vol. 432: N. Jones (Ed.), ESOP '90. Proceedings, 1990. IX, 436 pages. 1990.

Vol. 433: W. Schröder-Preikschat, W. Zimmer (Eds.), Progress in Distributed Operating Systems and Distributed Systems Management. Proceedings, 1989. V, 206 pages. 1990.

Vol. 435: G. Brassard (Ed.), Advances in Cryptology – CRYPTO '89. Proceedings, 1989. XIII, 634 pages. 1990.

Vol. 436: B. Steinholtz, A. Sølvberg, L. Bergman (Eds.), Advanced Information Systems Engineering. Proceedings, 1990. X, 392 pages. 1990.

Vol. 437: D. Kumar (Ed.), Current Trends in SNePS – Semantic Network Processing System. Proceedings, 1989. VII, 162 pages. 1990. (Subseries LNAI).

Vol. 438: D. H. Norrie, H.-W. Six (Eds.), Computer Assisted Learning – ICCAL '90. Proceedings, 1990. VII, 467 pages. 1990.

Vol. 439: P. Gorny, M. Tauber (Eds.), Visualization in Human-Computer Interaction. Proceedings, 1988. VI, 274 pages. 1990.

Vol. 440: E.Börger, H. Kleine Büning, M. M. Richter (Eds.), CSL '89. Proceedings, 1989. VI, 437 pages. 1990.

Vol. 441: T. Ito, R. H. Halstead, Jr. (Eds.), Parallel Lisp: Languages and Systems. Proceedings, 1989. XII, 364 pages. 1990.

Vol. 442: M. Main, A. Melton, M. Mislove, D. Schmidt (Eds.), Mathematical Foundations of Programming Semantics. Proceedings, 1989. VI, 439 pages. 1990.

Vol. 443: M. S. Paterson (Ed.), Automata, Languages and Programming. Proceedings, 1990. IX, 781 pages. 1990.

Vol. 444: S. Ramani, R. Chandrasekar, K. S. R. Anjaneyulu (Eds.), Knowledge Based Computer Systems. Proceedings, 1989. X, 546 pages. 1990. (Subseries LNAI).

Vol. 445: A. J. M. van Gasteren, On the Shape of Mathematical Arguments. VIII, 181 pages. 1990.

Vol. 446: L. Plümer, Termination Proofs for Logic Programs. VIII, 142 pages. 1990. (Subseries LNAI).

Vol. 447: J. R. Gilbert, R. Karlsson (Eds.), SWAT 90. 2nd Scandinavian Workshop on Algorithm Theory. Proceedings, 1990. VI, 417 pages. 1990.

Vol. 448: B. Simons, A. Spector (Eds.), Fault-Tolerant Distributed Computing. VI, 298 pages. 1990.

Vol. 449: M. E. Stickel (Ed.), 10th International Conference on Automated Deduction. Proceedings, 1990. XVI, 688 pages. 1990. (Subseries LNAI).

Vol. 450: T. Asano, T. Ibaraki, H. Imai, T. Nishizeki (Eds.), Algorithms. Proceedings, 1990. VIII, 479 pages. 1990.

Vol. 451: V. Mařík, O. Štěpánková, Z. Zdráhal (Eds.), Artificial Intelligence in Higher Education. Proceedings, 1989. IX, 247 pages. 1990. (Subseries LNAI).

Vol. 452: B. Rovan (Ed.), Mathematical Foundations of Computer Science 1990. Proceedings, 1990. VIII, 544 pages. 1990.

Vol. 453: J. Seberry, J. Pieprzyk (Eds.), Advances in Cryptology – AUSCRYPT '90. Proceedings, 1990. IX, 462 pages. 1990.

Vol. 454: V. Diekert, Combinatorics on Traces. XII, 165 pages. 1990.

Vol. 455: C. A. Floudas, P. M. Pardalos, A Collection of Test Problems for Constrained Global Optimization Algorithms. XIV, 180 pages. 1990.

Vol. 456: P. Deransart, J. Maluszyński (Eds.), Programming Language Implementation and Logic Programming. Proceedings, 1990. VIII, 401 pages. 1990.

Vol. 457: H. Burkhart (Ed.), CONPAR '90 – VAPP IV. Proceedings, 1990. XIV, 900 pages. 1990.

Vol. 458: J. C. M. Baeten, J. W. Klop (Eds.), CONCUR '90. Proceedings, 1990. VII, 537 pages. 1990.

Vol. 459: R. Studer (Ed.), Natural Language and Logic. Proceedings, 1989. VII, 252 pages. 1990. (Subseries LNAI).

Vol. 460: J. Uhl, H. A. Schmid, A Systematic Catalogue of Reusable Abstract Data Types. XII, 344 pages. 1990.